Cambridge
Collections

D1428724

The truth about love

a collection of writing on love through the ages

Edited by Stephen Siddall and Mary Ward

CAMBRIDGE
UNIVERSITY PRESS

CAMBRIDGE UNIVERSITY PRESS
Cambridge, New York, Melbourne, Madrid, Cape Town, Singapore, São Paulo, Delhi

Cambridge University Press
The Edinburgh Building, Cambridge CB2 8RU, UK

www.cambridge.org
Information on this title: www.cambridge.org/9780521748346

First published 2009

Printed in the United Kingdom at the University Press, Cambridge

A catalogue record for this publication is available from the British Library

ISBN 978-0-521-74834-6 paperback

Cover image: photography by Robert Doisneau / Rapho, Camera Press London

Contents

General introduction

O tell me the truth about love

In January 1938 the poet W. H. Auden wrote a collection entitled *12 Songs*. The twelfth (and so, presumably, his 'last word') contains the repeated line: 'O tell me the truth about love'. Yet the question implicit in this line remains unanswered. Auden is puzzled about the nature of love: he instinctively thinks about Cupid, the mischievous boy-god from renaissance art and love literature. And so Auden begins his poem with the line 'Some say that love's a little boy'.

Cupid's wings make him think of freedom, so he continues: 'And some say it's a bird'. He then refers to a popular song of his day: 'Some say it makes the world go round,' but the cliché unnerves him so he undermines it: 'And some say that's absurd'.

Auden's investigating persona continues to be jaunty, mocking but also insecure. There may be references to impending war: 'history books, patriotism, the transatlantic boats', but most of the allusions are to ordinary life in the 1930s and these too fail to reassure, not least because of the way Auden experiments with the rhyming of the word 'love'. It is partnered with 'fluff', 'stuff', 'enough' and 'rough', all either trival or unsettling in their context. Therefore he finds himself often repeating his pleading refrain: 'O tell me the truth about love.' His last verse is both thought-provoking and comically mundane:

When it comes will it come without warning
Just as I'm picking my nose?
Will it knock on my door in the morning,
Or tread in the bus on my toes?
Will it come like a change in the weather?
Will its greeting be courteous or rough?
Will it alter my life altogether?
O tell me the truth about love.

Over 300 years earlier Sir Walter Ralegh, the Elizabethan courtier-poet was more ambitious in his equally witty poem *Now what is love . . .* ?. Each verse begins with a question about how to define love: the next five lines give the answer, but so variously that the possibilities seem to cancel each other out. We can hardly be sure that the elusive essence of love ever can be categorised. Ralegh seems unsure too: the last line of each verse begins confidently but ends with a degree of doubt:

Now what is love, I pray thee tell?
It is that fountain and that well
Where pleasure and repentance dwell.
It is perhaps that sauncing bell
That tolls all into heaven or hell;
And this is love, as I hear tell.

Yet what is love, I pray thee say?
It is a work on holy day.
It is December matched with May,
When lusty bloods in fresh array
Hear ten months after of the play:
And this is love, as I hear say.

Yet what is love, I pray thee sain?
It is a sunshine mixed with rain.
It is a toothache, or like pain;
It is a game where none doth gain;
The lass saith No, and would full fain:
And this is love, as I hear sain.

Yet what is love, I pray thee say?
It is a yea, it is a nay,
A pretty kind of sporting fray;
It is a thing will soon away;
Then take the vantage while you may:
And this is love, as I hear say.

Yet what is love, I pray thee show?
A thing that creeps, it cannot go;
A prize that passeth to and fro;
A thing for one, a thing for mo;
And he that proves must find it so:
And this is love, sweet friend, I trow.

In the end, love is both subjective and widespread: 'A thing for one, a thing for mo'. At last Ralegh pretends he can be sure – but, in effect, his busy attempt at definition is to say that love can't be defined. And so, is the poem a witty confection, a project that is bound to fail and thus not worth the attempt? Well, like all good writing it engages the mind intelligently, it entertains, but it also wisely implies several paradoxes: that love enriches and humiliates, it delights, but causes a good deal of heart-ache, it is elusive, short-lived and occupies most people's minds much of the time.

Love also occupies writers. From the earliest myths to the most recently written piece of pulp fiction, there is no subject more thoroughly explored. Indeed, books and poems about war, religion, nature, society and many other topics are often partly about love too. The contemporary playwright David Hare, who writes about politics and ideas, has commented that he often includes a love story in his plays because everyone can relate to it, and so perhaps love may offer an inviting bridge to the more difficult aspects of his play.

Over time, some attitudes towards the representation of love have changed and developed, according to different social contexts and differing reader expectation. Love may be constant, 'an ever-fixed mark' (Shakespeare, Sonnet 116), or fickle and treacherous. Love can be both creative and destructive. Love is multi-faceted: it can be platonic; it can also engage the body (*eros*), mind (*caritas*) and soul (*agape*). These are Greek terms, used by philosophers to categorise love's nature and effects.

Love may last for an eternity, or it may consume and die in an instant. *Romeo and Juliet* is one of the world's great love stories, partly because of the paradox that vulnerable young people, living in a volatile and dangerous city, feel their love so intensely that they imagine infinity. Their imagination surpasses the fact of their brief mortality:

My bounty is as boundless as the sea
My love as deep; the more I give to thee
The more I have, for both are infinite.

Though we can all relate to love and to literature about love, people differ and lovers are not identical. Even when two lovers feel supremely together they may still love differently. This difference may be part of the joy of experiencing each other; conversely it may lead eventually to betrayal and separation.

The contexts for love stories in life and literature remind us that love is not simply a private relationship between two people. It takes its place in the real world, where others may observe and comment, expressing delight or disapproval. The image on the front cover of this book, *The Kiss by the Hôtel de Ville*, is about both the lovers and those who pass by in the street. Its immediate history is interesting: shot by the photographer Robert Doisneau in Paris in 1950, as part of a photoshoot on Parisian lovers for *Life* magazine, it was in fact staged; Doisneau claimed in 1992: 'I would have never dared to photograph people like that. Lovers kissing on the street, those couples are rarely legitimate.' The image has become iconic, appearing to epitomise the joy and spontaneity of love, and yet what we see with our eyes deceives. Being staged, it may be thought to be a sort of lie. But the image compels us through its emotional truth, which is paradoxically enhanced by the indifference of the passers-by.

The Kiss by Rodin.

The photograph has acquired a distinguished cultural history, as too has Rodin's *The Kiss* (see p. xii), a marble sculpture of two lovers entwined in a passionate embrace, flesh on flesh. This has become one of the most famous of all sculptures. Though it includes no sculptured observers, it invites us to peer, wander round and examine it from all angles – the most intimate of fictional moments made almost shockingly available to the world.

No doubt Rodin was trying to reproduce real life, but he was also prompted by cultural history. What was his inspiration for *The Kiss*? The answer lies in the 14th-century story of the lovers Paolo and Francesca. Their tragic story is narrated to the poet Dante as he visits the 5th Circle of Hell with his guide, Virgil, in *Inferno, The Divine Comedy* (1318). The 'lustful are forever buffeted by a violent storm', because they 'subjected reason to the rules of lust'. Dante sees Cleopatra, Helen of Troy, Paris, Dido and Tristan, but his attention is drawn to the two 'who go together there / And seem so lightly carried on the wind'.

Francesca had been married by political arrangement to Gianciotto Malatesta, but she fell in love with his brother, Paolo, whilst reading with him the story of the adulterous lovers Lancelot and Guinevere in the Arthurian legends. As they read, they often lifted their eyes from the text to gaze at each other. Francesca explains that once they reached the description of the longed-for kiss in the text, they read no more. Their adulterous love affair began when they read together a story about adultery. They were discovered, and stabbed to death by Gianciotto.

Francesca tells Dante that '*Amor* condusse noi ad un*a mor*te' (Love drew us onwards to consuming death). This short phrase, linguistically, shows how love and death are inseparable, that love inevitably leads to devouring death, but that within the word death (*morte*) is love (*amor*). Appropriately the lovers are forever entwined in a loving embrace, beyond death. Moreover, Dante, representing his readers as audience, experiences such increasing love and compassion for these doomed lovers that he finally collapses 'as bodies fall, for dead'. Francesca has informed Dante that:

There is no sorrow greater
Than, in times of misery, to hold at heart
The memory of happiness.

Dante's depiction of lovers forever tossed like birds in a tempestuous storm is a visual metaphor of the ceaseless nature of the turbulence of passion.

Paolo and Francesca's story has inspired writers, musicians and artists. Rodin's *The Kiss* depicts that moment when Paolo matched Lancelot's kiss 'trembling to my open mouth'. Rodin's assistant Jules Desbois commented that, like Paolo, Francesca 'is awake and filled with longing, as though the two made common cause to find their souls'. Ary Scheffer's painting (see below) shows the two lovers floating in the darkness towards the shadowy observers, Virgil and Dante. We, like Dante, suspend judgement, and the eye is drawn towards the compelling image of the lovers, brightly illuminated against the shadowy darkness of hell. The lovers appear to be flying unsupported, upon the wings of desire. They bear the wounds of love upon their flesh, a kind of secular stigmata. They are closely entwined, enveloped in a white sheet, which is a visual reminder of both passion and the grave, the bed sheet and the shroud. Therefore the lovers are joined for all eternity through love and in death.

Paolo and Francesca by Ary Scheffer.

Doisneau's iconic photograph, *The Kiss by the Hôtel de Ville*, similarly draws our attention to the part played by the passers-by, the witnesses. We as readers may read literature empathetically, like Dante, who fainted with sorrow on hearing the tragic tale of Paolo and Francesca, or we may stand apart, registering no emotion, as the detached passers-by in the photo, intent on their own business.

Therefore, like the photograph, the literature of love will be enriched if we understand something of its cultural, historical and philosophical background.

In the 5th century BC, the philosopher Plato explored 'the truth about love' through a series of questions and answers in two significant books, *Phaedrus* and *The Symposium*. *Phaedrus* is a conversation or dialogue between two men, Socrates the teacher and Phaedrus the pupil, out on a country ramble. They discuss love. What is desire? Is it wrong to pursue our desires without rational control? What is the relationship between reason and sensuality? Is love simply earthbound or is it something divine? In order to make these abstract truths more palatable, Plato's speakers jazz up the dialogue with startling images. The conflict between good and bad desires is likened to a charioteer trying to keep two horses under control. The bad horse, representing our ignoble desires, is ugly, sweaty and headstrong. The good horse is modest, restrained and beautiful. Other images include the physical sprouting of itchy, feathery wings – representing the awakening of true love and the realisation that there is a transcendent world of forms from which we came, 'trailing clouds of glory'.

The Romantic poets, particularly Blake and Shelley, were influenced by Platonic thought; so too were the metaphysical poets, especially John Donne, who relished the Platonic interplay between abstract thought and concrete imagery. Plato uses humour to convey profound truths. In *The Symposium* the dinner-party guests discuss love. The most extraordinary tale, a kind of creation myth, is expounded by Aristophanes. Also a blueprint for dating, it shows that we are all in search of the perfect partner who will complete us – our other half. Someone out there is waiting for us. We originally were circular beings with four arms and four legs, male, female and hermaphrodite. In order to punish us, Zeus chopped each spherical being in half. No one could reproduce. Everyone wandered miserably around looking for their other half until Zeus relented. This extraordinary tale implicitly influences much literature of pursuit and marriage. For example, Sue Bridehead in Thomas Hardy's *Jude the Obscure* feels that Jude completes her, and Hardy makes specific reference to this story, as does Milan Kundera in *The Unbearable Lightness of Being*.

Ovid, writing two thousand years ago in Rome, enjoyed fame and also notoriety as an expert in the truth about love. His *Ars Amatoria* is a practical guide to being a good lover. Advice is given to men and women alike, and always in the background – to enliven his writing and to provide racy examples – are the exploits of a galaxy of gods and goddesses; the Roman pantheon of gods. But Ovid is best known for his *Metamorphoses*, an astonishing anthology of myths and legends collected from all over the then-known world. Beginning with a creation myth, they extend beyond the present time into a glorious future. But what unites every single story is change – physical, bodily change – transformation or metamorphosis. Although love may not cause us to become bears, stars or laurel trees, love has transforming powers and in many stories about love you will read of emotional transformations. Silas Marner learns compassion through his love of the orphaned toddler, Eppie, and King Lear discovers through agonising mental and physical suffering both how to love and what it is to be loved completely by a daughter.

Petrarch (1304–1374), the Italian poet and father of the sonnet, took Ovid's story of Apollo and Daphne as a blueprint for his unrequited love for Laura, whom he first saw in church one Good Friday. He loved her passionately until her death; she never returned his love. Put briefly, Apollo, smitten with the golden arrow of desire, yearns to possess and love Daphne. But she has been penetrated by the leaden arrow of repulsion. She flees from him. He chases her. At the very moment before rape – help comes. She is transformed into a laurel tree; hair becomes tendrils and leaves, fingers twigs, arms branches, body trunk. Apollo must remain forever frustrated and may express his frustration, passion and desire only through the outpourings of his music – as Petrarch in his *Canzoniere*, the sonnets charting his unrequited love. This in turn inspired Elizabethan sonneteers: lovers burn and freeze alternately; Cupid's arrow wounds through the eye; imagery is hyperbolic – lovers are tossed on a sea of passion; the loved one is gloriously remote. Shakespeare was influenced by the Petrarchan tradition, and also enjoyed parodying its excesses in his sonnets and comedies. You will find that much of *Romeo and Juliet* has Petrarchan qualities: although Romeo pines for the disdainful Rosaline like a woebegone Petrarchan lover, his love for Juliet is idealised and transcendental, moving through death, beyond this world. And Juliet talks of cutting Romeo out into little stars after his death – a true metamorphosis, both Petrarchan and Ovidian.

Probably the greatest theological and literary influence is the Bible, a collection of books separated by hundreds of years. Myths are narrated, truths expounded, and the nature of love is defined, tested and celebrated. The book of Genesis begins with the story of the Garden of Eden, the Fall and the subsequent loss of paradise. Adam and Eve are expelled to an unstable world of pain, suffering and death. This event is at the heart of much love literature. Most famously, Milton's epic poem *Paradise Lost* recounts the story from many different points of view: Eve's, Adam's and Satan's – the eternal love triangle. But the influence of this story is all-pervasive. Adam and Eve were one flesh, thus every coupling enacts this; think of Cathy and Heathcliff's urgent desire to be united in *Wuthering Heights*. Dracula uses the language of Genesis as he bears down on his victim Mina, literally desiring to consume her flesh.

Yet the dark eroticism of Dracula seems pale beside another of the stories of the Bible – the Song of Songs, sometimes known as the Song of Solomon. Extraordinarily erotic and sensuous writing, this depicts the search of the bride for her bridegroom, her anticipation of joys to come, the promised ecstasy. Both bride and bridegroom delight in the glories of the body of the other. And this love is as strong as death: 'many waters cannot quench love; neither can the floods drown it.' So the book both celebrates sexual union and immortalises it. Many later works share this aim; for example, the 20th-century novelist D. H. Lawrence experiments in his writing about sex, giving it a transcendent, religious quality.

After great loss, death, love remains. Poetry in particular immortalises the lost beloved; Hardy's poems of 1912/13 resurrect his lately unloved wife Emma as an animated girl, riding the cliffs of Cornwall. The 21st-century poet Jackie Kay captures the moment when the living die in her tender poem *Darling* (2007): holding the hand of a loved one by her bedside, the speaker sings to her until she has 'slipped away, / already a slip of a girl again'. Her concluding stanza speaks eloquently to the reader. Death cannot quench love:

And what I didn't know or couldn't say then
Was that she hadn't really gone.
The dead don't go till you do, loved ones.
The dead are still here holding our hands.

How this book is organised

The anthology contains almost 80 extracts about love, ranging from Greek myth to the present day.

It is divided into seven sections, each beginning with an introduction. The texts and extracts are each introduced with a brief paragraph giving some contextual information about the work and the author.

The sections consider the following aspects of love:

1 Pursuit:	the thoughts and feelings of people when they fall in love and hope that their love will be returned.
2 Unrequited love:	the lover is distressed by lack of interest or a rejection.
3 Celebration:	the delight in love felt and shared.
4 Forbidden love:	love experienced in a context of disapproval or danger.
5 Family:	the variety of love that exists within a family.
6 Friendship:	the affection between friends has been described as the purest form of love.
7 Loss and betrayal:	love is vulnerable to death, absence or one partner falling out of love.

In each section the extracts are followed by a few questions that may stimulate group discussion or writing. For students preparing for exams, each set of questions includes this reminder:

In all of these questions (whether used for group discussion or for writing) you should consider:

a the ways the writers' choice of form, structure and language shape your responses to the extracts

b how your wider reading in the literature of love has contributed to your understanding and interpretation of the extracts.

Since so much writing explores so many different aspects of love, it is likely that whatever you read in this anthology will relate in some way to your own wider reading. Therefore, to stimulate your own further reading, each section ends with a few suggestions about what you may choose to read next. These pages refer to prose, poetry and drama from different periods, but – with so much wonderful writing available – they are bound to appear arbitrary. In fact, it could be valuable and interesting for you to compile your own further reading pages that may be totally different from ours – and just as valid.

1 Pursuit

At first glance, 'pursuit' may seem an unfeeling word for a lover's ardour, but love stories are many and various. They include the wish to possess and capture, but they may also describe the time, energy and dedication necessary to achieve the great prize of the beloved's favour.

Until about the middle of the 20th century the pursuer was likely to be male and, in earlier literature, if the roles were reversed then there was a basis for comedy, especially if the woman was too eager; an example is Lady Booby in Fielding's *Joseph Andrews* (published 1742, see extract p. 51). There is often comedy too if the man is ineffectual and the woman who refuses him confident, remote or witty. Love and lust are universal – everyone can relate to these feelings whether or not we share the social and gender assumptions that existed at the time of writing. In the best poems, novels and plays the nuances of feeling and circumstance make each story unique.

In primitive times man had to be a hunting animal. Later, even in more sophisticated societies, hunting for wild game was an aristocratic pastime. In war a medieval nobleman would fight for his feudal overlord, whilst in peacetime he would hunt by day and engage in civilised courtesies with women afterwards. Both activities were 'pursuits' in both senses of the word.

Pursuing the wrong woman might be dangerous. Sir Thomas Wyatt's (1503–1542) most famous sonnet begins: 'Whoso list[1] to hunt, I know where is an hind.'[2] This may sound like a nobleman's literal hunting, but Wyatt's 'hind' is Anne Boleyn, one of his former lovers, and she now 'belongs' to Henry VIII. The sestet warns off anyone whose courtesies might bring him too close to the dangerous prize:

---

[1]**list** wishes
[2]**hind** female deer

Who list her hunt (I put him out of doubt)
As well as I, may spend his time in vain,
And graven with diamonds in letters plain
There is written, her fair neck round about:
'Noli me tangere,[3] for Caesar's[4] I am,
And wild for to hold, though I seem tame.'

Sometimes the man simply exploits the woman. In Hardy's novel *Tess of the D'Urbervilles* (1891), Alec drives the vulnerable country girl Tess out to the aptly named 'Chase'. In the darkness and fog his seduction (or rape – Hardy leaves this ambiguous) is less of a love-pursuit and more of a wealthy young man's pastime: Alec plays at a gentleman's courtesies but his attitudes are selfish and exploitative. In *The Beaux' Stratagem* (1707, see extract p. 21) the pursuit is primarily of the woman's wealth but Farquhar's two well-named fortune-hunters, Aimwell and Archer, come to love and respect the women they have chosen. In this play all the women can look after their own interests, the confident men are often disconcerted, and the play ends with happy marriages – so most aspects of the pursuit are comic.

In traditional courtship the woman's influence civilises the man. For example, in Chaucer's *Troilus and Criseyde* (late 1380s, see extract p. 6) the young prince is arrogant, rough and sometimes discourteous, but, on seeing Criseyde and humbling himself to serve her, he becomes attentive to everyone's needs. The male lover was, paradoxically, elevated in virtue by becoming a servant to his lady and to the powerful God of Love. His devotion was called 'fin amour' (civilised love); this turned into a literary cult, much observed by courtier-poets. It has been noted that ardent love may even be a type of worship in which the lover uses words like 'mercy' and 'grace'.

The influence of 'fin amour' and its heightened language of courtesy can be seen in later love poetry: though the man took the initiative, it was the woman who held authority – at least, until marriage.

---

[3]***Noli me tangere*** do not touch me (originally said by Jesus to Mary Magdalen after his resurrection)

[4]**Caesar's** belonging to the emperor (in this case, the king, Henry VIII; Anne Boleyn 'belongs' to him)

At this point the love story would end rather than describe the realities of life, where men held most of the advantages.

The final extract in this section, *The Lover: a Ballad* (p. 54), was written in the 18th century; it celebrates a woman's feisty independence, unusual for those times but easily recognised today, especially in the work of female novelists such as A. S. Byatt, Jeanette Winterson, Angela Carter and Toni Morrison.

All in Green

by E. E. Cummings

Cummings (1894–1962) was born in Cambridge, Massachusetts and educated at Harvard. His literary output was wide, ranging through politics, satire, travel writing, plays and romantic lyrical verse. His early work was noted for its technical skill and experiments in typography as well as for its musical grace. He is known for not always using upper-case letters in his poems.

All in green went my love riding
on a great horse of gold
into the silver dawn.

four lean hounds crouched low and smiling
the merry deer ran before.

Fleeter be they than dappled dreams
the swift sweet deer
the red rare deer.

Four red roebuck at white water
the cruel bugle sang before.

Horn at hip went my love riding
riding the echo down
into the silver dawn.

four lean hounds crouched low and smiling
the level meadows ran before.

Softer be they than slippered sleep
the lean lithe deer
the fleet flown deer.

Four fleet does at a gold valley
the famished arrows sang before.

Bow at belt went my love riding
riding the mountain down
into the silver dawn.

four lean hounds crouched low and smiling
the sheer peaks ran before.

Paler be they than daunting death
the sleek slim deer
the tall tense deer.

Four tall stags at a green mountain
the lucky hunter sang before.

All in green went my love riding
on a great horse of gold
into the silver dawn.

four lean hounds crouched low and smiling
my heart fell dead before.

Troilus and Criseyde

by Geoffrey Chaucer

This famous story from the Trojan Wars interested several writers (see Shakespeare's treatment on p. 119). The young prince Troilus falls in love with Criseyde, and her uncle Pandarus brings them together. In this extract Chaucer (c.1343–1400) tells of Troilus promising Criseyde his faithful love and service.

In chaunged vois, right for his verray drede,
Which vois ek quook, and therto his manere
Goodly abaist,[1] and now his hewes[2] rede,
Now pale, unto Criseyde, his lady dere,
With look down cast and humble iyolden chere,[3]
Lo, the alderfirste word that hym asterte
Was, twyes, 'Mercy, mercy, swete herte!'

And stynte[4] a while, and whan he myghte out brynge,
The nexte word was, 'God woot, for I have,
As ferforthly as I have had konnynge,[5]
Ben youres al, God so my soule save,
And shal, til that I, woful wight, be grave!
And though I dar, ne kan, unto yow pleyne,
Iwis, I suffre nought the lasse peyne.

'Thus muche as now, O wommanliche wif,[6]
I may out brynge, and if this yow displese,
That shal I wreke upon myn owen lif[7]

---

[1]**Goodly abaist** totally humbled
[2]**hewes** complexion
[3]**humble iyolden chere** keeping his behaviour modest
[4]**stynte** broke off
[5]**konnynge** knowledge
[6]**wif** lady
[7]**wreke upon myn owen lif** kill myself

Right soone, I trowe, and do youre herte an ese,
If with my deth youre wreththe I may apese.[8]
But syn that ye han herd me somwhat seye,
Now recche[9] I nevere how soone that I deye.'

Therwith his manly sorwe to biholde,
It myghte han mad an herte of stoon to rewe;[10]
And Pandare wep as he to water wolde,
And poked evere his nece new and newe,
And seyde, 'Wo bygon ben hertes trewe![11]
For love of God, make of this thing an ende,
Or sle[12] us both at ones, er ye wende.'[13]

'I! what?' quod she, 'by God and by my trouthe,
I not nat what ye wilne that I seye.'
'I! what?' quod he, 'that ye han on hym routhe,[14]
For Goddes love, and doth hym nought to deye.'
'Now thanne thus,' quod she, 'I wolde hym preye
To telle me the fyn of his entente.[15]
Yet wist I nevere wel what that he mente.'

'What that I mene, O swete herte deere?'
Quod Troilus, 'O goodly, fresshe free,
That with the stremes of youre eyen cleere
Ye wolde somtyme frendly on me see,
And thanne agreen that I may ben he,
Withouten braunche of vice on any wise,
In trouthe alwey to don yow my servise,

---

[8]**youre wreththe I may apese** I may soften your displeasure
[9]**recche** care
[10]**rewe** pity
[11]**Wo bygon ben hertes trewe!** What suffering true lovers have to endure!
[12]**sle** kill
[13]**er ye wende** lit. before you go
[14]**routhe** pity
[15]**fyn of his entente** (lit. the end of his purpose) everything he wishes

'As to my lady right and chief resort,
With al my wit[16] and al my diligence;
And I to han, right as yow list, comfort,
Under yowre yerde,[17] egal to myn offence,
As deth, if that I breke youre defence;
And that ye deigne[18] me so muche honoure,
Me to comanden aught in any houre;

'And I to ben youre verray, humble, trewe,
Secret, and in my paynes pacient,
And evere mo desiren fresshly newe
To serve, and ben ay ylike diligent,
And with good herte al holly youre talent[19]
Receyven wel, how sore that me smerte, –
Lo, this mene I, myn owen swete herte.'

---

[16]**wit** judgement
[17]**yerde** discipline
[18]**deigne** allow
[19]**talent** wishes

Free Fall

by William Golding

William Golding (1911–1993) achieved immediate success in 1954 with *Lord of the Flies*, his first novel. In it, as in many of his later works, Golding explores the nature and origins of cruelty.

In *Free Fall* Sammy Mountjoy, his destructive 'hero', loses his innocence; he tries to find out when and how this happened by reviewing his life from childhood. In this extract he recalls his late adolescence, when he is a student at art school and sets out to seduce Beatrice, a very innocent young girl.

That night I wrote Beatrice a letter . . . I begged her to read the letter carefully – not knowing how common this opening was in such a letter – not knowing that there were thousands of young men in London that night writing just such letters to just such altars . . . I told her that I was a helpless victim, that pride had prevented me from making this clear to her, but she was the sun and moon for me, that without her I should die, that I did not expect much – only that she should agree to some special relationship between us that would give me more standing than these acquaintances so casually blessed. For she might come to care for me, I said, in my bourgeois pamphlet,[1] she might even – for I have loved you from the first day and I always shall.

Two o'clock in the morning and autumn mist, London fog about. I sneaked out of the house for the family I lived with were supposed to report my movements to the authorities. I rode off, through the night, not daring to lose a post. First one policeman stopped me and took my name and address and then two stopped me. The third time I was tired enough to be honest and I told the statue in the blue coat that I was in love

[1]**bourgeois pamphlet** conventional letter

so he waved me on and wished me luck. At last I came to her door, pushed the package through and heard it fall. I was saying to myself as I nodded on the bike: at least I have been honest, been honest, I don't know what to do.

How do they react in themselves, these soft, cloven creatures? Where is the dial that marks their degrees of feeling? I had had my sex already. The party had seen to that, Sheila, dark and dirty. We had given each other a little furtive pleasure like handing round a bag of toffees. It was also our absurd declaration of independence . . . It was freedom. But these other contained, untouched girls – how do they feel and think? Or are they . . . a clear bubble blown about, vulnerable but unwounded? Surely she must have known! But how did the situation present itself? Granted the whole physical process appears horrible and unmentionable – for so it did, I know that – what then does love appear to be? Is it an abstract thing with as little humanity as the dancing advertisements of Piccadilly? Or does love immediately imply a white wedding, a house? She had dressed and undressed herself, tended her delicate body year in year out. Did she never think with faster pulse and breath – he is in love, he wants to do – that – to me? Perhaps now with the spread of enlightenment virginity has lost sacred caste and girls go eager to swim. It was, after all, a social habit. She was lower middle class where the instinct or habit was to keep what you had intact. It was a class in those days of great power and stability, ignoble and ungenerous. I cannot tell what flutter if any I made in her dovecote, could not, cannot, knew and know nothing about her. But she read the letter.

This time I did not pretend to be riding by. I sat my saddle, one hand on the handle-bars one foot on the pavement. I watched them tumble out of the double doors and she came with them. The blessed damozels had been tipped off because they marched away without a giggle. I looked her in the eye and burned with the shame of my confession.

'You read my letter?'

They were not terms on which she blushed. Without a word we went to Lyons[2] and sat in silence.

'Well?'

She did pinken a bit then, she spoke softly and gently as to an invalid.

'I don't know what to say, Sammy.'

'I meant every word of it. You've' – spread hands – 'got me. I'm defeated.'

'How?'

'It's a kind of competition.'

But I saw that her eyes were still empty of understanding.

'Forget it, Beatrice. If you can't understand – look. Have goodwill. You see? Give me a chance to – *am* I so awful? I know I'm nothing to look at, but I do' – deep breath – 'I do – you know how I feel.'

Silence.

'Well?'

'Your course. It won't last for ever. Then you won't come this way.'

'My course? What? Oh – that! I mean I thought if you and I – we could go walking in the country and then you could – I'm quite harmless really.'

'Your course!'

'So you guessed, did you? I'm cutting the Art School at this moment. There are some things that are more important.'

'Sammy!'

Now the untroubled pools began to fill. There was wonder and awe and a trace of speculation. Did she think to herself; it is true, he is in love, he has done a real thing for me? I am that, after all, which can be loved. I am not entirely empty. I have a stature like the others. I am human?

'You'll come? Say you'll come, Beatrice!'

She was commendably virtuous on every level. She would come; but I must promise – not in exchange, for that would be

---

[2]**Lyons** Lyons Corner House was a chain of popular tea-rooms in the 1950s

bargaining - must promise I would not cut the art school any more. I think she began to see herself as a centre of power, as an influence for good; but her interest in my future gave me such delight that I did not analyse it.

Not on Sunday. On Saturday. She couldn't come on Sunday, she said, with a kind of mild surprise that anyone should expect her to. And so I met my first, indeed, my only rival. That surprised me then and surprises me now; first, that I should rage so at this invisible rival, second, that I had none physical. She was so sweet, so unique, so beautiful - or did I invent her beauty? Had all young men been as I, the ways where she went would have been crowded. Did no other man have as I this unquenchable desire to know, to be someone else, to understand; was mine the only mixture near her of worship and jealousy and musky tumescence? Were there others, is it the common experience to be granted a favour, and at once to be a tumult of delight and gratitude for the granting and wild rage because the favour had to be asked for?

We walked on the downs in grey weather and I shook out my talent before her. I impressed myself. When I described the inner compulsion that drove me to paint I felt full of my own genius. But to Beatrice, of course, I was describing a disease which stood between me and a respectable, prosperous life. Or so I think; for all these are guesses. Part of the reality of my life is that I do not understand it. Moreover she did not make things easy for she hardly spoke at all. All I know is that I must have succeeded in giving her a picture of a stormy interior, an object of some awe and pity. Yet the truth was on a smaller scale altogether, the wound less tragic and paradoxically less easily healed.

'Well? What do you think?'

Silence; averted profile. We were coming down from the ridge, about to plunge into wet woods. We stopped where they began and I took her hand. The rags of my self-respect fell from me. Nothing venture, nothing win.

'Aren't you sorry for me?'

She let her hand lie in mine. It was the first time in my life I had touched her. I heard the little word float away, carried by the wind.

'Maybe.'

Her head turned, her face was only a few inches from mine. I leaned forward and gently and chastely kissed her on the lips.

We must have gone on and I must have talked yet the words are gone. All I remember is my astonishment.

Not quite all. For I remember the substance of my discovery. I was, by that mutely invited salute, admitted to the status of boy friend. The perquisites[3] of this position were two. First, I had a claim on her time and she would not go out with any other male. Second, I was entitled to a similar strictly chaste salute on rare occasions and also on saying good night. I am nearly sure that at that moment Beatrice meant her gesture as prophylactic.[4] Boy friends were nice boys and therefore – so her reasoning may have gone – if Sammy is a boy friend it will make him nice. It will make him normal. Dear Beatrice!

---

[3]**perquisites** customary benefits
[4]**prophylactic** medicine to prevent disease

Maud

by Alfred Lord Tennyson

Tennyson (1809–1892) became Poet Laureate in 1850 and was a favourite of Queen Victoria.

The gloomy narrator of *Maud* tells of his family disasters and how he courted the beautiful daughter of a lord, his surprise at winning her, her brother's hostility, and the narrator's flight abroad and eventual madness. As a whole *Maud* is a disturbing poem, criticised in its day for being neurotic, obscure and fragmented, but it also displays Tennyson's great musical talents as a lyric poet.

VIII

She came to the village church,
And sat by a pillar alone;
An angel watching an urn
Wept over her, carved in stone;
And once, but once, she lifted her eyes,
And suddenly, sweetly, strangely blushed
To find they were met by my own;
And suddenly, sweetly, my heart beat stronger
And thicker, until I heard no longer
The snowy-banded, dilettante,
Delicate-handed priest intone;
And thought, is it pride, and mused and sighed
'No surely, now it cannot be pride.'

XXII

Come into the garden, Maud,
   For the black bat, night, has flown,
Come into the garden, Maud,
   I am here at the gate alone;
And the woodbine spices are wafted abroad,
   And the musk of the rose is blown.

For a breeze of morning moves,
   And the planet of Love is on high,
Beginning to faint in the light that she loves
   On a bed of daffodil sky,
To faint in the light of the sun she loves,
   To faint in his light, and to die.

All night have the roses heard
   The flute, violin, bassoon;
All night has the casement jessamine[1] stirred
   To the dancers dancing in tune;
Till a silence fell with the waking bird,
   And a hush with the setting moon.

I said to the lily, 'There is but one
   With whom she has heart to be gay.
When will the dancers leave her alone?
   She is weary of dance and play.'
Now half to the setting moon are gone,
   And half to the rising day;
Low on the sand and loud on the stone
   The last wheel echoes away.

I said to the rose, 'The brief night goes
   In babble and revel and wine.
O young lord-lover, what sighs are those,
   For one that will never be thine?
But mine, but mine,' so I sware to the rose,
   'For ever and ever, mine.'

---

[1]**jessamine** jasmine

And the soul of the rose went into my blood,
As the music clashed in the hall;
And long by the garden lake I stood,
For I heard your rivulet fall
From the lake to the meadow and on to the wood,
Our wood, that is dearer than all;

From the meadow your walks have left so sweet
That whenever a March-wind sighs
He sets the jewel-print of your feet
In violets blue as your eyes,
To the woody hollows in which we meet
And the valleys of Paradise.

The slender acacia would not shake
One long milk-bloom on the tree;
The white lake-blossom fell into the lake
As the pimpernel[2] dozed on the lea;
But the rose was awake all night for your sake,
Knowing your promise to me;
The lilies and roses were all awake,
They sighed for the dawn and thee.

Queen rose of the rosebud garden of girls,
Come hither, the dances are done,
In gloss of satin and glimmer of pearls,
Queen lily and rose in one;
Shine out, little head, sunning over with curls,
To the flowers, and be their sun.

[2]**pimpernel** small plant found in cornfields, often with bright red flowers

There has fallen a splendid tear
   From the passion-flower at the gate.
She is coming, my dove, my dear;
   She is coming, my life, my fate;
The red rose cries, 'She is near, she is near;'
   And the white rose weeps, 'She is late;'
The larkspur listens, 'I hear, I hear;'
   And the lily whispers, 'I wait.'

She is coming, my own, my sweet;
   Were it ever so airy a tread,
My heart would hear her and beat,
   Were it earth in an earthy bed;
My dust would hear her and beat,
   Had I lain for a century dead;
Would start and tremble under her feet,
   And blossom in purple and red.

The True History of the Kelly Gang

by Peter Carey

Peter Carey (born 1943) is one of the foremost contemporary Australian novelists. He combines realism and the surreal; he is also a lively satirist, often with a disturbing strain of black comedy. His novel *Oscar and Lucinda* won the Booker prize in 1988.

The True History of the Kelly Gang is based on the life of the great 19th-century Australian outlaw, Ned Kelly, whose early life is full of petty crime and protecting his younger brother from being persecuted by landowners and sheriffs. In this extract he meets a young girl, Mary Hearn. He later marries her; she supports him, shares his life, and eventually urges him to perpetuate his legend by writing his story.

2 much younger ladies soon come into the room if they had been sleeping they give no sign of weariness their eyes was bright & their hair were coifed.[1] One were a tall pretty blonde very jolly and bosomy she immediately begun waltzing with Fitzpatrick though there were no music none at all.

The 2nd girl could be no more than 5 ft. tall but her beauty were much finer more delicate her hair were the colour of a crow's wings glistening it would reflect the colour of the sky. Her back were slender with a lovely sweep to it her shoulders was straight her head held high. When she come into my arms she smelled of soap and pine trees and I judged she were 16 or 17 yr. of age.

I confessed immediately I could not dance and she said she would teach me and she fit into my arms as light as a summer breeze. Her eyes were green her skin v. white as it is with girls not long off the boat from home and she and her friend begun to sing and sway it being too late to play the piano Dee Dah Dee Dah.

---

[1]**coifed** carefully arranged

She said her name were Mary Hearn and she had come from the village of Templecrone just this past year she said I were a marvellous student did ever anyone learn the steps so rapidly? I were suddenly more happy than I had ever hoped to be.

Having been 2 days in the saddle I now wished out loud I had a clean shirt and had combed the burrs out of my hair but she said I shouldnt worry for her own da were a blacksmith and farrier back home so the smell of horses made me most familiar and she lay her glossy head against my chest and we danced around the room with Mrs Robinson sitting in her chair knitting a long pink scarf.

No matter what skullduggery and death Fitzy later caused no matter how great a coward & liar he proved himself I still believe he never wanted no more than this in life and when he danced with that bosomy Belinda at Mrs Robinson's there were no malice in him.

We all collapsed out of breath on the pretty sofas they was upholstered in expensive velvet with red & yellow roses in panels at the back and even little cloths to keep the hair oil from staining.

Then Fitzpatrick brought out them parcels and the girls was excited and wondering what could be inside although they knew very well of course.

As the whole world now understands Fitzpatrick were a very poor policeman but he might have worked in a haberdashery and made a honest living off it. He presented one dress to Belinda while I give the other to Mary Hearn and both girls cried out in happiness Mary kissing me on both my cheeks.

The girls departed to try on their gifts so Mrs Robinson brought out the cold leg of lamb cutting us great slabs I were very hungry but knew I must attend to my horse who had not been watered yet. Coming back inside the house I heard my name called out Ned Kelly Ned Kelly.

I followed the call along the passage it were very dark I come around a dogleg and there I found an open door and

Mary Hearn standing in candlelight she were holding the back of the dress together with her hand.

Ned you'll hook me up.

She turned and took her hand away the dress sliding from her to the floor she tasted like butter shortbread I told her what a sweet & pretty thing she were and she put her hand across my mouth and buried her face into my beard.

My daughter I cannot guess how old you are so I ask you not to read no more until you have children of your own even then perhaps you will be like me you will not wish to see inside your parents' door. But do not burn this or destroy what follows I will want it for myself to remember what a joy it were to fall in love.

Then we was playing what they call THE GAME you never knew so many hooks and buttons and sweet smelling things we took them off her one by one until she lay across her bed there were no sin for so did God make her skin so white her hair as black as night her eyes green and her lips smiling. She were a teacher with a mighty vocation pulling and dragging when I took her she were slender and strong as a deer her breasts small but very full she threw back her head offering her pale throat to me I run her to ground I took her breasts took them in my mouth sucking & suckling I didnt know whose milk I stole but she were crying out and holding my hair it were the best thing that happened to me in my life.

We lay close together afterwards and smiled at each other and it were only when her babe awoke that I were upset. I had not known she were the mother of a child and I were ashamed to have acted thus.

Leaving well ahead of dawn I set off back across the rich flats heading up towards the distant Wombat Ranges they was beyond sight of the streets of Benalla. 2 days later I turned down beside Bullock Creek I were not prepared for what I seen.

The Beaux' Stratagem

by George Farquhar

George Farquhar, born in Ireland and educated at Trinity College Dublin, moved to London to advance his career in the theatre. *The Beaux' Stratagem* (first performed in 1707) was his last play and he died in poverty a few months later. The plot is based on Aimwell and Archer, two dashing but penniless young men, travelling the country looking for a wealthy young woman for one of them to marry. In each town they alternately play the role of master and servant. In Lichfield Archer is the servant and he amuses himself by flirting with the landlord's daughter in the pub where they are lodging.

ARCHER Come, my dear, have you conned over the catechise[1] I taught you last night?

CHERRY Come, question me.

ARCHER What is love?

CHERRY Love is I know not what, it comes I know not how, and goes I know not when.

ARCHER Very well, an apt scholar. – *(Chucks her under the chin.)* Where does love enter?

CHERRY Into the eyes.

ARCHER And where go out?

CHERRY I won't tell ye.

ARCHER What are objects of that passion?

CHERRY Youth, beauty, and clean linen.

ARCHER The reason?

CHERRY The two first are fashionable in nature, and the third at court.

ARCHER That's my dear. – What are the signs and tokens of that passion?

---

[1]**catechise** catechism, question-and-answer instruction, typically for knowledge of religious doctrine

CHERRY A stealing look, a stammering tongue, words improbable, designs impossible, and actions impracticable.

ARCHER That's my good child! Kiss me. – What must a lover do to obtain his mistress?

CHERRY He must adore the person that disdains him, he must bribe the chambermaid that betrays him, and court the footman that laughs at him. He must – he must –

ARCHER Nay, child, I must whip you if you don't mind your lesson; he must treat his –

CHERRY O, ay! – He must treat his enemies with respect, his friends with indifference, and all the world with contempt; he must suffer much, and fear more; he must desire much, and hope little; in short, he must embrace his ruin, and throw himself away.

ARCHER Had ever man so hopeful a pupil as mine? – Come, my dear, why is love called a riddle?

CHERRY Because, being blind, he leads those that see, and, though a child, he governs a man.

ARCHER Mighty well! – And why is love pictured blind?

CHERRY Because the painters, out of the weakness or privilege of their art, chose to hide those eyes that they could not draw.

ARCHER That's my dear little scholar; kiss me again. – And why should love, that's a child, govern a man?

CHERRY Because that a child is the end of love.

ARCHER And so ends love's catechism. – And now, my dear, we'll go in, and make my master's bed.

Emma

by Jane Austen

Jane Austen (1775–1817) lived in Hampshire, Bath and Winchester and wrote with great wit and insight about family life within her own social class. In Emma Woodhouse she created her most confident heroine. She is young, attractive and wealthy and she likes to manage other people's lives. She has been busy trying to marry off her pretty and naïve friend Harriet Smith to Mr Elton, the social-climbing vicar of the parish. After a Christmas ball Emma finds herself in the carriage alone with him.

The carriage came; and Mr Woodhouse, always the first object on such occasions, was carefully attended to his own by Mr Knightley and Mr Weston; but not all that either could say could prevent some renewal of alarm at the sight of the snow which had actually fallen, and the discovery of a much darker night than he had been prepared for. 'He was afraid they should have a very bad drive. He was afraid poor Isabella would not like it. And there would be poor Emma in the carriage behind. He did not know what they had best do. They must keep as much together as they could;' and James was talked to, and given a charge to go very slow, and wait for the other carriage.

Isabella stepped in after her father; John Knightley forgetting that he did not belong to their party, stept in after his wife very naturally; so that Emma found, on being escorted and followed into the second carriage by Mr Elton, that the door was to be lawfully shut on them, and that they were to have a *tête-à-tête*[1] drive. It would not have been the awkwardness of a moment, it would have been rather a pleasure, previous to the suspicions of this very day; she could have talked to him of Harriet, and the three-quarters of a mile would have seemed but one. But now, she would rather it had not happened. She

---

[1]***tête-à-tête*** private

believed he had been drinking too much of Mr Weston's good wine, and felt sure that he would want to be talking nonsense.

To restrain him as much as might be, by her own manners, she was immediately preparing to speak, with exquisite calmness and gravity, of the weather and the night; but scarcely had she begun, scarcely had they passed the sweep-gate and joined the other carriage, than she found her subject cut up – her hand seized – her attention demanded, and Mr Elton actually making violent love to her: availing himself of the precious opportunity, declaring sentiments which must be already well known, hoping – fearing – adoring – ready to die if she refused him; but flattering himself that his ardent attachment and unequalled love and unexampled passion could not fail of having some effect, and, in short, very much resolved on being seriously accepted as soon as possible. It really was so. Without scruple – without apology – without much apparent diffidence, Mr Elton, the lover of Harriet, was professing himself *her* lover. She tried to stop him; but vainly; he would go on, and say it all. Angry as she was, the thought of the moment made her resolve to restrain herself when she did speak. She felt that half this folly must be drunkenness, and therefore could hope that it might belong only to the passing hour. Accordingly, with a mixture of the serious and the playful, which she hoped would best suit his half-and-half state, she replied:

'I am very much astonished, Mr Elton. This to *me*! You forget yourself; you take me for my friend; any message to Miss Smith I shall be happy to deliver; but no more of this to *me*, if you please.'

'Miss Smith! message to Miss Smith! What could she possibly mean?' And he repeated her words with such assurance of accent, such boastful pretence of amazement, that she could not help replying with quickness:

'Mr Elton, this is the most extraordinary conduct! and I can account for it only in one way; you are not yourself, or you could not speak either to me or of Harriet in such a manner. Command yourself enough to say no more, and I will endeavour to forget it.'

But Mr Elton had only drunk wine enough to elevate his spirits, not at all to confuse his intellects. He perfectly knew his own meaning; and having warmly protested against her suspicion as most injurious, and slightly touched upon his respect for Miss Smith as her friend, but acknowledging his wonder that Miss Smith should be mentioned at all, he resumed the subject of his own passion, and was very urgent for a favourable answer.

As she thought less of his inebriety, she thought more of his inconstancy and presumption, and with fewer struggles for politeness, replied:

'It is impossible for me to doubt any longer. You have made yourself too clear. Mr Elton, my astonishment is much beyond anything I can express. After such behaviour as I have witnessed during the last month, to Miss Smith – such attentions as I have been in the daily habit of observing – to be addressing me in this manner: this is an unsteadiness of character, indeed, which I had not supposed possible. Believe me, sir, I am far, very far, from gratified in being the object of such professions.'

'Good Heaven!' cried Mr Elton, 'what can be the meaning of this? Miss Smith! I never thought of Miss Smith in the whole course of my existence; never paid her any attentions, but as your friend; never cared whether she were dead or alive, but as your friend. If she has fancied otherwise, her own wishes have misled her, and I am very sorry, extremely sorry. But, Miss Smith, indeed! Oh, Miss Woodhouse, who can think of Miss Smith when Miss Woodhouse is near? No, upon my honour, there is no unsteadiness of character. I have thought only of you. I protest against having paid the smallest attention to any one else. Everything that I have said or done, for many weeks past, has been with the sole view of marking my adoration of yourself. You cannot really seriously doubt it. No' (in an accent meant to be insinuating), 'I am sure you have seen and understood me.'

It would be impossible to say what Emma felt on hearing this; which of all her unpleasant sensations was uppermost. She was too completely overpowered to be immediately able to reply; and two moments of silence being ample encouragement for Mr Elton's sanguine state of mind, he tried to take her hand again, as he joyously exclaimed:

'Charming Miss Woodhouse! allow me to interpret this interesting silence. It confesses that you have long understood me.'

'No, sir,' cried Emma, 'it confesses no such thing. So far from having long understood you I have been in a most complete error with respect to your views, till this moment. As to myself, I am very sorry that you should have been giving way to any feelings. Nothing could be further from my wishes - your attachment to my friend Harriet - your pursuit of her (pursuit it appeared) gave me great pleasure, and I have been very earnestly wishing you success; but had I supposed that she were not your attraction to Hartfield, I should certainly have thought you judged ill in making your visits so frequent. Am I to believe that you have never sought to recommend yourself particularly to Miss Smith - that you have never thought seriously of her?'

'Never, madam,' cried he, affronted in his turn; 'never, I assure you. *I* think seriously of Miss Smith! Miss Smith is a very good sort of girl: and I should be happy to see her respectably settled. I wish her extremely well; and, no doubt, there are men who might not object to - Everybody has their level; but as for myself, I am not, I think, quite so much at a loss. I need not so totally despair of an equal alliance as to be addressing myself to Miss Smith! No, madam, my visits to Hartfield have been for yourself only; and the encouragement I received - '

'Encouragement! I give you encouragement! Sir, you have been entirely mistaken in supposing it. I have seen you only as the admirer of my friend. In no other light could you have been more to me than a common acquaintance. I am exceedingly sorry; but it is well that the mistake ends where it does. Had the same behaviour continued, Miss Smith might have been led into a misconception of your views; not being aware, probably, any more than myself, of the very great inequality which you are so sensible of. But, as it is, the disappointment is single, and, I trust, will not be lasting. I have no thoughts of matrimony at present.'

He was too angry to say another word, her manner too decided to invite supplication; and in this state of swelling resentment, and mutually deep mortification, they had to continue together a few minutes longer, for the fears of Mr Woodhouse had confined them to a foot-pace. If there had not been so much anger, there would have been desperate awkwardness; but their straightforward emotions left no room for the little zigzags of embarrassment. Without knowing when the carriage turned into Vicarage Lane, or when it stopped, they found themselves, all at once, at the door of his house; and he was out before another syllable passed. Emma then felt it indispensable to wish him a good night. The compliment was just returned, coldly and proudly; and, under indescribable irritation of spirits, she was then conveyed to Hartfield.

Samuel Pepys

by Claire Tomalin

Claire Tomalin (born 1943) is best known for her scholarly and sensitive biographies. This biography of the 17th-century diarist Samuel Pepys won the Whitbread Book of the year in 2002.

Pepys (1633–1703) kept a diary, chiefly of his busy life in London. A fellow-diarist, John Evelyn, remembered him as 'a very worthy, industrious and curious person, none in England exceeding him in knowledge of the navy . . . universally beloved, hospitable, generous, learned in many things, skilled in music.'

In chapter 4 Tomalin describes Pepys's courtship and marriage to his young wife.

Pepys wooed the woman who was to be his wife with passion. Thirteen years after his wooing, he relived what he had felt during that time in a moment of intense, recaptured emotion. It came to him as he listened to music in the theatre. The music, he wrote in his Diary, was 'so sweet . . . that it made me really sick, just as I have formerly been when in love with my wife'. Memory and music had merged into one another. 'It ravished me' and 'wrapped up my soul' and 'I remained all night transported so as I could not believe that ever any music hath that real command over the soul of a man as this did upon me'. The music that brought about this magical effect was played, improbably perhaps to some modern ears, on recorders, and, although he does not say so, it accompanied the appearance of Nell Gwyn,[1] as she made a carefully stage-managed descent from the flies to the stage, bearing a basket of fruit and flowers and playing the part of a winged angel. In Pepys's collection of prints there is one of Nell Gwyn wearing little more than a pair of wings, and, though she would have worn rather more on the stage, there was no hiding the fact that she was the most

[1]**Nell Gwyn** famous London actress and mistress to Charles II

celebrated erotic icon of the London theatre. The angel in Dekker and Massinger's *The Virgin Martyr*, the play Pepys was attending, comes on disguised as a boy during the first four acts and appears in heavenly form only in the last; and it could be that her provokingly desirable appearance, as well as the music, was responsible for plunging Pepys into the past in this Proustian[2] way, and reheating the memory of his old love and longing for the body of his Elizabeth.

The sickness of love and the sickness of the stone[3] were the two preoccupations of his early twenties. To speak of love as a mixture of sweetness and sickness as he did is a striking conceit; clearly for him, at twenty-two, it had been an overpowering experience. So much so that it led him to fly in the face of what every intelligent clerk about town knew: that marriage was meant to be a step on the social ladder, and that a bride should bring some money and a worthwhile family alliance; it should not simply be a matter of running passionately after a woman with your nose in her smock. Pepys lost his good sense in his desire for Elizabeth. Nothing is known of how they met, whether in a bookshop or any other sort of shop, or through a friend; he may simply have got into conversation with her in the street. She was pretty enough to catch the eye, with her bright, definite face surrounded by curls, prominent eyes and expressive mouth; and she was a lively talker in two languages, which may have been what first caught the fancy of a man who loved to practise his own skills as a linguist. In the year he met her he bought himself a French *Nouveau Testament*. Being foreign marked her off from other young women. She had lived in Paris, her father was French, and both her parents could boast of a higher social standing than Pepys himself. Alexandre le Marchant de St Michel came of a noble family in the Anjou, and her English mother also had grandly connected, landowning

---

[2]**Proustian** involuntary memory (from the French author Marcel Proust)
[3]**the stone** Pepys suffered from a stone in his kidneys

parents. All this sounded impressive, although in fact they were virtually destitute and friendless when Pepys met her.

Never mind that. He wanted Elizabeth for herself. The pain of his illness, and the question mark it set over his future, can only have sharpened his determination to possess her as soon as he could. If life was to give him no more than this, then at least he would have had her. Whether his wooing was an honourable one from the start or not, it became so. He persuaded himself that he could support a bride on his scant earnings, take her to live in the Montagu lodgings in Whitehall and put everything else out of his mind. He did not discuss his marital intentions with his employer or, it would seem, in any serious manner with her family or his own. There was no question on either side of a marriage settlement.

Elizabeth was fourteen, the same age as his sister Pall, but the two girls were as unlike as it was possible to be and notably failed to become friends, then or at any later time. Pall was only just literate and, according to her brother, far from lovely, 'full of Freckles and not handsome in face', whereas Elizabeth was vivacious as well as attractive, took trouble with her appearance and her clothes, and had acquired some education and polish in spite of her parents' difficulties – she was a reader as well as a talker. Sam took trouble with his love letters; although none survive, the words of a young Cambridge contemporary wooing his future wife suggest the style of the times:

Endeared Sweetheart, When I was last with you there fell into my Bosom such a spark of Love that nothing will quench it but Yourself. The Nature of this Love, is, I hope sincere, the measure of it great, and as far as I know my own Heart it is right and genuine. The very bare probability of success ravished my Heart with Joy . . . I hope the Lord has given You in part your father's Spirit, and has made You all glorious within, he has beautified your Body, very pleasant are You to me. You are in my Heart to live and die in waiting on You; and I extremely please Myself in loving You, and I like my Affections the better because they tell me they are only placed upon You . . . sweet Mrs Betty as I have given my Heart to You, You ought in return to give me Yours, and You cannot in Equity deny it me.

Whether or not Pepys wrote love letters as frank and delightful as this one, Elizabeth found him an eloquent and persuasive lover, and she was ready to be wooed and won.

Betrayal

by Harold Pinter

Harold Pinter (1930–2008) published poetry in periodicals before he wrote his first play in 1957. Since then he has been acclaimed as one of the greatest contemporary playwrights, noted for the colloquial surface of his dialogue. However, he also conveys an underlying menace in many of his characters and dramatises the difficulty of communication even in apparently close relationships.

In *Betrayal*, his play about adultery and its unexpected consequences, he reverses chronology: scene one takes place in 1977 and concludes the story; scene 9 (this extract) is set in 1968, when the story begins. Jerry, invited to a party by his best friend Robert, waits in the bedroom for Robert's wife Emma.

1968

Scene Nine: Robert and Emma's House. Bedroom. 1968. Winter.

The room is dimly lit. JERRY *is sitting in the shadows. Faint music through the door.*

The door opens. Light. Music. EMMA *comes in, closes the door. She goes towards the mirror, sees* JERRY.

EMMA Good God.

JERRY I've been waiting for you.

EMMA What do you mean?

JERRY I knew you'd come.
He drinks.

EMMA I've just come in to comb my hair.
He stands.

JERRY I knew you'd have to. I knew you'd have to comb your hair. I knew you'd have to get away from the party.
She goes to the mirror, combs her hair.
He watches her.
You're a beautiful hostess.

EMMA Aren't you enjoying the party?

JERRY You're beautiful.

He goes to her.

Listen. I've been watching you all night. I must tell you, I want to tell you, I have to tell you –

EMMA Please –

JERRY You're incredible.

EMMA You're drunk.

JERRY Nevertheless.

He holds her.

EMMA Jerry.

JERRY I was best man at your wedding. I saw you in white. I watched you glide by in white.

EMMA I wasn't in white.

JERRY You know what should have happened?

EMMA What?

JERRY I should have had you, in your white, before the wedding. I should have blackened you, in your white wedding dress, blackened you in your bridal dress, before ushering you into your wedding, as your best man.

EMMA My husband's best man. Your best friend's best man.

JERRY No. Your best man.

EMMA I must get back.

JERRY You're lovely. I'm crazy about you. All these words I'm using, don't you see, they've never been said before. Can't you see? I'm crazy about you. It's a whirlwind. Have you ever been to the Sahara Desert? Listen to me. It's true. Listen. You overwhelm me. You're so lovely.

EMMA I'm not.

JERRY You're so beautiful. Look at the way you look at me.

EMMA I'm not . . . looking at you.

JERRY Look at the way you're looking at me. I can't wait for you, I'm bowled over, I'm totally knocked out, you dazzle me, you jewel, my jewel, I can't ever sleep again, no, listen, it's the truth, I won't walk, I'll be a cripple, I'll descend, I'll diminish, into total paralysis, my life is in your hands, that's what you're banishing me to, a state of catatonia,[1] do you know the state of catatonia? do you? do you? the state of . . . where the reigning prince is the prince of emptiness, the prince of absence, the prince of desolation. I love you.

EMMA My husband is at the other side of that door.

JERRY Everyone knows. The world knows. It knows. But they'll never know, they'll never know, they're in a different world. I adore you. I'm madly in love with you. I can't believe that what anyone is at this moment saying has ever happened has ever happened. Nothing has ever happened. Nothing. This is the only thing that has ever happened. Your eyes kill me. I'm lost. You're wonderful.

EMMA No.

JERRY Yes.

He kisses her.
She breaks away.
He kisses her.
Laughter off.
She breaks away.
Door opens. ROBERT.

EMMA Your best friend is drunk.

JERRY As you are my best and oldest friend and, in the present instance, my host, I decided to take this opportunity to tell your wife how beautiful she was.

ROBERT Quite right.

JERRY It is quite right, to . . . to face up to the facts . . . and to offer a token, without blush, a token of one's unalloyed appreciation, no holds barred.

---

[1]**catatonia** psychological illness, linked with schizophrenia, including immobility with periods of violence

ROBERT Absolutely.

JERRY And how wonderful for you that this is so, that this is the case, that her beauty is the case.

ROBERT Quite right.

JERRY *moves to* ROBERT *and takes hold of his elbow.*

JERRY I speak as your oldest friend. Your best man.

ROBERT You are, actually.

He clasps JERRY*'s shoulder, briefly, turns, leaves the room.*

EMMA *moves towards the door.* JERRY *grasps her arm.*

She stops still.

They stand still, looking at each other.

Go, Lovely Rose!

by Edmund Waller

Edmund Waller (1606–1687) was involved in the dangerous politics of the Civil War: he was a member of parliament and supported Charles I; later he was pardoned by Cromwell and restored to favour with the restoration of the monarchy under Charles II. His poems were first published in 1645.

Go, Lovely Rose!, his best-known poem, follows the tradition of 'carpe diem' (a Latin phrase meaning 'seize the day'). The poet/lover, usually male, urges the girl to recognise that her beauty won't last and that life is short, and she should love him before time overtakes them both.

Go, lovely rose!
Tell her that wastes her time and me
That now she knows,
When I resemble her to thee,
How sweet and fair she seems to be.

Tell her that's young,
And shuns to have her graces spied,
That hadst thou sprung
In deserts where no men abide,
Thou must have uncommended died.

Small is the worth
Of beauty from the light retired;
Bid her come forth,
Suffer herself to be desired,
And not blush so to be admired.

Then die, that she
The common fate of all things rare
May read in thee;
How small a part of time they share,
That are so wondrous sweet and fair!

Half of a Yellow Sun

by Chimamanda Ngozi Adichie

Half of a Yellow Sun is dedicated to the memories of both the author's grandfathers, who were amongst the million who died in the Nigerian–Biafran War (1967–1970), and of her grandmothers, who survived the war. Chimamanda Ngozi Adichie (born 1977) traces the lives of two sisters and their lovers during the Biafran War as well as the years immediately preceding the war. The houseboy Ugwu, according to Adichie, 'connects all the characters'. In this extract, taken from the beginning of the novel, he meets his master's beautiful girlfriend for the first time. In an interview the author stated that 'this is a book about love. War is not just a time when people died, but a time when people laughed and loved and came together.'

He had been with Master for four months when Master told him, 'A special woman is coming for the weekend. Very special. You make sure the house is clean. I'll order the food from the staff club.'

'But, sah, I can cook,' Ugwu said, with a sad premonition.

'She's just come back from London, my good man, and she likes her rice a certain way. Fried rice, I think. I'm not sure you could make something suitable.' Master turned to walk away.

'I can make that, sah,' Ugwu said quickly, although he had no idea what fried rice was. 'Let me make the rice, and you get the chicken from the staff club.'

'Artful negotiation,' Master said in English. 'All right, then. You make the rice.'

'Yes, sah,' Ugwu said. Later, he cleaned the rooms and scrubbed the toilet carefully, as he always did, but Master looked at them and said they were not clean enough and went out and bought another jar of Vim powder and asked, sharply, why Ugwu didn't clean the spaces between the tiles. Ugwu cleaned them again. He scrubbed until sweat crawled down the sides of his face, until his arm ached. And on Saturday, he bristled as he cooked. Master had never complained about his work before. It was this woman's fault, this woman that Master considered too special even for him to cook for. Just come back from London, indeed.

When the doorbell rang, he muttered a curse under his breath about her stomach swelling from eating faeces. He heard Master's raised voice, excited and childlike, followed by a long silence and he imagined their hug, and her ugly body pressed to Master's. Then he heard her voice. He stood still. He had always thought that Master's English could not be compared to anybody's, not Professor Ezeka, whose English one could hardly hear, or Okeoma, who spoke English as if he were speaking Igbo, with the same cadences and pauses, or Patel, whose English was a faded lilt. Not even the white man Professor Lehman, with his words forced out through his nose, sounded as dignified as Master. Master's English was music, but what Ugwu was hearing now, from this woman, was magic. Here was a superior tongue, a luminous language, the kind of English he heard on Master's radio, rolling out with clipped precision. It reminded him of slicing a yam with a newly sharpened knife, the easy perfection in every slice.

'Ugwu!' Master called. 'Bring Coke!'

Ugwu walked out to the living room. She smelt of coconuts. He greeted her, his 'Good afternoon' a mumble, his eyes on the floor.

'*Kedu?*' she asked.

'I'm well, mah.' He still did not look at her. As he uncorked the bottle, she laughed at something Master said. Ugwu was about to pour the cold Coke into her glass when she touched his hand and said, '*Rapuba*, don't worry about that.'

Her hand was lightly moist. 'Yes, mah.'

'Your master has told me how well you take care of him, Ugwu,' she said. Her Igbo words were softer than her English, and he was disappointed at how easily they came out. He wished she would stumble in her Igbo; he had not expected English that perfect to sit beside equally perfect Igbo.

'Yes, mah,' he mumbled. His eyes were still focused on the floor.

'What have you cooked us, my good man?' Master asked, as if he did not know. He sounded annoyingly jaunty.

'I serve now, sah,' Ugwu said, in English, and then wished he had said *I am serving now*, because it sounded better, because it would impress her more. As he set the table, he kept from glancing at the living room, although he could hear her laughter and Master's voice, with its irritating new timbre.

He finally looked at her as she and Master sat down at the table. Her oval face was smooth like an egg, the lush colour of rain-drenched earth, and her eyes were large and slanted and she looked like she was not supposed to be walking and talking like everyone else; she should be in a glass case like the one in Master's study, where people could admire her curvy, fleshy body, where she would be preserved untainted. Her hair was long; each of the plaits that hung down to her neck ended in a soft fuzz. She smiled easily; her teeth were the same bright white of her eyes. He did not know how long he stood staring at her until Master said, 'Ugwu usually does a lot better than this. He makes a fantastic stew.'

'It's quite tasteless, which is better than bad-tasting, of course,' she said, and smiled at Master before turning to Ugwu. 'I'll show you how to cook rice properly, Ugwu, without using so much oil.'

'Yes, mah,' Ugwu said. He had invented what he imagined was fried rice, frying the rice in groundnut oil, and had half-hoped it would send them both to the toilet in a hurry. Now, though, he wanted to cook a perfect meal, a savoury *jollof* rice or his special stew with *arigbe*, to show her how well he could cook. He delayed washing up so that the running water would not drown out her voice. When he served them tea, he took his time rearranging the biscuits on the saucer so that he could linger and listen to her, until Master said, 'That's quite all right, my good man.' Her name was Olanna. But Master said it only once; he mostly called her *nkem*, my own. They talked about the quarrel between the Sardauna and the premier of the Western Region, and then Master said something about waiting until she moved to Nsukka and how it was only a few weeks away after all. Ugwu held his breath to make sure he had heard clearly. Master was laughing now, saying, 'But we will live here together, *nkem*, and you can keep the Elias Avenue flat as well.'

She would move to Nsukka. She would live in this house. Ugwu walked away from the door and stared at the pot on the stove. His life would change. He would learn to cook fried rice and he would have to use less oil and he would take orders from her. He felt sad, and yet his sadness was incomplete; he felt expectant, too, an excitement he did not entirely understand.

That evening, he was washing Master's linen in the backyard, near the lemon tree, when he looked up from the basin of soapy water and saw her standing by the back door, watching him. At first, he was sure it was his imagination, because the people he thought the most about often appeared to him in visions. He had imaginary conversations with Anulika all the time, and, right after he touched himself at night, Nnesinachi would appear briefly with a mysterious smile on her face. But Olanna was really at the door. She was walking across the yard towards him. She had only a wrapper tied around her chest, and as she walked, he imagined that she was a yellow cashew, shapely and ripe.

'Mah? You want anything?' he asked. He knew that if he reached out and touched her face, it would feel like butter, the kind Master unwrapped from a paper packet and spread on his bread.

'Let me help you with that.' She pointed at the bedsheet he was rinsing, and slowly he took the dripping sheet out. She held one end and moved back. 'Turn yours that way,' she said.

He twisted his end of the sheet to his right while she twisted to her right, and they watched as the water was squeezed out. The sheet was slippery.

'Thank, mah,' he said.

She smiled. Her smile made him feel taller. 'Oh, look, those pawpaws are almost ripe. *Lotekwa*, don't forget to pluck them.'

There was something polished about her voice, about her; she was like the stone that lay right below a gushing spring, rubbed smooth by years and years of sparkling water, and looking at her was similar to finding that stone, knowing that there were so few like it. He watched her walk back indoors.

He did not want to share the job of caring for Master with anyone, did not want to disrupt the balance of his life with Master, and yet it was suddenly unbearable to think of not seeing her again. Later, after dinner, he tiptoed to Master's bedroom and rested his ear on the door. She was moaning loudly, sounds that seemed so unlike her, so uncontrolled and stirring and throaty. He stood there for a long time, until the moans stopped, and then he went back to his room.

Paradise Lost

by John Milton

John Milton (1608–1674) supported the anti-royalists and worked as a secretary to Oliver Cromwell in the English Civil War. He developed a great skill in writing lyrical poetry but felt a vocation to create a great epic poem in English to match the work of Homer and Virgil. *Paradise Lost* describes the creation of the world and the Fall of Adam and Eve, through which Milton aims to 'justify the works of God to men'. This extract is taken from Book 9, in which Satan, embodied in the serpent, speaks to Eve alone in the Garden of Eden. He intends to tempt her into eating from the forbidden tree, so disobeying God. To reach this point he first uses the language of flattery and seduction.

With tract oblique
At first, as one who sought access, but feard
To interrupt, side-long he works his way.
As when a Ship by skilful Stearsman wrought
Nigh Rivers mouth or Foreland, where the Wind
Veres oft, as oft so steers, and shifts her Saile;
So varied hee, and of his tortuous Traine
Curld many a wanton wreath in sight of Eve,
To lure her Eye; shee busied heard the sound
Of rusling Leaves, but minded not, as us'd
To such disport before her through the Field,
From every Beast, more duteous at her call
Then at Circean[1] call the Herd disguis'd.
Hee boulder now, uncalld before her stood;
But as in gaze admiring: Oft he bowd
His turret Crest, and sleek enameld Neck,
Fawning, and lickd the ground whereon she trod.
His gentle dumb expression turnd at length

---

[1]**Circean** of the witch, Circe, in Greek mythology, who transformed her enemies into animals through the use of magical potions.

The Eye of Eve to mark his play; hee glad
Of her attention gaind, with Serpent Tongue
Organic, or impulse of vocal Air,
His fraudulent temptation thus began.
   Wonder not, sovran Mistress, if perhaps
Thou canst, who art sole Wonder, much less arm
Thy looks, the Heav'n of mildness, with disdain,
Displeas'd that I approach thee thus, and gaze
Insatiat, I thus single, nor have feard
Thy awful brow, more awful thus retir'd.
Fairest resemblance of thy Maker faire,
Thee all things living gaze on, all things thine
By gift, and thy Celestial Beautie adore
With ravishment beheld, there best beheld
Where universally admir'd; but here
In this enclosure wild, these Beasts among,
Beholders rude, and shallow to discerne
Half what in thee is fair, one man except,
Who sees thee? (and what is one?) who shouldst be seen
A Goddess among Gods, ador'd and serv'd
By Angels numberless, thy daily Train.

The Line of Beauty

by Alan Hollinghurst

Alan Hollinghurst (born 1954) won the Man Booker Prize with this novel, which tells of 20 year-old Nick Guest beginning to come to terms with his homosexuality. He is living with the prosperous London family of an MP, Gerald Fedden, his wife Rachel and their son, Nick's schoolfriend Toby. Most of the family are away and Nick is 'Looking after the Cat', i.e. keeping an eye on Toby's volatile sister Catherine. Nick has responded to an ad placed in the newspaper by Leo: 'Black guy, late 20s, v. good-looking, interests cinema, music, politics, seeks intelligent like-minded guy 18–40'.

Nick had never been on a date with a man before, and was much less experienced than Catherine imagined. In the course of their long conversations about men he had let one or two of his fantasies assume the status of fact, had lied a little, and had left some of Catherine's assumptions about him unchallenged. His confessed but entirely imaginary seductions took on – partly through the special effort required to invent them and repeat them consistently – the quality of real memories. He sometimes had the sense, from a hint of reserve in people he was talking to, that while they didn't believe him they saw he was beginning to believe himself. He had only come out fully in his last year at Oxford, and had used his new licence mainly to flirt with straight boys. His heart was given to Toby, with whom flirting would have been inappropriate, almost sacrilegious.[1] He wasn't quite ready to accept the fact that if he was going to have a lover it wouldn't be Toby, or any other drunk straight boy hopping the fence, it would be a gay lover – that compromised thing that he himself would then become. Proper queens, whom he applauded and feared and hesitantly imitated, seemed often to find something wrong with him, pretty and clever though he

---

[1]**sacrilegious** violating what is sacred

was. At any rate they didn't want to go to bed with him, and he was free to wander back, in inseparable relief and discouragement, to his inner theatre of sexual make-believe. There the show never ended and the actors never tired and a certain staleness of repetition was the only hazard. So the meeting with Leo, pursued through all the obstacles of the system which alone made it possible, was momentous for Nick. Pausing for a last hopeful gaze into the gilt arch of the hall mirror, which monitored all comings and goings, he found it reluctant to give its approval; when he pulled the door shut and set off along the street he felt giddily alone, and had to remind himself he was doing all this for pleasure. It had taken on the mood of a pointless dare.

As he hurried down the hill he started focusing again on his Interests and Ambitions, the rather surprising topic for the meeting. He saw that interests weren't always a sexy thing. A shared passion for a subject, large or small, could quickly put two strangers into a special state of subdued rapture and rivalry, distantly resembling love; but you had to hit on the subject. As for ambitions, he felt it was hard to announce them without sounding either self-deluding or feeble, and in fact unambitious. Gerald could say, 'I want to be Home Secretary,' and have people smiling but conceding the possibility. Whereas Nick's ambition was to be loved by a handsome black man in his late twenties with a racing bike and a job in local government. This was the one thing he wasn't going to be able to admit to Leo himself.

He fixed his thoughts for the hundredth time on the little back bar of the Chepstow Castle, which he had chosen for its shadowy semi-privacy – a space incuriously glanced into by people being served in the public bar, but barely used on summer evenings when everyone stood outside on the pavement. There was an amber light in there, among the old whisky mirrors and photographs of horse-drawn drays. He saw himself sitting shoulder to shoulder with Leo, their hands joined in secret on the dusty moquette.

As he approached the pub he registered a black man at the edge of the crowd of drinkers, then knew it was Leo, then pretended he hadn't seen him. So he was quite small; and he'd grown a kind of beard. Why was he waiting in the street? Nick was already beside him and looked again, very nervously, and saw his questioning smile.

'If you don't want to know me . . . ' Leo said.

Nick staggered and laughed and stuck out his hand. 'I thought you'd be inside.'

Leo nodded, and looked down the street. 'This way I can see you coming.'

'Ah . . . ' Nick laughed again.

'Besides, I wasn't sure about the bike, in this area.' And there the bike was, refined, weightless, priceless, the bike of the future, shackled to the nearest lamp-post.

'Oh, I'm sure it will be fine.' Nick frowned and gazed. He was surprised that Leo thought this a bad area. Of course he thought it was rather dangerous himself; and three or four corners away there were pubs he knew he could never enter, so bad were their names, and so intense the mana of their glimpsed interiors. But here . . . . A tall Rastafarian[2] strolled by, and his roll of the head was a greeting to Leo, who nodded and then looked away with what seemed to Nick a guarded admission of kinship.

'We'll have a little chat outside, eh?'

Nick went in to get the drinks. He stood at the counter looking through to the back bar – where in fact there were several people talking, perhaps one of those groups that meet in a pub, and the room was brighter than he remembered it or would have wanted it. Everything seemed to be a bit different. Leo was only having a Coke, but Nick needed courage for the evening and his own identical-looking drink had a double rum in it. He had never drunk rum before, and was always aston-

---

[2]**Rastafarian** recent monotheistic religion, which believes that Haile Selassie, Emperor of Ethiopia, is a messiah

ished that anyone liked Coke. His mind held the floating image of the man he had longed to meet, whom he had touched for a moment and left outside in all his disconcerting reality. He was too sexy, he was too much what he wanted, in his falling-down jeans and his tight blue shirt. Nick was worried by his obvious intention to seduce, or at least to show his capacity for seduction. He took the drinks out with a light tremble.

There wasn't anywhere to sit down, so they stood and leaned against a brown-tiled window sill; in the opaque lower half of the window the word SPIRITS was etched in fancy Victorian capitals, their serifs[3] spiralling out in interlacing tendrils. Leo looked at Nick frankly, since that was what he was here for, and Nick grinned and blushed, which made Leo smile too, for a moment.

Nick said, 'You're growing a beard, I see.'

'Yeah – sensitive skin . . . it's a bloodbath when I shave. Literally,' said Leo, with a quick glance that showed Nick that he liked to make his point. 'Then if I don't shave, I get these ingrowing hairs, fucking murder, have to pick the ends out with a pin.' He stroked his stubbly jaw with a small fine hand, and Nick saw that he had those shaving-bumps he had half-noticed on other black men. 'I tend to leave it for four days, say, five days, maybe, then have a good shave: try and avoid both problems that way.'

'Right . . . ' said Nick, and smiled, partly because he was learning something interesting.

'Most of them still recognize me, though,' said Leo, and gave a wink.

'No, it wasn't that,' said Nick, who was too shy to explain his own shyness. His glance slipped up and down between Leo's loose crotch and the neat shallow cushion of his hair, and tended to avoid his handsome face. He was taking Leo's word for it that he was handsome, but it didn't quite cover the

---

[3]**serifs** the decorative lines added to letters (for example, T) in certain font styles

continuing shock of what was beautiful, strange, and even ugly about him. The phrase 'most of them' slowly took on meaning in his mind. 'Anyway,' he said, and took a quick sip of his drink, which had a reassuring burn to it. 'I suppose you've had lots of replies.' Sometimes when he was nervous he asked questions to which he would rather not have known the answers.

Leo made a little puff of comic exhaustion. 'Yeah . . . yeah, I'm not answering some of them. It's a joke. They don't include a picture, or if they do they look horrible. Or they're ninety-nine years old. I even had a thing from a woman, a lesbian woman admittedly, with a view to would I father her child.' Leo frowned indignantly but there was something sly and flattered in his look too. 'And some of the stuff they write. It's disgusting! It's not like I'm just looking for a bonk, is it? This is something a bit different.'

'Quite,' said Nick – though bonk was a troublingly casual way of referring to something which preoccupied him so much.

'This dog's been round the block a few times,' Leo said, and looked off down the street as if he might spot himself coming home. 'Anyway, you looked nice. You've got nice writing.'

'Thanks. So have you.'

Leo took in the compliment with a nod. 'And you can spell,' he said.

Nick laughed. 'Yes, I'm good at that.' He'd been afraid that his own little letter sounded pedantic and virginal, but it seemed he'd got it about right. He didn't remember it calling for any great virtuosity of spelling. 'I always have trouble with "moccasin",' he said.

'Ah, there you are . . . ' said Leo, with a wary chuckle, before changing the subject. 'It's nice where you live,' he said.

'Oh . . . yes . . . ' said Nick, as if he couldn't quite remember where it was.

'I went by there the other day, on the bike. I nearly rang your bell.'

'Mm – you should have. I've had the place virtually to myself.' He felt sick at the thought of the missed chance.

'Yeah? I saw this girl going in . . . '

'Oh, that was probably only Catherine.'

Leo nodded. 'Catherine. She's your sister, yeah?'

'No, I don't have a sister. She's actually the sister of my friend Toby.' Nick smiled and stared: 'It's not my house.'

'Oh . . . ' said Leo. 'Oh.'

'God, I don't come from that sort of background. No, I just live there. It belongs to Toby's parents. I've just got a tiny little room up in the attic.' Nick was rather surprised to hear himself throwing his whole fantasy of belonging there out of the window.

Leo looked a bit disappointed. He said, 'Right . . . ' and shook his head slowly.

'I mean they're very good friends, they're a sort of second family to me, but I probably won't be there for long. It's just to help me out, while I'm getting started at university.'

'And I thought I'd got myself a nice little rich boy,' Leo said. And perhaps he meant it, Nick couldn't be sure, they were total strangers after all, though a minute before he'd imagined them naked together in the Feddens' emperor-size bed. Was that why his letter did the trick – the address, the Babylonian notepaper?

'Sorry,' he said, with a hint of humour. He drank some more of the sweet strong rum and Coke, so obviously not his kind of drink. The refined blue of the dusk sky was already showing its old lonely reach.

Leo laughed. 'I'm only kidding you!'

'I know,' Nick said, with a little smile, as Leo reached out and squeezed his shoulder, just by his shirt collar, and slowly let go. Nick reacted with his own quick pat at Leo's side. He was absurdly relieved. A charge passed into him through Leo's fingers, and he saw the two of them kissing passionately, in a rush of imagination that was as palpable as this awkward pavement rendezvous.

'Still, your friends must be rich,' Leo said.

Nick was careful not to deny this. 'Oh, they're rolling in money.'

'Yeah . . . ' Leo crooned, with a fixed smile; he might have been savouring the fact or condemning it. Nick saw further questions coming, and decided at once he wouldn't tell him about Gerald. The evening demanded enough courage as it was. A Tory MP would shadow their meeting like an unwelcome chaperon, and Leo would get on his bike and leave them to it. He could say something about Rachel's family, perhaps, if an explanation was called for. But in fact Leo emptied his glass and said, 'Same again?'

Nick hastily finished his own drink, and said, 'Thanks. Or maybe this time I'll have a shot of rum in it.'

Joseph Andrews

by Henry Fielding

In *Joseph Andrews*, Henry Fielding (1707–1754) was writing partly to parody Samuel Richardson's novel *Pamela*, which praises the virtue of a servant girl who rejects sexual pressure from her employer. Fielding invents a brother for Pamela; he too values his 'virtue'. Fielding has thus reversed the gender roles: in this extract it is the woman who has the greater age, status, power and worldly experience. Lady Booby is recently widowed and should be showing all the grave decorum of grief which society requires, but she has fallen in lust with her handsome young servant, Joseph.

At this time an accident happened which put a stop to those agreeable walks, which probably would have soon puffed up the cheeks of Fame, and caused her to blow her brazen trumpet through the town; and this was no other than the death of Sir Thomas Booby, who, departing this life, left his disconsolate lady confined to her house, as closely as if she herself had been attacked by some violent disease. During the first six days the poor lady admitted none but Mrs. Slipslop, and three female friends, who made a party at cards: but on the seventh she ordered Joey, whom, for a good reason, we shall hereafter call JOSEPH, to bring up her tea-kettle. The lady being in bed, called Joseph to her, bade him sit down, and, having accidentally laid her hand on his, she asked him if he had ever been in love. Joseph answered, with some confusion, it was time enough for one so young as himself to think on such things. 'As young as you are,' replied the lady, 'I am convinced you are no stranger to that passion. Come, Joey,' says she, 'tell me truly, who is the happy girl whose eyes have made a conquest of you?' Joseph returned, that all the women he had ever seen were equally indifferent to him. 'Oh then,' said the lady, 'you are a general lover. Indeed, you handsome fellows, like handsome women, are very long and difficult in fixing; but yet you shall never persuade me that your heart is so insusceptible of affection; I rather impute what you say to your secrecy, a very commendable quality, and what I am far from being angry with you for. Nothing can be more unworthy in a young man, than to betray any intimacies with the ladies.' 'Ladies! madam,' said Joseph, 'I am sure I never had the impudence to think of any that deserve that name.' 'Don't pretend to too much modesty,' said she, 'for that sometimes may be impertinent: but pray answer me this question. Suppose a lady should happen to like you; suppose she should prefer you to all your sex, and admit you to the same familiarities as you might have hoped for if you had been born her equal, are you certain that no vanity could tempt you to discover her? Answer me honestly, Joseph; have you so much more sense and so much more virtue than you handsome young fellows generally have, who make no scruple of sacrificing our dear reputation to your pride, without considering the great obligation we lay on you by our condescension and confidence? Can you keep a secret, my Joey?' 'Madam,' says he, 'I hope your ladyship can't tax me with ever betraying the secrets of the family; and I hope, if you was to turn me away, I might have that character of you.' 'I don't intend to turn you away, Joey,' said she, and sighed; 'I am afraid it is not in my power.' She then raised herself a little in her bed, and discovered one of the whitest necks that ever was seen; at which Joseph blushed. 'La!' says she, in an affected surprise, 'what am I doing? I have trusted myself with a man alone, naked in bed; suppose you should have any wicked intentions upon my honour, how should I defend myself?' Joseph protested that he never had the least evil design against her. 'No,' says she, 'perhaps you may not call your designs wicked; and perhaps they are not so.' – He swore they were not. 'You misunderstand me,' says she; 'I mean if they were against my honour, they may not be wicked; but the world calls them so. But then, say you, the world will never know anything of the matter; yet would not that be trusting to your secrecy? Must not my reputation be then in your power? Would you not then be my master?' Joseph begged her ladyship to be comforted; for that he would never imagine the least wicked thing against her, and that he had rather die a thousand deaths than give her any reason to suspect him. 'Yes,' said she, 'I must have reason to suspect you. Are you not a man? and, without vanity, I may pretend to some charms. But perhaps you may fear I should prosecute you; indeed I hope you do; and yet Heaven knows I should never have the confidence to appear before a court of justice; and you know, Joey, I am of a forgiving temper. Tell me, Joey, don't you think I should forgive you?' – 'Indeed, madam,' says Joseph, 'I will never do anything to disoblige your ladyship.' – 'How,' says she, 'do you think it would not disoblige me then? Do you think I would willingly suffer you?' – 'I don't understand you, madam,' says Joseph. – 'Don't you?' said she, 'then you are either a fool, or pretend to be so; I find I was mistaken in you. So get you downstairs, and never let me see your face again; your pretended innocence cannot impose on me.' – 'Madam,' said Joseph, 'I would not have your ladyship think any evil of me. I have always endeavoured to be a dutiful servant both to you and my master.' – 'O thou villain!' answered my lady; 'why didst thou mention the name of that dear man, unless to torment me, to bring his precious memory to my mind?' (and then she burst into a fit of tears.) 'Get thee from my sight! I shall never endure thee more.' At which words she turned away from him; and Joseph retreated from the room in a most disconsolate condition, and writ that letter which the reader will find in the next chapter.

The Lover: a Ballad

by Lady Mary Wortley Montague

Lady Mary Pierrepont (1689–1762) married Lord Wortley Montague, who became ambassador to Turkey. She travelled with him and was soon well known for her letters and travel writing. On their return to London in 1717 she became famous for her wit and intellect. In 1739 the couple left England and spent 23 years in France and Italy. This satirical ballad mocks the social expectation that women should simply conform to the conditions of male-dominated courtship.

At length, by so much importunity[1] pressed,
Take, Molly, at once, the inside of my breast;
This stupid indifference so often you blame
Is not owing to nature, to fear, or to shame:
I am not as cold as a virgin in lead,
Nor is Sunday's sermon so strong in my head:
I know but too well how time flies along,
That we live but few years, and yet fewer are young.

But I hate to be cheated, and never will buy
Long years of repentance for moments of joy.
Oh! was there a man (but where shall I find
Good sense and good nature so equally joined?)
Would value his pleasure, contribute to mine;
Not meanly would boast, nor lewdly design;
Not over severe, yet not stupidly vain,
For I would have the power, though not give the pain.

No pedant, yet learnèd; not rake-helly[2] gay,
Or laughing, because he has nothing to say;
To all my whole sex obliging and free,

---

[1]**importunity** urging
[2]**rake-helly** adverb coined from 'rake-hell', a debauched man

Yet never be fond of any but me;
In public, preserve the decorums are just,[3]
And show in his eyes he is true to his trust;
Then rarely approach, and respectfully bow,
Yet not fulsomely pert, nor yet foppishly[4] low.

But when the long hours of public are past,
And we meet with champagne and a chicken at last,
May every fond pleasure that hour endear;
Be banished afar both discretion and fear.
Forgetting or scorning the airs of the crowd,
He may cease to be formal, and I to be proud,
Till lost in the joy, we confess that we live,
And he may be rude, and yet I may forgive.

And that my delight may be solidly fixed,
Let the friend and the lover be handsomely mixed;
In whose tender bosom my soul might confide,
Whose kindness can soothe me, whose counsel could guide.
From such a dear lover, as here I describe,
No danger should fright me, no millions should bribe;
But till this astonishing creature I know,
As I long have lived chaste, I will keep myself so.

I never will share with the wanton coquette,[5]
Or be caught by a vain affectation of wit.
The toasters and songsters may try all their art,
But never shall enter the pass of my heart.
I loathe the lewd rake, the dressed fopling despise:
Before such pursuers the nice virgin flies:
And as Ovid has sweetly in parables told,
We harden like trees, and like rivers are cold.

---

[3]**preserve the decorums are just** follow the etiquette that is appropriate
[4]**foppishly** foolishly
[5]**coquette** flirt

Questions

In all of these questions you should consider:

a the ways the writers' choice of form, structure and language shape your responses to the extracts

b how your wider reading in the literature of love has contributed to your understanding and interpretation of the extracts.

1 Examine the language used by the man to express devotion and commitment to the woman. Consider especially the extracts by Chaucer, Milton and Austen and compare the authors' methods.

2 Both Cummings and Tennyson celebrate a woman's beauty and the impact she has on a man. Compare the poets' use of imagery and rhythmical verse to show their heightened feelings.

3 What is persuasive about Waller's brief lyric *Go, Lovely Rose!*? Why do you think the speaker addresses the rose rather than the woman?

4 Jane Austen is known for her comic and ironical writing. In this extract, which of the two characters – Emma or Mr Elton – is more of a comic target? Give reasons and evidence for your views.

5 How does Fielding make Lady Booby a comic character?

6 Sammy in the extract from *Free Fall*, Archer in *The Beaux' Stratagem*, Jerry in *Betrayal* and Leo in *The Line of Beauty* all use language for the purpose of seduction. In what ways do you find their approaches persuasive? In what ways are they disagreeable?

7 Which of the arguments that Lady Mary Wortley Montague makes in her ballad do you find most convincing and why?

Further reading

- Chaucer's *Troilus and Criseyde* (extract p. 6) is an extended story, often very moving. In shorter poems such as *The Franklin's Tale* and the *Parlement of Foulys* Chaucer tells more tales of dedicated lovers; in *The Knight's Tale*, written in high style, he describes two noblemen competing for the same woman – a story parodied in the more robust and earthy *Miller's Tale*.
- If you enjoy shorter poems, you will find beautiful lyrics and sequences of sonnets written in the English renaissance of the 16th and early 17th centuries by Shakespeare, Spenser, Wyatt, Surrey, Daniel, Drayton and many others.
- Elizabethan and Jacobean playwrights (around 1580–1620) borrowed old stories, largely English and Italian, to dramatise the pursuit of love: Shakespeare's *Romeo and Juliet* and *Antony and Cleopatra* are both about doomed lovers; in *As You Like It*, *Much Ado about Nothing* and *A Midsummer Night's Dream* the lovers overcome their difficulties and find their reward.
- If wit and city comedy are to your taste, you might try Restoration comedy (plays written around 1700 by Wycherley, Congreve, Vanbrugh and Etherege): men with charm and panache achieve the great prize of the beautiful and often wealthy heroine, whereas those who are foppish, stupid and ineffectual gain nothing but mockery.
- Some of the great novelists, with their extended narrative scope, can explore the complications of a love pursuit. Henry Fielding wrote *Tom Jones* soon after his great comic success with *Joseph Andrews* (see p. 51); it is packed even more with robust events. The extract from *Emma* (p. 23), with its gentler comedy and psychological delicacy, may encourage you to try Austen's other novels, particularly *Pride and Prejudice* or *Persuasion*. Though the men take the initiatives in courtship, Austen's stories are told through the women and their feelings.
- Some 20th-century novels, such as Faulks's *Birdsong* or de Bernieres's *Captain Corelli's Mandolin* use war as a background to the love story; in some, such as Pat Barker's *Life Class*, the war is so much in the foreground that it seems to alter the lover's identity and complicate the pursuit.

2 Unrequited love

The phrase 'unrequited love' describes love that is not returned or reciprocated, a desire unfulfilled, or passion unconsummated. Yet it may be 'better to have loved and lost / than never to have loved at all' (Tennyson, *In Memoriam*). Indeed, Charles Ryder discovers in Evelyn Waugh's *Brideshead Revisited* that 'to know and to love another human being is the root of all wisdom'. Perhaps the very act of loving confers on the lover a state of grace, whether or not it is returned or fulfilled. Yeats embraces the state of loving unreservedly in his poem *The Folly of Being Comforted* (p. 81). Those who attempt to distract or console him, he states, are misguided, offering cheap reassurance.

Much writing in the literature of love is about the search to find the appropriate words to convey love: this journey has been described by some critical theorists as 'the Postmodern sublime'. This phrase indicates both the despair of ever finding language adequate to experience – a Postmodern problem – and also a yearning for something that has never been possessed – 'the sublime'. In the story from Ovid's *Metamorphoses*, adapted by the poet Ted Hughes (p. 61), the nymph Echo burns with desire for the exquisitely beautiful young man, Narcissus, but the only way she can communicate this passion is by echoing his words. She is as much deprived of love as she is of the power to communicate. She has experienced the glory of the vision, the sublime, but words fail her.

On the other hand, Judith, the Cambridge-educated heroine in Rosamond Lehmann's novel *Dusty Answer*, is confident that she can communicate her love for her childhood friend Roddy after a romantic night with him on the river. She is articulate and clever. She has a voice. Her love must be told and she hastens to write him a passionate love letter that very evening. But she has failed to pick up on warning signals such as Roddy's teasing comment that she is a 'tiger for conversation', and this effusive outpouring of her love for him misfires disastrously (p. 68).

In *The Glass Menagerie* by Tennessee Williams, Laura has silently adored Jim since her schooldays. In the extract from the final scene (p. 73), Jim encourages her to give a voice to this love: 'Let yourself go, now, Laura, just let yourself go'. And this letting go and articulating her love is a necessary healing, even though she has to release him because he is already engaged. Jim helps her to embrace (and face) the pain of unrequited love whilst simultaneously showing her that she is loved. Neither Echo nor Judith receives this warm generosity. Language fails them.

Unrequited love is about absence. The loved one is not present so how can love possibly be consummated? The speakers in the sonnets by Sidney and Barnfield ache for actual physical contact, to touch, hold and caress the beloved, and they envy the material world which comes into daily contact with their loved one. In Sidney's poem, the 'dear one', Stella, pays more attention to her pet dog than to the devoted Astrophel; Barnfield enjoys the homoerotic conceit of wishing that he was his (male) lover's pillow, enveloped in endless sexual pleasure. Carol Ann Duffy, writing four centuries later, develops the transgressive[1] (here both sexual and socio-economic) nature of this desire. The speaker in the dramatic monologue *Warming her Pearls* is a lady's maid, who has worn her mistress' pearls all day close to her skin. She intimately desires her mistress, 'burning' alone at night when the pearls are removed.

Finally, the potentially absurd position of the unrequited lover may be comically humorous to those around. In *Cold Comfort Farm* Stella Gibbons parodies[2] its excesses (p. 87). She craftily juxtaposes the release of the bull Big Business, who has suddenly bellowed his 'thick, dark-red note', with the unwelcome arrival of the surly rejected lover, Urk, who is bedecked with dead animals.

---

[1]**transgressive** deviating from custom or law
[2]**parodies** imitates in a mocking way

Tales from Ovid: Echo and Narcissus

by Ted Hughes

Ted Hughes (1930–1998) was renowned for the passion and violence within his poetry, which depicts the startling unpredictability of the natural world. He became Poet Laureate in 1984. In the year before his death, he adapted 24 tales from Ovid's *Metamorphoses* in free verse. The tales tell of how passion 'combusts, or levitates, or mutates' so that bodies are 'changed [. . .] into other bodies'. The nymph Echo is besotted with the handsome youth Narcissus. But he is not interested.

The moment Echo saw Narcissus
She was in love. She followed him
Like a starving wolf
Following a stag too strong to be tackled.
And like a cat in winter at a fire
She could not edge close enough
To what singed her, and would burn her.
She almost burst
With longing to call out to him and somehow
Let him know what she felt.
But she had to wait
For some other to speak
So she could snatch their last words
With whatever sense they might lend her.

It so happened, Narcissus
Had strayed apart
From his companions.
He hallooed them: 'Where are you?
I'm here.' And Echo
Caught at the syllables as if they were precious:
'I'm here,' she cried, 'I'm here' and 'I'm here' and 'I'm here.'

Narcissus looked around wildly.
'I'll stay here,' he shouted.
'You come to me.' And 'Come to me,'
Shouted Echo. 'Come to me,
To me, to me, to me.'
Narcissus stood baffled,
Whether to stay or go. He began to run,
Calling as he ran: 'Stay there.' But Echo
Cried back, weeping to utter it, 'Stay there,
Stay there, stay there, stay there.'
Narcissus stopped and listened. Then, more quietly,
'Let's meet halfway. Come.' And Echo
Eagerly repeated it: 'Come.'

But when she emerged from the undergrowth
Her expression pleading,
Her arms raised to embrace him,
Narcissus turned and ran.
'No,' he cried 'no, I would sooner be dead
Than let you touch me.' Echo collapsed in sobs,
As her voice lurched among the mountains:
'Touch me, touch me, touch me, touch me.'

Echo moped under the leaves.
Humiliated, she hid
In the deep woods. From that day
Like a hurt lynx, for her
Any cave was a good home.
But love was fixed in her body
Like a barbed arrow. There it festered
With his rejection. Sleeplessly
She brooded over the pain,
Wasting away as she suffered,
The petal of her beauty
Fading and shrivelling, falling from her –
Leaving her voice and bones.

Her bones, they say, turned
Into stone, sinking into the humus.
Her voice roamed off by itself,
Unseen in the forest, unseen
On the empty mountainside –
Though all could hear it
Living the only life left to Echo.

Venus and Adonis

by William Shakespeare

Shakespeare (1564–1616) made his reputation with this poem, which ranks alongside Marlowe's *Hero and Leander* for its new and erotic treatment of an old legend. Venus, the goddess of love, falls in love with a beautiful young man, Adonis. She begs to meet him again, but he is devoted to hunting. The next day she hears the baying of his hounds and finds him killed by the boar he was chasing. In this extract from early in the poem there is sensuality, comedy and pathos in the way she tries to seduce Adonis.

'I have been wooed, as I entreat thee now,
Even by the stern and direful god of war,
Whose sinewy neck in battle ne'er did bow,
Who conquers where he comes in every jar;[1]
Yet hath he been my captive and my slave,
And begged for that which thou unasked shalt have.

'Over my altars hath he hung his lance,
His batt'red shield, his uncontrollèd crest,
And for my sake hath learned to sport and dance,
To toy, to wanton,[2] dally, smile and jest,
Scorning his churlish drum and ensign red,
Making my arms his field, his tent my bed.

'Thus he that overruled I overswayèd,
Leading him prisoner in a red rose chain;
Strong-tempered steel his stronger strength obeyèd,
Yet was he servile to my coy disdain.
O be not proud, nor brag not of thy might,
For mast'ring her that foiled the god of fight.

---

[1]**jar** combat
[2]**wanton** play flirtatiously

'Touch but my lips with those fair lips of thine –
Though mine be not so fair, yet are they red –
The kiss shall be thine own as well as mine.
What see'st thou in the ground? Hold up thy head.
  Look in mine eye-balls, there thy beauty lies:
  Then why not lips on lips, since eyes in eyes?

'Art thou ashamed to kiss? Then wink[3] again,
And I will wink; so shall the day seem night.
Love keeps his revels where there are but twain;
Be bold to play, our sport is not in sight.
  These blue-veined violets whereon we lean
  Never can blab, nor know not what we mean.

'The tender spring upon thy tempting lip
Shows thee unripe; yet mayst thou well be tasted.
Make use of time, let not advantage slip;
Beauty within itself should not be wasted.
  Fair flowers that are not gathered in their prime
  Rot, and consume themselves in little time.

'Were I hard-favoured,[4] foul, or wrinkled-old,
Ill-nurtured, crookèd, churlish, harsh in voice,
O'er-worn, despisèd, rheumatic, and cold,
Thick-sighted, barren, lean, and lacking juice –
  Then mightst thou pause, for then I were not for thee;
  But having no defects, why dost abhor me?

'Thou canst not see one wrinkle in my brow,
Mine eyes are grey and bright and quick in turning,
My beauty as the spring doth yearly grow,
My flesh is soft and plump, my marrow[5] burning.

---

[3]**wink** close (your) eyes
[4]**hard-favoured** harsh in appearance
[5]**marrow** sexual essence

My smooth moist hand, were it with thy hand felt,
Would in thy palm dissolve, or seem to melt.

'Bid me discourse, I will enchant thine ear,
Or like a fairy trip[6] upon the green,
Or like a nymph with long dishevelled hair
Dance on the sands, and yet no footing seen.
Love is a spirit all compact of[7] fire,
Not gross to sink, but light and will aspire.

'Witness this primrose bank whereon I lie:
These forceless flowers like sturdy trees support me;
Two strengthless doves[8] will draw me through the sky
From morn till night, even where I list to sport me.
Is love so light, sweet boy, and may it be
That thou should think it heavy unto thee?

'Is thine own heart to thine own face affected?[9]
Can thy right hand seize love upon thy left?
Then woo thyself, be of thyself rejected;
Steal thine own freedom, and complain on theft.
Narcissus so himself himself forsook,
And died to kiss his shadow in the brook.

'Torches are made to light, jewels to wear,
Dainties[10] to taste, fresh beauty for the use,
Herbs for their smell, and sappy plants to bear:
Things growing to themselves are growth's abuse.
Seeds spring from seeds, and beauty breedeth beauty;
Thou wast begot, to get[11] it is thy duty.

---

[6]**trip** dance lightly
[7]**compact of** composed of
[8]**doves** associated with Venus because they drew her chariot
[9]**affected** attracted
[10]**Dainties** sweet and delicate food
[11]**get** beget, give birth to

'Upon the earth's increase why shouldst thou feed,
Unless the earth with thy increase be fed?
By law of nature thou art bound to breed,
That thine may live when thou thyself art dead;
And so in spite of death thou dost survive,
In that thy likeness still is left alive.'

By this the love-sick queen began to sweat,
For where they lay the shadow had forsook them,
And Titan,[12] tirèd in the midday heat,
With burning eye did hotly overlook them,
Wishing Adonis had his team[13] to guide,
So he were like him and by Venus' side.

And now Adonis, with a lazy sprite
And with a heavy, dark, disliking eye,
His low'ring brows o'erwhelming his fair sight
Like misty vapours when they blot the sky,
Souring his cheeks cries, 'Fie, no more of love!
The sun doth burn my face, I must remove.'

[12]**Titan** the sun god
[13]**team** of horses who draw Titan's chariot

Dusty Answer

by Rosamond Lehmann

In 1936 Rosamond Lehmann caused controversy by describing an abortion in her novel *The Weather in the Streets*; her second novel, *A Note in Music*, was outspoken in its frank depiction of homosexuality. In her autobiographical writing, *The Swan in the Evening* (1967), she writes about the tragedy of her daughter Sally's sudden death, and her desire to communicate with her daughter beyond the grave.

Her first novel, *Dusty Answer*, is partially based on Lehmann's own experiences as an undergraduate at Girton. It describes Judy's journey into womanhood; her emotional and sexual awakening. In this extract Judy has spent an evening with her cousin Roddy on the river. Desperate to communicate the strength of her feelings, she sends him a letter the next morning.

It was on the next evening that she awoke to the realization that Roddy had not come – might not – certainly would not now. He was going away. He, who always found self-expression, explanations, so difficult, would be at a loss to know what to say when he too woke up. He who never made plans would be helpless when it came to making any which should include her too in the future. Last night he had been dumb, he had sighed and sighed, whispered inarticulately: he would find it hard to be the first to break silence, to endeavour to re-establish the balance of real life between them. She would write him a letter, tell him all; yes, she would tell him all. Her love for him need no longer be like a half-shameful secret. If she posted a letter tonight, he would get it tomorrow morning, just before he left.

She wrote:

Roddy, this is to say good-bye once more and to send you all my love till we meet again. I do love you, indeed, in every sort of way, and to any degree you can possibly imagine; and beyond that more, more, more, unimaginably. The more my love for you annihilates me, the more it becomes a sense of inexhaustible power.

Do you love me, Roddy? Tell me again that you do; and don't think me importunate.

I am so wrapped round and rich in my thoughts of you that at the moment I feel I can endure your absence. I almost welcome it because it will give me time to sit alone, and begin to realize my happiness. So that when you come back – Oh Roddy, come back soon!

I have loved you ever since I first saw you when we were little, I suppose, – only you, always you. I'm not likely ever to stop loving you. Thank God I can tell you so at last. Will you go on loving me? Am I to go on loving you? Oh but you won't say no, after last night. If you don't want to be tied quite yet, I shall understand. I can wait years quite happily, if you love me. Roddy I am yours. Last night I gave you what has always belonged to you. But I can't think about last night yet. It is too close and tremendous and shattering. I gasp and nearly faint when I try to recall it. I dissolve.

When I came back to my room in the dawn I stared and stared at my face in the glass, wondering how it was I could recognize it. How is it I look the same, and move, eat, speak, much as usual?

Ought I to have been more coy, more reluctant last night? Would it have been more fitting – would you have respected me more? Was I too bold? Oh, that is foolishness: I had no will but yours.

But because I love you so much I am a little fearful. So write to me quickly and tell me what to think, feel, do. I shall dream till then.

There is so much more to tell you, and yet it is all the same really. My darling, I love you!

Judy.

She posted it. Next morning she hurriedly dressed and ran downstairs in the sudden expectation of finding a letter from him; but there was none.

Now he would have got hers . . . Now he would have read it . . . Now he would be walking to the station . . .

She heard the train steam out; and doubt and sorrow came like a cloud upon her; but only for a little while.

In the cool of the evening she wandered down to the river and sat beside it dreaming. She dreamt happily of Jennifer. She would be able to love Jennifer peacefully now, think of her without that ache, see her again, perhaps, with all the old restlessness assuaged. Jennifer's letter would surely come soon now . . .

If Roddy were to ask her to come away with him at once, for ever, she would take just the copper bowl from her table and spring to him, and leave all the rest of the past without a pang.

Perhaps Roddy had written her a letter just before he had gone away; and if so it might have come by the evening post. She left the river and went to seek it.

Who could it be coming towards her down the little pathway which led from the station to the bottom of the garden and then on to the blue gate in the wall of the garden next door? She stood still under the overhanging lilacs and may-trees, her heart pounding, her limbs melting. It was Roddy, in a white shirt and white flannels, – coming from the station. He caught sight of her, seemed to hesitate, came on till he was close to her; and she had the strangest feeling that he intended to pass right by her as if he did not see her . . . What was the word for his face? Smooth: yes, smooth as a stone. She had never before noticed what a smooth face he had; but she could not see him clearly because of the beating of her pulses.

'Roddy!'

He lifted his eyebrows.

'Oh, hullo, Judith.'

'I thought you'd gone away.'

'I'm going tomorrow. A girl I know rang up this morning to suggest coming down for the day, so I waited. I've just seen her off.'

A girl he knew . . . Roddy had always had this curious facility in the dealing of verbal wounds.

'I see . . . How nice.'

A face smooth and cold as a stone. Not the faintest expression in it. Had he bidden the girl he knew good-bye with a face like this? No, it had certainly been twinkling and teasing then.

'Well I must get on.' He looked up the path as if meditating immediate escape; then said, without looking at her, and in a frozen voice: 'I got a letter from you this morning.'

'Oh you did get it?'

There could never have been a more foolish-sounding bleat. In the ensuing silence she added feebly: 'Shall you – answer it – some time?'

'I thought the best thing I could do was to leave it unanswered.'

'Oh . . . '

Because of course it had been so improper, so altogether monstrous to write like that . . .

'Well,' she said. 'I thought . . . I'm sorry.'

She ought to apologize to him, because he had meant to go away without saying anything, and she had come on him unawares and spoilt his escape.

'I was very much surprised at the way you wrote,' he said.

'How do you mean, surprised, Roddy?' she said timidly.

She had known all along in the deepest layer of her consciousness that something like this would happen. Permanent happiness had never been for her.

It was not much of a shock. In a moment that night was a far, unreal memory.

'Well' – he hesitated. 'If a man wants to ask a girl to – marry him he generally asks her himself – do you see?'

'You mean – it was outrageous of me not to wait – to write like that?'

'I thought it a little odd.'

'Oh, but Roddy, surely – surely that's one of those worn-out conventions . . . Surely a woman has a perfect right to say she – loves a man – if she wants to – it's simply a question of having the courage . . . I can't see why not . . . I've always believed one should . . . '

It was no good trying to expostulate, to bluff like that, with his dead face confronting her. He would not be taken in by any such lying gallantries. How did one combat people whose features never gave way by so much as a quiver? She leaned against the wooden fence and tried to fix her eyes upon the may-tree opposite. Very far, but clear, she heard her mother at the other end of the garden, calling her name: but that was another Judith.

Raining in My Heart by Rabindra Singh (2003); a young man broods over pictures of Marilyn Monroe.

The Glass Menagerie

by Tennessee Williams

Tennessee Williams (1911–1983) gained instant success with this early play. There are autobiographical elements: Tom has much in common with the author and Laura is based on his sister, Rose.

In this extract Tom, instructed by his mother, brings a gentleman caller home for Laura. It is Jim, for whom Laura has nursed a quiet passion since their last years at school together. When the pair are left alone, Jim coaxes the gentle and reclusive Laura out of her shyness. She begins to blossom.

JIM I guess you think I think a lot of myself!

LAURA No – o-o-o, I –

JIM Now how about you? Isn't there something you take
more interest in than anything else?

LAURA Well, I do – as I said – have my – glass collection –

A peal of girlish laughter from the kitchen.

JIM I'm not right sure I know what you're talking about.
What kind of glass is it?

LAURA Little articles of it, they're ornaments mostly!
Most of them are little animals made out of glass,
the tiniest little animals in the world. Mother calls
them a glass menagerie!
Here's an example of one, if you'd like to see it!
This one is one of the oldest. It's nearly thirteen.

Music: 'The Glass Menagerie'.
He stretches out his hand.

Oh, be careful – if you breathe, it breaks!

JIM I'd better not take it. I'm pretty clumsy with things.

LAURA Go on, I trust you with him!

Places it in his palm.

There now – you're holding him gently!
Hold him over the light, he loves the light! You see
how the light shines through him?

JIM It sure does shine!

LAURA I shouldn't be partial, but he is my favourite one.

JIM What kind of a thing is this one supposed to be?

LAURA Haven't you noticed the single horn on his forehead?

JIM A unicorn, huh?

LAURA Mmmm-hmmm!

JIM Unicorns, aren't they extinct in the modern world?

LAURA I know!

JIM Poor little fellow, he must feel sort of lonesome.

LAURA *(Smiling)* Well, if he does he doesn't complain about it. He stays on a shelf with some horses that don't have horns and all of them seem to get along nicely together.

JIM How do you know?

LAURA *(Lightly)* I haven't heard any arguments among them!

JIM *(Grinning)* No arguments, huh? Well, that's a pretty good sign! Where shall I set him?

LAURA Put him on the table. They all like a change of scenery once in a while!

JIM *(Stretching)* Well, well, well, well –
Look how big my shadow is when I stretch!

LAURA Oh, oh, yes – it stretches across the ceiling!

JIM *(Crossing to door)* I think it's stopped raining. *(Opens fire-escape door.)* Where does the music come from?

LAURA From the Paradise Dance Hall across the alley.

JIM How about cutting the rug a little, Miss Wingfield?

LAURA Oh –

JIM Or is your programme filled up? Let me have a look at it. *(Grasps imaginary card.)* Why, every dance is taken! I'll just have to scratch some out. *(Waltz music: 'La Golondrina'.)* Ahhh, a waltz! *(He executes some sweeping turns by himself then holds his arms toward* LAURA.*)*

LAURA *(Breathlessly)* I – can't dance!

JIM There you go, that inferiority stuff! Come on, try!

LAURA Oh, but I'd step on you!

JIM I'm not made out of glass.

LAURA How – how – how do we start?

JIM Just leave it to me. You hold your arms out a little.

LAURA Like this?

JIM A little bit higher. Right. Now don't tighten up, that's the main thing about it – relax.

LAURA *(Laughing breathlessly)* It's hard not to. I'm afraid you can't budge me.

JIM What do you bet I can't? *(He swings her into motion.)*

LAURA Goodness, yes, you can!

JIM Let yourself go, now, Laura, just let yourself go.

LAURA I'm –

JIM Come on!

LAURA Trying!

JIM Not so stiff – Easy does it!

LAURA I know but I'm –

JIM Loosen th' backbone! There now, that's a lot better.

LAURA Am I?

JIM Lots, lots better! *(He moves her about the room in a clumsy waltz.)*

LAURA Oh, my!

JIM Ha-ha!

LAURA Oh, my goodness!

JIM Ha-ha-ha! *(They suddenly bump into the table.* JIM *stops.)* What did we hit on?

LAURA Table.

JIM Did something fall off it? I think –

LAURA Yes.

JIM I hope that it wasn't the little glass horse with the horn!

LAURA Yes.

JIM Aw, aw, aw. Is it broken?

LAURA Now it is just like all the other horses.
JIM It's lost its –
LAURA Horn!
It doesn't matter. Maybe it's a blessing in disguise.
JIM You'll never forgive me. I bet that that was your favourite piece of glass.
LAURA I don't have favourites much. It's no tragedy, Freckles.
Glass breaks so easily. No matter how careful you are.
The traffic jars the shelves and things fall off them.
JIM Still I'm awfully sorry that I was the cause.
LAURA *(Smiling)* I'll just imagine he had an operation.
The horn was removed to make him feel less – freakish!

They both laugh.

Now he will feel more at home with the other horses,
the ones that don't have horns. . . .
JIM Ha-ha, that's very funny!

Suddenly serious.

I'm glad to see that you have a sense of humour.
You know – you're – well – very different!
Surprisingly different from anyone else I know!

His voice becomes soft and hesitant with a genuine feeling.

Do you mind me telling you that?

LAURA *is abashed beyond speech.*

I mean it in a nice way . . .

LAURA *nods shyly, looking away.*

You make me feel sort of – I don't know how to put it!
I'm usually pretty good at expressing things, but –
This is something that I don't know how to say!

LAURA *touches her throat and clears it – turns the broken unicorn in her hands.*

Even softer.

Has anyone ever told you that you were pretty?

Pause: music.

LAURA *looks up slowly, with wonder, and shakes her head.*

Well, you are! In a very different way from anyone else. And all the nicer because of the difference, too.

His voice becomes low and husky. LAURA *turns away, nearly faint with the novelty of her emotions.*

I wish that you were my sister. I'd teach you to have some confidence in yourself. The different people are not like other people, but being different is nothing to be ashamed of. Because other people are not such wonderful people. They're one hundred times one thousand. You're one times one! They walk all over the earth. You just stay here. They're common as – weeds, but – you – well, you're – *Blue Roses!*

Image on screen: blue roses. Music changes.

LAURA But blue is wrong for – roses . . .

JIM It's right for you! – You're – pretty!

LAURA In what respect am I pretty?

JIM In all respects – believe me! Your eyes – your hair – are pretty! Your hands are pretty!

He catches hold of her hand.

You think I'm making this up because I'm invited to dinner and have to be nice. Oh, I could do that! I could put on an act for you, Laura, and say lots of things without being very sincere. But this time I am. I'm talking to you sincerely. I happened to notice you had this inferiority complex that keeps you from feeling comfortable with people. Somebody needs to build your confidence up and make you proud instead of shy and turning away and – blushing – Somebody – ought to –

Ought to – *kiss* you, Laura!

His hand slips slowly up her arm to her shoulder.

Music swells tumultuously.

He suddenly turns her about and kisses her on the lips.

When he releases her, LAURA *sinks on the sofa with a bright, dazed look.*

JIM *backs away and fishes in his pocket for a cigarette.*

Legend on screen: 'souvenir'.

Stumble-john!

He lights the cigarette, avoiding her look.

There is a peal of girlish laughter from AMANDA *in the kitchen.*

LAURA *slowly raises and opens her hand. It still contains the little broken glass animal. She looks at it with a tender, bewildered expression.*

Stumble-john!
I shouldn't have done that – That was way off the beam.
You don't smoke, do you?

She looks up, smiling, not hearing the question.

He sits beside her a little gingerly. She looks at him speechlessly – waiting.

He coughs decorously and moves a little farther aside as he considers the situation and senses her feelings, dimly, with perturbation.

Gently.

Would you – care for a – mint?

She doesn't seem to hear him but her look grows brighter even.

Peppermint – Life-Saver?
My pocket's a regular drug store – wherever I go . . .

He pops a mint in his mouth. Then gulps and decides to make a clean breast of it. He speaks slowly and gingerly.

Laura, you know, if I had a sister like you, I'd do the same thing as Tom. I'd bring out fellows and – introduce her to them. The right type of boys of a type to – appreciate her.
Only – well – he made a mistake about me.
Maybe I've got no call to be saying this. That may not have been the idea in having me over. But what if it was? There's nothing wrong about that. The only trouble is that in my case – I'm not in a situation to – do the right thing.

I can't take down your number and say I'll phone.
I can't call up next week and – ask for a date.
I thought I had better explain the situation in case you – misunderstand it and – hurt your feelings . . .

Pause.

Slowly, very slowly, LAURA*'s look changes, her eyes returning slowly from his to the ornament in her palm.*

AMANDA *utters another gay laugh in the kitchen.*

LAURA *(faintly)* You – won't – call again?

JIM No, Laura, I can't.

He rises from the sofa.

As I was just explaining, I've – got strings on me.
Laura, I've – been going steady!
I go out all of the time with a girl named Betty. She's a home-girl like you, and Catholic, and Irish, and in a great many ways we – get along fine.
I met her last summer on a moonlight boat trip up the river to Alton, on the *Majestic*.
Well – right away from the start it was – love!

Legend: 'Love!'

LAURA *sways slightly forward and grips the arm of the sofa. He fails to notice, now enrapt in his own comfortable being.*

Being in love has made a new man of me!

Leaning stiffly forward, clutching the arm of the sofa, LAURA *struggles visibly with her storm. But* JIM *is oblivious, she is a long way off.*

The power of love is really pretty tremendous!
Love is something that – changes the whole world, Laura!

The storm abates a little and LAURA *leans back. He notices her again.*

It happened that Betty's aunt took sick, she got a wire and had to go to Centralia. So Tom – when he asked me to dinner – I naturally just accepted the invitation, not knowing that you – that he – that I –

He stops awkwardly.

Huh – I'm a stumble-john!

He flops back on the sofa.

The holy candles in the altar of LAURA*'s face have been snuffed out. There is a look of almost infinite desolation.*

JIM *glances at her uneasily.*

I wish that you would – say something. *(She bites her lip which was trembling and then bravely smiles. She opens her hand again on the broken glass ornament. Then she gently takes his hand and raises it level with her own. She carefully places the unicorn in the palm of his hand, then pushes his fingers closed upon it.)* What are you – doing that for? You want me to have him? Laura? *(She nods.)* What for?

LAURA A – souvenir . . .

She rises unsteadily and crouches beside the victrola to wind it up.

Legend on screen: 'Things have a way of turning out so badly!'

The Folly of Being Comforted

by W. B. Yeats

The Irish poet W. B. Yeats (1865–1939) loved the beautiful revolutionary Maud Gonne, throughout his life. They never married, and she inspired much of his most tender love poetry, including *The Cloths of Heaven*. This poem rejects the notion that his unrequited love will hurt less as time passes.

One that is ever kind said yesterday:
'Your well-beloved's hair has threads of grey,
And little shadows come about her eyes;
Time can but make it easier to be wise
Though now it seems impossible, and so
All that you need is patience.'
Heart cries, 'No,
I have not a crumb of comfort, not a grain.
Time can but make her beauty over again:
Because of that great nobleness of hers
The fire that stirs about her, when she stirs,
Burns but more clearly. O she had not these ways
When all the wild summer was in her gaze.'

O heart! O heart! if she'd but turn her head.
You'd know the folly of being comforted.

The Waves

by Virginia Woolf

Boldly experimental in her writing, the novelist and critic Virginia Woolf (1882–1941) was at the forefront of the Modernist movement. Conventional plotting and characterisation are replaced by impressionistic writing and subtly indirect narration. Woolf suffered bouts of severe depression throughout her life, and in 1941 she drowned herself in the river Ouse.

In *The Waves*, Woolf tells the life stories of six different characters from childhood to maturity. Their inner lives are the focus of the novel, depicted through each person's 'stream of consciousness', the outpouring of every thought, feeling and sensation as it occurs. Here, at the beginning of the novel, the six young children are playing outside. Susan sees Jinny kiss Louis.

'I was running,' said Jinny, 'after breakfast. I saw leaves moving in a hole in the hedge. I thought, "That is a bird on its nest." I parted them and looked; but there was no bird on a nest. The leaves went on moving. I was frightened. I ran past Susan, past Rhoda, and Neville and Bernard in the tool-house talking. I cried as I ran, faster and faster. What moved the leaves? What moves my heart, my legs? And I dashed in here, seeing you green as a bush, like a branch, very still, Louis, with your eyes fixed. "Is he dead?" I thought, and kissed you, with my heart jumping under my pink frock like the leaves, which go on moving, though there is nothing to move them. Now I smell geraniums; I smell earth mould. I dance. I ripple. I am thrown over you like a net of light. I lie quivering flung over you.'

'Through the chink in the hedge,' said Susan, 'I saw her kiss him. I raised my head from my flowerpot and looked through a chink in the hedge. I saw her kiss him. I saw them, Jinny and Louis, kissing. Now I will wrap my agony inside my pocket-handkerchief. It shall be screwed tight into a ball. I will go to the beech wood alone, before lessons. I will not sit at a table, doing sums. I will not sit next Jinny and next Louis. I will take my anguish and lay it upon the roots under the beech trees. I will examine it and take it between my fingers. They will not find me. I shall eat nuts and peer for eggs through the brambles and my hair will be matted and I shall sleep under hedges and drink water from ditches and die there.'

'Susan has passed us,' said Bernard. 'She has passed the tool-house door with her handkerchief screwed into a ball. She was not crying, but her eyes, which are so beautiful, were narrow as cats' eyes before they spring. I shall follow her, Neville. I shall go gently behind her, to be at hand, with my curiosity, to comfort her when she bursts out in a rage and thinks, "I am alone."

'Now she walks across the field with a swing, nonchalantly, to deceive us. Then she comes to the dip; she thinks she is unseen; she begins to run with her fists clenched in front of her. Her nails meet in the ball of her pocket-handkerchief. She is making for the beech woods out of the light. She spreads her arms as she comes to them and takes to the shade like a swimmer. But she is blind after the light and trips and flings herself down on the roots under the trees, where the light seems to pant in and out, in and out. The branches heave up and down. There is agitation and trouble here. There is gloom. The light is fitful. There is anguish here. The roots make a skeleton on the ground, with dead leaves heaped in the angles. Susan has spread her anguish out. Her pocket-handkerchief is laid on the roots of the beech trees and she sobs, sitting crumpled where she has fallen.'

'I saw her kiss him,' said Susan. 'I looked between the leaves and saw her. She danced in flecked with diamonds light as dust. And I am squat, Bernard, I am short. I have eyes that look close to the ground and see insects in the grass. The yellow warmth in my side turned to stone when I saw Jinny kiss Louis. I shall eat grass and die in a ditch in the brown water where dead leaves have rotted.'

If to Love

by Pierre de Ronsard

Pierre de Ronsard (1524–1585) is now recognised as one of the most influential of French poets. However, he had intended to follow a career as a courtier and soldier, but his increasing deafness prevented him from realising this ambition. Instead, he turned to literature, subsequently becoming the leader of the Pleiade (named after the stars, the Pleiades), a group of seven writers who strove to disseminate the influence of the 14th-century Italian poet Petrarch amongst French writers. His *Sonnets pour Hélène* inspired several English sonnet writers in the same century. This sonnet, unusually, has sixteen lines. The translation is by D. B. Wyndham Lewis.

English translation

If to love, Madam, is to dream and long
and brood by day and night on means of pleasing you,
to be forgetful of all else, to wish to do nothing else
but adore and serve the beauty that wounds me,
If to love is to pursue a happiness which flies me,
to lose myself in loneliness, to suffer much pain,
to fear greatly and to hold my tongue,
to weep, to beg for pity, and to see myself sent away,
If to love is to live in you more than in myself,
to hide great weariness under a mask of joy,
to feel in the depths of my soul the odds against which I fight,
to be hot and cold as the fever of love takes me,
To be ashamed, when I speak to you, to confess my pain –
if that is to love, then I love you furiously,
I love you, knowing full well my pain is deadly.
The heart says so often enough; the tongue is silent.

Original French

Si c'est aimer, Madame, et de jour et de nuict,
Resver, songer, penser le moyen de vous plaire,
Oublier toute chose, et ne vouloir rien faire
Qu'adorer et servir la beauté qui me nuit,
Si c'est aimer, de suivre un bonheur qui me fuit,
De me perdre moymesme et d'estre solitaire,
Souffrir beaucoup de mal, beaucoup craindre et me taire,
Pleurer, crier mercy, et m'en voir esconduit,
Si c'est aimer, de vivre en vous plus qu'en moymesme,
Cacher d'un front joyeux une langueur extresme,
Sentir au fond de l'àme un combat inegal,
Chaud, froid, comme la fievre amoureuse me traitte,
Honteux, parlant à vous, de confesser mon mal:
Si cela c'est aimer, furieux je vous aime,
Je vous aime, et sçay bien que mon mal est fatal,
Le coeur le dit assez, mai la langue est muette.

Astrophel and Stella

by Sir Philip Sidney

In his sonnet sequence, Sir Philip Sidney (1554–1586) traces Astrophel (the star lover)'s unrequited love for Stella (the star).The only event in the whole sequence is a kiss, snatched whilst she is asleep. As in Ronsard's sonnet (p. 84), Petrarch's influence is self-evident: the extended conceit, the blazon, the military metaphors, and above all, the poet's plight. Like Petrarch and his Laura, Astrophel loves – but the love is not returned. Here he envies Stella's dog.

Deare, why make you more of a dog then me?
  If he do love, I burne, I burne in love:
  If he waite well, I never thence would move:
If he be faire, yet but a dog can be.
Litle he is, so litle worth is he;
  He barks; my songs thine owne voyce oft doth prove:
  Bid'n, perhaps he fetcheth thee a glove,
But I, unbid, fetch even my soule to thee.
  Yet while I languish, him that bosome clips,[1]
That lap doth lap, nay lets, in spite of spite,
This sowre-breath'd mate tast of those sugred lips.
Alas, if you graunt only such delight
  To witlesse things, then *Love* I hope (since wit
  Becomes a clog) will soone ease me of it.

---

[1]**clips** embraces

Cold Comfort Farm

by Stella Gibbons

Writing about the origins of *Cold Comfort Farm*, Stella Gibbons (1902–1989) stated that 'it is quite time that the earthy and passionate novel was parodied.' Flora Poste, on visiting her relatives, the Starkadders, at Cold Comfort Farm, determines to bring them properly into the 20th century. This extract juxtaposes the letting out of the bull, Big Business, with the arrival of Urk, Elfine's intended. Both Big Business and Urk suffer from unconsummated desire.

It was half past eight. Mrs Beetle had finished sweeping the floor and was shaking the mat out in the yard, in the sunshine. (It always surprised Flora to see the sun shining into the yard at Cold Comfort; she had a feeling that the rays ought to be short-circuited just outside the wall by the atmosphere of the farmhouse.)

'Ni smorning,' screamed Mrs Beetle, adding that we could do with a bit of it.

Flora smilingly agreed and went across to the cupboard to take down her own little green teapot (a present from Mrs Smiling) and tin of China tea. She glanced out into the yard and was pleased to see that none of the male Starkadders were about. Elfine was out on a walk. Judith was probably lying despairingly across her bed, looking with leaden eyes at the ceiling across which the first flies of the year were beginning monotonously to circle and crawl.

The bull suddenly bellowed his thick, dark-red note. Flora paused, with the teapot in her hand, and looked thoughtfully out across the yard towards his shed.

'Mrs Beetle,' she said firmly, 'the bull ought to be let out. Could you help me do it? Are you afraid of bulls?'

[. . .] Big Business bellowed again. It was a harsh, mournful sound; there were old swamps and rotting horns buried in it.

Flora ran across the yard and pushed open the gate leading into the big field facing the farm, fastening it back. Then she took down the bull-prong, or whatever it called itself, and, standing at a comfortable distance from the shed, manoeuvred the catch back, and saw the door swing open.

Out came Big Business. It was a much less dramatic affair than she had supposed it would be. He stood for a second or two bewildered by the light, with his big head swaying stupidly. Flora stood quite still.

'Eeee-yer! Go on, yer old brute!' shrieked Mrs Beetle.

The bull lumbered off across the yard, still with his head down, towards the gate. Flora followed cautiously, holding the bull-prong. Mrs Beetle screeched to her for the dear's sake to be careful. Once Big Business half turned towards her, and she made a determined movement with the prong. Then, to her relief, he went through the gate into the grassy field, and she swung it to and shut it before he had time to turn round.

[. . .] To her dismay, just as the figure of the postman appeared at that point of the path where it curved over the hill towards the farm-house, it was joined by another figure. Flora craned her eyes above her cup to see who it might be. It was somebody who was hung about with a good many dead rabbits and pheasants in one way and another, so that his features were obscured from view. He stopped, said something to the postman, and Flora saw something white pass from hand to hand. The rabbit-festooned Starkadder, whoever he might be, had forestalled her. She bit crossly into a piece of toast and continued to observe the approaching figure. He soon came close enough for her to see that it was Urk.

She was much disconcerted. It could not have been worse.

'Turns you up, don't it, seein' ter-day's dinner come in 'anging round someone's neck like that?' observed Mrs Beetle, who was loading a tray with food to take up to Mrs Doom. 'Termorrer's, too, for all I know, and the day after's. Give me cold storage, any day.'

Urk opened the door of the kitchen and came slowly into the room.

He had been shooting rabbits. His narrow nostrils were slightly distended to inhale the blood-odour from the seventeen which hung round his neck. Their cold fur brushed his hands lightly and imploringly like little pleas for mercy, and his buttocks were softly brushed by the draggled tail-feathers of five pheasants which hung from the pheasant-belt encircling his waist. He felt the weight of the twenty-five dead animals he bore (for there was a shrew or two in his breast pocket) pulling him down, like heavy, dark-blooded roots into the dumb soil. He was drowsy with killing, in the mood of a lion lying on a hippopotamus with its mouth full.

He held the letters in front of him, looking down at them with a sleepy stare. Flora saw, with a start of indignation, that his thumb had left a red mark upon an envelope addressed in Charles's neat hand.

This was quite intolerable. She rose quickly to her feet, holding out her hand.

'My letters, please,' she said, crisply.

[. . .] 'Ye're smart, aren't yer? Think I don't know what's going on . . . wi' books from London and all that rot. Now you listen to me. She's mine, I tell you . . . mine. She's my woman, same as a hen belongs to a cock, and no one don't have her except me, ye see? She were promised to me the day she were born, by her Grandmother. I put a cross in water-vole's blood on her feedin'-bottle when she was an hour old, to mark her for mine, and held her up so's she might see it and know she was mine . . . And every year since then, on her birthday, I've taken her up to Ticklepenny's Corner and we've hung over th' old well until we see a water-vole, and I've said to her, I've said, "Remember". And all she would say was: "What, Cousin Urk?" But she knows all right. She knows. When the water-voles mate under the may trees this summer I'll make her mine. Dick Hawk-Monitor . . . what's he? A bit of a boy? Playin' at horses in a red coat, like his daddy afore him. Many a time I've lay and laughed at 'em . . . fools. Me and the water-voles, we can afford to wait for what we want. So you heed what I say, miss. Elfine's mine. I doan't mind her bein' a bit above me' (here his voice thickened in a manner which caused Mrs Beetle to make a sound resembling 't-t-t-t-'), ''cause a man likes his piece to be a bit dainty. But she's mine –'

'We heard,' said Flora; 'you said it before.'

'– and God help the man or woman who tries to take her from me. Me and the water-voles, we'll get her back.'

'Are those water-voles round your neck?' asked Flora, interestedly. 'I've never seen any before. What a lot of them all at once!'

He turned from her, with a peculiar stooping, stealthy, swooping movement, and padded out of the kitchen.

'Well, I never,' said Mrs Beetle, loudly; 'there's a narsty temper for you.'

Sonnet 8: Sometimes I Wish . . .

by Richard Barnfield

Richard Barnfield (1574–1620) was a prolific poet; indeed, some of his writing was misattributed to Shakespeare. He too wrote a sonnet sequence and, like Shakespeare, addressed his sonnets to a man, here the mythological youth Ganymede. Always cruel and distant, Ganymede repels his ardent admirer.

Sometimes I wish that I his pillow were,
So might I steale a kisse, and yet not seene,
So might I gaze upon his sleeping eine,[1]
Although I did it with a panting feare:
But when I well consider how vaine my wish is,
Ah foolish Bees (thinke I) that doe not sucke
His lips for hony; but poore flowers doe plucke
Which have no sweet in them: when his sole kisses,
Are able to revive a dying soule.
Kisse him, but sting him not, for if you doe,
His angry voice your flying will pursue:
But when they heare his tongue, what can controule,
Their back-returne? for then they plaine may see,
How hony-combs from his lips dropping bee.

---

[1]**eine** eyes

Warming Her Pearls

by Carol Ann Duffy

Carol Ann Duffy is probably Britain's most accessible and well-known female poet. Described as 'poems for people who don't like poetry', her works challenge and surprise her readers. Her dramatic monologues liberate a range of suppressed female voices; here the maid exploits her servile position to gain intimate physical contact with her mistress, by 'warming her pearls' close to her body.

(for Judith Radstone)

Next to my own skin, her pearls. My mistress
bids me wear them, warm them, until evening
when I'll brush her hair. At six, I place them
round her cool, white throat. All day I think of her,

resting in the Yellow Room, contemplating silk
or taffeta, which gown tonight? She fans herself
whilst I work willingly, my slow heat entering
each pearl. Slack on my neck, her rope.

She's beautiful. I dream about her
in my attic bed; picture her dancing
with tall men, puzzled by my faint, persistent scent
beneath her French perfume, her milky stones.

I dust her shoulders with a rabbit's foot,
watch the soft blush seep through her skin
like an indolent sigh. In her looking-glass
my red lips part as though I want to speak.

Full moon. Her carriage brings her home. I see
her every movement in my head . . . . Undressing,
taking off her jewels, her slim hand reaching
for the case, slipping naked into bed, the way

she always does . . . . And I lie here awake,
knowing the pearls are cooling even now
in the room where my mistress sleeps. All night
I feel their absence and I burn.

Questions

In all of these questions you should consider:

a the ways the writers' choice of form, structure and language shape your responses to the extracts

b how your wider reading in the literature of love has contributed to your understanding and interpretation of the extracts.

1 How does Ted Hughes express passionate feelings in *Echo and Narcissus*? Consider the differences between the presentation of self-love and that of love for the other.

2 Compare the failures of communication in *Echo and Narcissus* and *Dusty Answer*. To what extent do you sympathise with the female characters?

3 Consider the presentation of Laura in the extract from *The Glass Menagerie*. In what ways does Tennessee Williams make this both dramatic and sensitive?

4 How does Yeats convey the experience of unrequited love through time? Compare this poem with the extract from *The Glass Menagerie*. How far do you consider that each writer makes pain bearable?

5 In the extract from *The Waves*, do you find Virginia Woolf serious, comic or both in the ways she presents the sufferings of childhood? How does the author convey the sense of being a child?

6 Compare the presentation of unconsummated desire in the three sonnets – by Ronsard, Sidney and Barnfield.

7 In what ways does Stella Gibbons make the extract from *Cold Comfort Farm* comic? Compare this extract with Sidney's sonnet. Do they have anything in common?

8 Which unrequited lover represented in this section do you find to be the most sympathetic and why?

Further reading

- Having read Ronsard's sonnet, you might like to trace Petrarch's influence over the sonneteers of Elizabethan England: Sidney, Spenser, Daniel and, to some extent, Shakespeare. The Elizabethan poets, particularly Wyatt and Ralegh, enjoyed dramatising the fiction of the unobtainable Virgin Queen within their poetry, for example Ralegh's poem *The Ocean's Love to Cynthia*.
- If you enjoyed reading Barnfield's sonnet, it is worth considering the presentation of homoerotic love in Shakespeare's sonnets. How do his sonnets addressed to the young man differ in tone from the later sonnets to the 'dark lady'?
- Shakespeare's plays are full of those who love, but in vain. Sometimes this is comic, sometimes tragic: for example, consider the deranged love tangle in *A Midsummer Night's Dream*, Viola and Orsino in *Twelfth Night* and Ophelia in *Hamlet*.
- In John Milton's 17th-century epic poem *Paradise Lost*, we find Satan burning within his 'hot hell' as he desires the unfallen Eve: his 'love' morphs into virulent poison. He is both the archetypal demon and the doomed lover, perpetually frustrated.
- Charlotte Brontë knew in her own life what it was to love both passionately and hopelessly, and she communicates this through both her poetry and her novels, particularly *Villette*. Her sister Emily's novel *Wuthering Heights* contains two of literature's most famous lovers, Cathy and Heathcliff. But they never consummate their love.
- The literature of the 19th century is a rich source of unrequited love. Thomas Hardy's novels, in particular, convey the yearning of those who love, apparently without hope. Consider Gabriel Oak's passion for Bathsheba in *Far from the Madding Crowd* and Elizabeth-Jane's for Farfrae in *The Mayor of Casterbridge*.
- If you enjoyed *Warming Her Pearls* you may like to read the best-selling novel by Sarah Waters, *Tipping the Velvet*, which depicts a lesbian relationship. The tension between mistress and servant is explored in *Rebecca* by Daphne du Maurier (1938), a dark mystery of repressed desire.
- Unrequited lovers may be generous, like Laura in *The Glass Menagerie*, or they may brood and plot revenge like the rejected Abigail in *The Crucible* by Arthur Miller. She lies in order to inflict pain on the man she loves.

3 Celebration

When the longing, wondering, heart-ache and anticipation are over – and the love is mutual – then the romantic story can reach its conclusion. Lovers, audience and readers are rewarded with marriage. Fielding's *Tom Jones*, Congreve's *The Way of the World*, George Eliot's *Middlemarch*, Jane Austen's *Pride and Prejudice* are profound, at times even comic, explorations of love; each works through a complicated emotional journey and marriage is a destination that feels satisfying, both morally and aesthetically. Sometimes, as in Shakespeare's comedies, there are several marriages; *As You Like It* celebrates no fewer than four.

In *East Coker* from his *Four Quartets* (1935–42) T. S. Eliot sees something ancient and holy in this coming together, celebrated in the music of the dance, which echoes the medieval belief in heavenly concord and matches the rhythms of the seasons:

In that open field
If you do not come too close, if you do not come too close,
On a summer midnight, you can hear the music
Of the weak pipe and the little drum
And see them dancing around the bonfire
The association of man and woman
In daunsinge, signifying matrimonie –
A dignified and commodious sacrament.
Two and two, necessarye coniunction,
Holding eche other by the hand or the arm
Which betokeneth concorde.

In all of these examples there is public celebration, as well as the individual and mutual joy of two lovers. Marriage is a social institution as well as a private contract. The language of a Christian wedding service also suggests that marriage is not a conclusion, the end of a romantic story, but the beginning of a couple's new life. Children may be born into the marriage and they will take the story into an unknown future, as yet unwritten.

Of course, marriage is not the only way of celebrating the fulfilment of lovers. Several of the extracts in this section neither declare nor imply a marriage. Fulfilment comes in different ways, not always the young love of so much romantic fiction, not always between a man and a woman. But whether the end of a story or its beginning, whether Christian or not, whether marriage or simple togetherness, a lover's delight is frequently celebrated in literature. And, as for any extreme experience, a writer may find that the language available seems to crack and falter. The sense of exaltation makes the moment seem unique: since it feels that no one can ever have experienced this intense happiness before, the stock of words and syntax from normal life can't do justice to it.

In *Loving in Truth,* the Elizabethan sonneteer Sir Philip Sidney finds himself with pen in hand but unable to express his love for Stella, his lady. His 'Muse' watches the struggle to devise fine words and witty inventions and finally urges the lover to 'look in thy heart and write.' Perhaps simple honesty will succeed where the poet's craft has failed? But Sidney may also be teasing his readers: he knows that using language, however simple, to convey deep feeling, is a skilled and complicated task. Does he really believe that, in order to write, all a lover needs to do is 'look in thy heart', or is this advice in fact a clever poet's disingenuous pretence? Many poets have extended their craft to include music: Thomas Carew (p. 103), like many before and since, called his poem *A Song*. Others, like Browning (p. 110), are left with unanswered questions.

Sometimes the only way to convey a love is to compare it to another, such as that between celebrated lovers from history or mythology. Sometimes a writer will take the comparison further by reversing it, and have the characters claim that they are the lovers that others will be compared to. For example, Shakespeare's Troilus and Cressida (p. 119) imagine themselves immortalised for their fidelity; future poets will need their names in order to find the telling simile that can't be bettered. John Donne goes even further in his poem *The*

Canonization: the two lovers will be made saints and all future worshippers of love and in love will look up to heaven to learn 'the truth about love':

. . . 'You whom reverend love
Made one another's hermitage
You, to whom love was peace, that now is rage;
Who did the whole world's soul contract, and drove
Into the glasses of your eyes
(So made such mirrors and such spies
That they did all to you epitomize,)
Countries, towns, courts: beg from above
A pattern of your love!'

Joyful and assertive hyperbole can surely go no further than this.

Comeclose and Sleepnow

by Roger McGough

McGough is associated with Liverpool, where he was born in 1937 and became a member of the music/poetry group The Scaffold. His witty, energetic way with words is also evident in his frequent work for radio.

it is afterwards
and you talk on tiptoe
happy to be part
of the darkness
lips becoming limp
a prelude to tiredness.
Comeclose and Sleepnow
for in the morning
when a policeman
disguised as the sun
creeps into the room
and your mother
disguised as birds
calls from the trees
you will put on a dress of guilt
and shoes with broken high ideals
and refusing coffee
run
alltheway
home

The Good-Morrow

by John Donne

John Donne (1572–1631) was a leading practitioner of what became known as 'metaphysical poetry'. Many of his earlier poems, like *The Good-Morrow*, are about love; these appear in his collection of *Songs and Sonets* [*sic*]. After he was ordained in 1615, he became one of the most famous preachers in London and wrote most of his religious poems and sermons. Whether secular or religious, his work is passionate, intellectual and self-dramatising. He often catches the moment of strong feeling and uses surprising images and allusions to convey it.

I wonder, by my troth, what thou and I
Did, till we lov'd? were we not wean'd till then?
But suck'd on country pleasures, childishly?
Or snorted we in the Seven Sleepers'[1] den?
'Twas so; but this,[2] all pleasures fancies be:
If ever any beauty I did see,
Which I desir'd, and got, 'twas but a dream of thee.

And now good-morrow to our waking souls,
Which watch not one another out of fear;
For love, all love of other sights controls,
And makes one little room, an everywhere.
Let sea-discoverers to new worlds have gone,
Let maps to others, worlds on worlds have shown,
Let us possess one world, each hath one, and is one.

---

[1]**Seven Sleepers'** legendary Christians imprisoned for 200 years, who woke into a new life
[2]**but this** apart from this

My face in thine eye, thine in mine appears,
And true plain hearts do in the faces rest;
Where can we find two better hemispheres,
Without sharp North, without declining West?
Whatever dies, was not mix'd equally;
If our two loves be one, or, thou and I
Love just alike in all, none of these loves can die.

A Song

by Thomas Carew

Carew (1594/5–1640) was influenced by John Donne, for whom he wrote an elegy, published with Donne's poems in 1633. His own poems were published in 1640. He was favoured by Charles I and, along with his friend Sir John Suckling, became one of the major Cavalier poets.

Ask me no more where Jove bestows,
When June is past, the fading rose;
For in your beauty's orient deep
These flowers, as in their causes, sleep.

Ask me no more whither doth stray
The golden atoms of the day;
For in pure love heaven did prepare
Those powders to enrich your hair.

Ask me no more whither doth haste
The nightingale, when May is past;
For in your sweet dividing throat
She winters, and keeps warm her note.

Ask me no more where those stars light,
That downwards fall in dead of night;
For in your eyes they sit, and there
Fixed become as in their sphere.

Ask me no more if east or west
The phœnix[1] builds her spicy nest;
For unto you at last she flies,
And in your fragrant bosom dies.

---

[1]**phoenix** legendary Arabian bird, reborn from its own ashes on a pyre of sweet spices

Letter to Lord Alfred Douglas, c.1891

from Oscar Wilde

Oscar Wilde (1854–1900) was famous for his flamboyant life as well as for his wit as a playwright and poet. He fell in love with the young Lord Alfred Douglas, whose father the Marquess of Queensberry opposed him in a court case, which led to Wilde's imprisonment in 1895 for homosexuality. After two years he was released and lived in France until his death.

My own dear boy – Your sonnet is quite lovely and it is a marvel that those red roseleaf lips of yours should be made no less for the music of song than for the madness of kissing. Your slim gilt soul walks between passion and poetry. I know that Hyacinthus, whom Apollo loved so madly, was you in Greek days. Why are you alone in London, and when do you go to Salisbury? Do go there and cool your hands in the grey twilight of Gothic things, and come here whenever you like. It is a lovely place; it only lacks you, but go to Salisbury first. Always with undying love.

Yours,
Oscar

Letter to her husband, 1920

from Zelda Fitzgerald

Zelda Sayre was married to the novelist Scott Fitzgerald (1896–1940), author of *The Great Gatsby*. Together they were leading figures in the party-going, extravagant American 'Jazz Age'. Their marriage was said to be tempestuous. She suffered from schizophrenia and was eventually committed to a sanatorium, where she died in a fire.

I look down the tracks and see you coming – and out of every haze & mist your darling rumpled trousers are hurrying to me – Without you, dearest dearest I couldn't see or hear or feel or think – or live – I love you so and I'm never in all our lives going to let us be apart another night. It's like begging for mercy of a storm or killing Beauty or growing old, without you. I want to kiss you so – and in the back where your dear hair starts and your chest – I love you – and I can't tell you how much – To think that I'll *die* without your knowing – Goofo, you've *got* to try [to] feel how much I do – how inanimate I am when you're gone – I can't even hate these damnable people – Nobodys got any right to live but us – and they're dirtying up our world and I can't hate them because I want you so – Come Quick – Come Quick to me – I could never do without you if you hated me and were covered with sores like a leper – if you ran away with another woman and starved me and beat me – I still would want you *I know* –

Lover, Lover, Darling –
Your Wife

Letter to Victor Hugo, 1833

from Juliette Drouet

The actress Juliette Drouet was the mistress of Victor Hugo (1802–1885), the French romantic poet and novelist. She acted as his secretary and regular travelling companion for most of his life.

To my beloved,

I have left you, my beloved. May the memory of my love follow and comfort you during our separation. If you only knew how much I love you, how essential you are to my life, you would not dare to stay away for an instant, you would always remain by my side, your heart pressed close to my heart, your soul to my soul.

It is now eleven o'clock in the evening. I have not seen you. I am waiting for you with great impatience, as I will wait for you always. It seems a whole century since I last saw you, since I last looked upon your features and became intoxicated with your gaze. Given my ill-luck, I shall probably not see you tonight.

Oh! come back, my love, my life, come back.

If you knew how I long for you, how the memory of last night leaves me delirious with joy and full of desire. How I long to give myself up in ecstasy to your sweet breath and to those kisses from your lips which fill me with delight!

My Victor, forgive me all my extravagances. They are a further token of my love. Love me. I need your love as a touchstone of my existence. It is the sun which breathes life into me.

I am going to bed. I shall fall asleep praying of you. My need to see you happy gives me faith.

My last waking thoughts, and all my dreams, are of you.

Juliette

Journal entry, 19 April 1956

by Sylvia Plath

The American poet Sylvia Plath (1932–1963) was born in Boston, and educated at Smith College, Massachusetts, and Cambridge University, where she met the poet Ted Hughes. They married on 16 June 1956; she described him as 'that big, dark, hunky boy'. Her feelings were intense and often troubled and she committed suicide in the bleak winter of 1963. Throughout her life she kept a journal.

Although Plath admired Hughes even before she first sought him out at a party in February 1956, their story is no fairy tale. In this extract, we see that Plath is concerned that her history of depression will come out and that she still has feelings for her previous lover Richard Sassoon.

Re Ted: you have accepted his being; you were desperate for this and you know what you must pay: utter vigilance in Cambridge (rumor will be legion, but there must be no proof; never drink, keep calm); loss of Richard and whistling void in guts when he leaves you with memory of his big iron violent virile body, incredible tendernesses & rich voice which makes poems & quirked people & music. Knowledge of his utter big luck & power & blast by it as he goes on, beyond – <u>the first</u> to keep on beyond – to hundreds of other women, other poems – 'I can make more love the more I make love.' If Richard's tenderness & virility & aesthetic rapport made you despair of going & finding one after him, you will <u>never</u> find a huge derrick-striding Ted with poems & richness – he makes you feel small, too-secure: he is not tender and has no love for you. Only a body – a girl-poet, an interlude – Consider yourself lucky to have been stabbed by him; <u>never complain</u> or <u>be bitter</u> or ask for more than normal human consideration as an integrated being. <u>Let him go</u>. Have the guts. Make him happy: cook, play, read, but don't loose others – work for Krook, Varsity & home – keep other cups & flagons full – never accuse or nag – let him run, reap, rip – and glory in the temporary sun of his ruthless force –

A Pink Wool Knitted Dress

by Ted Hughes

Ted Hughes (1930–1998), a Yorkshireman, was educated at Cambridge. In 1984 he became Poet Laureate. Most of his poems celebrate the beauty and violence of the natural world, but in the last year of his life he dedicated a collection of poems entitled *Birthday Letters* to his children, Frieda and Nicholas. These poems chart his courtship of and marriage to their mother, the poet Sylvia Plath. *A Pink Wool Knitted Dress* describes their actual wedding.

In your pink wool knitted dress
Before anything had smudged anything
You stood at the altar. Bloomsday.

Rain – so that a just-bought umbrella
Was the only furnishing about me
Newer than three years inured.
My tie – sole, drab, veteran RAF black –
Was the used-up symbol of a tie.
My cord jacket – thrice-dyed black, exhausted,
Just hanging on to itself.

I was a post-war, utility son-in-law!
Not quite the Frog-Prince. Maybe the Swineherd
Stealing this daughter's pedigree dreams
From under her watchtowered searchlit future.

No ceremony could conscript me
Out of my uniform. I wore my whole wardrobe –
Except for the odd, spare, identical item.
My wedding, like Nature, wanted to hide.
However – if we were going to be married
It had better be Westminster Abbey. Why not?
The Dean told us why not. That is how
I learned that I had a Parish Church.

St George of the Chimney Sweeps.
So we squeezed into marriage finally.
Your mother, brave even in this
US Foreign Affairs gamble,
Acted all bridesmaids and all guests,
Even – magnanimity – represented

My family
Who had heard nothing about it.
I had invited only their ancestors.
I had not even confided my theft of you
To a closest friend. For Best Man – my squire
To hold the meanwhile rings –
We requisitioned the sexton. Twist of the outrage:
He was packing children into a bus,
Taking them to the Zoo – in that downpour!
All the prison animals had to be patient
While we married.
                                        You were transfigured.
So slender and new and naked,
A nodding spray of wet lilac.
You shook, you sobbed with joy, you were ocean depth
Brimming with God.
You said you saw the heavens open
And show riches, ready to drop upon us.
Levitated beside you, I stood subjected
To a strange tense: the spellbound future.

In that echo-gaunt, weekday chancel
I see you
Wrestling to contain your flames
In your pink wool knitted dress
And in your eye-pupils – great cut jewels
Jostling their tear-flames, truly like big jewels
Shaken in a dice-cup and held up to me.

Two in the Campagna

by Robert Browning

Browning (1812–1889) was a playwright and poet, influenced by the romantics, Shelley, Byron and Keats. He admired the poems of Elizabeth Barrett, and met her in 1845. In 1846 they eloped to Italy after marrying in London – in secret because of her father's objections. Browning continued to spend much of his time in Italy after his wife's death in 1861.

I wonder do you feel to-day
   As I have felt since, hand in hand,
We sat down on the grass, to stray
   In spirit better through the land,
This morn of Rome and May?

For me, I touched a thought, I know,
   Has tantalized me many times,
(Like turns of thread the spiders throw
   Mocking across our path) for rhymes
To catch at and let go.

Help me to hold it: first it left
   The yellowing fennel, run to seed
There, branching from the brickwork's cleft,
   Some old tomb's ruin: yonder weed
Took up the floating weft,

Where one small orange cup amassed
   Five beetles, – blind and green they grope
Among the honey-meal, – and last,
   Everywhere on the grassy slope
I traced it. Hold it fast!

The champaign[1] with its endless fleece
   Of feathery grasses everywhere!
Silence and passion, joy and peace,
   An everlasting wash of air –
Rome's ghost since her decease.

Such life here, through such lengths of hours,
   Such miracles performed in play,
Such primal naked forms of flowers,
   Such letting Nature have her way
While Heaven looks from its towers.

How say you? Let us, O my dove,
   Let us be unashamed of soul,
As earth lies bare to heaven above.
   How is it under our control
To love or not to love?

I would that you were all to me,
   You that are just so much, no more –
Nor yours, nor mine, – nor slave nor free!
   Where does the fault lie? what the core
Of the wound, since wound must be?

I would I could adopt your will,
   See with your eyes, and set my heart
Beating by yours, and drink my fill
   At your soul's springs, – your part, my part
In life, for good and ill.

---

[1]**champaign** open countryside

No. I yearn upward – touch you close,
   Then stand away. I kiss your cheek,
Catch your soul's warmth, – I pluck the rose
   And love it more than tongue can speak –
Then the good minute goes.

Already how am I so far
   Out of that minute? Must I go
Still like the thistle-ball, no bar,
   Onward, whenever light winds blow,
Fixed by no friendly star?

Just when I seemed about to learn!
   Where is the thread now? Off again!
The old trick! Only I discern –
   Infinite passion, and the pain
Of finite hearts that yearn.

I Like it to Rain

by Nii Ayikwei Parkes

Nii Ayikwei Parkes, a Ghanaian writer, is also a performer and has led workshops in Africa, the Americas and Europe. He writes mainly in English, but occasionally in French and his native Ga. His first collection of poetry *Eyes of a Boy, Lips of a Man* was published in 1999. Since then he has written jazz-inspired poems and short stories and was a 2005 associate writer-in-residence for BBC Radio 3.

Sometimes I like it to rain
Heavy, relentless and loud,
So you burrow into me like pain,
And inhale me slow and free.

I like the clouds to stretch
And darken, and shadow the world
As water mimics prison bars,
And we bond like inmates.
For at these times the sun
Restrains its prying eyes,
Neighbours melt in the gloom,
And we are alone in love

It is morning,
But neither day nor night;
You are neither you nor I
I am neither prisoner nor free.

Anna Karenina

by Leo Tolstoy

Tolstoy (1828–1910), one of the greatest Russian writers, known especially for his epic novel *War and Peace*, became a powerful moral authority after several of his works were criticised for their unorthodox moral positions. *Anna Karenina* is about the illicit love of a married woman for an army officer; it examines her adultery and the destruction of her marriage. Meanwhile, the two other major characters, Constantine Levin and Kitty Shcherbatsky, have moved tentatively in an opposite direction – towards engagement and, in this extract, to their wedding day. This translation was made by Louise and Aylmer Maude in 1918.

The clergy put on their vestments and the priest and deacon came forward to the lectern that stood near the entrance doors. The priest turned to Levin and said something that Levin did not hear.

'Take the bride's hand and lead her,' said the best man.

For a long time Levin could not be made to understand what he had to do, and they were a long while trying to set him right. Just as they were going to give it up because he would either use the wrong hand or else take her by the wrong one, he at last comprehended that he with his right hand, without changing his position, must take her by her right hand. When at last he had taken her hand properly, the priest went a few steps in front of them and halted at the lectern. The crowd of friends and relatives, their voices buzzing and the ladies' trains rustling, moved after them. Someone stooped down to arrange the bride's veil. The church became so quiet that the drops of wax were heard falling from the candles.

The old priest, with his sacerdotal[1] headgear and his locks of grey hair, glistening like silver, combed back behind his ears,

---

[1]**sacerdotal** priestly

drew his small old hands out from beneath his vestments of heavy silver cloth with a large gold cross on the back, and began turning over some pages on the lectern.

Oblonsky stepped up cautiously, whispered something to him, made a sign to Levin, and stepped back again.

The priest lit two wax candles decorated with flowers, and holding them askew in his left hand so that the wax kept slowly dripping, turned to the young couple. It was the same priest who had heard Levin's confession. He looked wearily and sadly at the bride and bridegroom, sighed, and disengaging his right hand from the vestments, held it up in blessing over the bridegroom, and then over the bride; only in his manner when he placed his fingers on Kitty's bowed head there was a shade of tenderness. Then he gave them the candles, took the censer, and slowly stepped away from them.

'Is it really true?' thought Levin, and glanced round at his bride. He could see her profile slightly from above, and by the just perceptible movements of her lips and eyelashes he knew she was aware of his look. She did not turn, but her high frilled collar moved, rising to her pink little ear. He saw that a sigh had been suppressed within her breast and that the little hand in its long glove holding the candle trembled. All the worry about his shirt, his lateness, the conversation of their relatives, their displeasure at his ridiculous mishap, suddenly vanished from his mind and he felt happy though scared.

The handsome, tall senior deacon in a silver cloth alb,[2] his curled hair parted down the middle, came briskly forward lifting his stole with a practised movement of two fingers, and stopped opposite the priest.

'Bless us, Lord!' slowly succeeding one another, and vibratingly resonant, came the solemn tones.

'Blessed be our God, now and hereafter, for ever and ever!' replied the old priest meekly, in a sing-song voice, continuing to turn something over on the lectern. Then, harmoniously filling

[2]**alb** long vestment, pale in colour

the whole church from windows to vaulted roof, a full chord sung by the invisible choir rose, swelled, hung for a moment, and softly died away.

There were prayers as usual for the world above, for salvation, for the Synod,[3] for the Emperor, and also for the servants of God that day wedded, Constantine and Catherine.

'Let us pray to the Lord that He may send them perfect love, peace and help!' the whole church seemed to breathe with the senior deacon's voice.

Levin listened to the words and was struck by them. 'How did they find out that it is help, exactly help that I need?' he wondered, remembering his late fears and doubts. 'What do I know? What can I do in this awful matter without help? Help is exactly what I need now!'

When the deacon had finished the prayer for the Imperial family, the priest holding a book turned to the bride and bridegroom.

'Eternal God who joinest them that were separate,' he read in his mild sing-song voice, 'and hast ordained for them an indissoluble union in love; Thou who didst bless Isaac and Rebecca[4] and hast kept Thy promise to their heirs, bless these Thy servants, Constantine and Catherine, and lead them on the path of righteousness! Most merciful God, Lover of Man, we praise Thee! Glory be to the Father, and to the Son, and to the Holy Ghost, now and hereafter and for ever and ever!'

'Amen!' from the invisible choir, again floated through the air.

'"Joinest them that were separate"' – what a depth of meaning is in those words, and how well they fit in with what I am feeling at this moment!' thought Levin. 'Does she feel the same?'

Looking round he met her eyes. From the expression in them he concluded that she understood them as he did; but

---

[3]**Synod** church council

[4]**Isaac and Rebecca** Abraham's son Isaac married Rebecca (Genesis chapter 24)

this was not so. She understood hardly anything of the service and was not even listening to the words of the ceremony. She could neither listen nor understand, so deep was the one feeling that filled her soul and became ever stronger and stronger. It was a feeling of joy at the fruition of what had been for the last month and a half going on in her soul, of that which for those six weeks had gladdened and tortured her. On the day when, in the ballroom of the house in Arbat Street, she in her brown dress had gone up to him and silently plighted herself to him, on that day and in that hour a complete rupture seemed to have taken place within her soul between her former life and this other new and entirely unknown life - although in fact the old life still went on. Those six weeks had been the most blissful and at the same time the most trying of her life. The whole of her life, all her desires and hopes, were concentrated on this one man, still incomprehensible to her, to whom she was bound by a feeling - even more incomprehensible than the man himself - which now attracted and now repelled her. Meantime she went on living under the conditions of her old life and was horrified at herself: at her utter and unconquerable indifference to all her past, the things, habits and people who had loved and still loved her, to her mother who was hurt by her indifference, to her dear, affectionate father whom she had previously loved more than anyone else on earth. At one moment she was horrified at this indifference, and the next moment rejoiced at that which caused her indifference. She could not think of or desire anything but life with this man; but, as that life had not yet begun, she could not even clearly picture it to herself. There was only anticipation, fear and joy at something new and unknown; and now at any moment the anticipation and uncertainty, and the remorse at repudiating her former life, would all come to an end and something new would begin. This new life could not help being terrible in consequence of its incertitude, but terrible or not it was already an accomplished fact within her soul six weeks ago, and was now only being sanctified.

Again turning to the reading-desk the priest with some difficulty picked up Kitty's little ring, and asking Levin for his hand put the ring on the tip of his finger. 'The servant of God, Constantine, is betrothed to the servant of God, Catherine,' and having put a big ring on Kitty's slender, rosy finger, pathetic in its weakness, the priest repeated the same words.

Several times the couple tried to guess what was expected of them, and blundered each time, the priest prompting them in whispers. When what was necessary had at length been complied with, he made the sign of the cross over them with the rings and again gave the larger one to Kitty and the little one to Levin, and again they blundered and passed the rings twice backwards and forwards without doing what was necessary.

Dolly, Chirikov and Oblonsky came forward to help them. The result was some confusion, whispering and smiles, but the expression of solemn emotion on the young couple's faces did not change; on the contrary, while they fumbled with their hands they looked even more solemn and serious than before, and the smile with which Oblonsky whispered to them to put on their rings involuntarily died on his lips. He felt that any kind of smile would hurt their feelings.

'Thou hast from the beginning created them male and female,' read the priest when they had exchanged rings. 'Through Thee the wife is knit to the husband for a helpmeet and to procreate the human race. Therefore, O God our Lord, who sentest down Thy truth upon Thy heritage, and gavest Thy promises to our fathers from generation to generation of Thy chosen people, look down upon Thy servant Constantine and Thy servant Catherine and strengthen them in their union with faith and concord in truth and love . . . '

Levin felt more and more that his ideas of marriage and his dreams of how he would arrange his life had been but childishness, and that this was something he had never understood and was now still further from understanding, although it was happening to him; and in his breast a tremor rose higher and higher, and the unruly tears came to his eyes.

Troilus and Cressida

by William Shakespeare

Shakespeare (1564–1616) probably read Homer's account of the Trojan War in a translation by his contemporary, Chapman, and the love story of Troilus and Cressida in Chaucer's great narrative poem. His play explores disillusion and deceit in both the politics of the war and the failure of love. Cressida's uncle Pandarus brings her to the young prince Troilus, they fall passionately in love and, in this extract, they speak of their unwavering commitment. This scene is especially poignant in the light of Cressida's later betrayal of Troilus, with the Greek leader Diomede.

CRESSIDA Prince Troilus, I have loved you night and day
For many weary months.
TROILUS Why was my Cressid then so hard to win?
CRESSIDA Hard to seem won; but I was won, my lord,
With the first glance that ever – pardon me;
If I confess much, you will play the tyrant.
I love you now; but not, till now, so much
But I might master it. In faith, I lie!
My thoughts were like unbridled children, grown
Too headstrong for their mother. See, we fools!
Why have I blabbed? Who shall be true to us,
When we are so unsecret to ourselves?
But, though I loved you well, I wooed you not;
And yet, good faith, I wished myself a man,
Or that we women had men's privilege
Of speaking first. Sweet, bid me hold my tongue;
For in this rapture I shall surely speak
The thing I shall repent. See, see, your silence,
Cunning in dumbness, from my weakness draws
My very soul of counsel! Stop my mouth.

TROILUS And shall, albeit sweet music issues thence. *(kisses her)*
PANDARUS Pretty, i'faith.
CRESSIDA My lord, I do beseech you, pardon me:
'Twas not my purpose thus to beg a kiss.
I am ashamed. O heavens! what have I done?
For this time will I take my leave, my lord.
TROILUS Your leave, sweet Cressid?
PANDARUS Leave! An you take leave till tomorrow morning –
CRESSIDA Pray you, content you.
TROILUS What offends you, lady?
CRESSIDA Sir, mine own company.
TROILUS You cannot shun yourself.
CRESSIDA Let me go and try.
I have a kind of self resides with you,
But an unkind self that itself will leave
To be another's fool. I would be gone.
Where is my wit? I know not what I speak.
TROILUS Well know they what they speak that speak so wisely.
CRESSIDA Perchance, my lord, I show more craft than love,
And fell so roundly[1] to a large confession
To angle for your thoughts; but you are wise,
Or else you love not: for to be wise and love
Exceeds man's might; that dwells with gods above.
TROILUS O that I thought it could be in a woman –
As, if it can, I will presume in you –
To feed for aye[2] her lamp and flame of love;
To keep her constancy in plight[3] and youth,
Outliving beauties outward, with a mind
That doth renew swifter than blood decays!

---

[1]**roundly** directly, straight out
[2]**for aye** for ever
[3]**plight** healthy condition

Or that persuasion could but thus convince me
That my integrity and truth to you
Might be affronted[4] with the match and weight
Of such a winnowed[5] purity in love –
How were I then uplifted! But, alas,
I am as true as truth's simplicity,
And simpler than the infancy of truth!

CRESSIDA In that I'll war with you.

TROILUS O virtuous fight,
When right with right wars who shall be most right!
True swains[6] in love shall in the world to come
Approve their truths by Troilus. When their rhymes,
Full of protest, of oath, and big compare,[7]
Want similes, truth tired with iteration[8] –
'As true as steel, as plantage to the moon,
As sun to day, as turtle[9] to her mate,
As iron to adamant,[10] as earth to th'centre' –
Yet, after all comparisons of truth,
As truth's authentic author to be cited,
'As true as Troilus' shall crown up the verse
And sanctify the numbers.[11]

CRESSIDA Prophet may you be!
If I be false, or swerve a hair from truth,
When time is old and hath forgot itself,

---

[4]**affronted** equally faced
[5]**winnowed** sifted (i.e. any impurities have been blown away)
[6]**swains** shepherds (conventionally poet-lovers)
[7]**compare** comparison
[8]**iteration** being repeated
[9]**turtle** turtle-dove, famous for fidelity
[10]**adamant** legendary substance of great magnetism and hardness
[11]**numbers** verses

When waterdrops have worn the stones of Troy,
And blind oblivion swallowed cities up,
And mighty states characterless are grated[12]
To dusty nothing, yet let memory,
From false to false, among false maids in love,
Upbraid[13] my falsehood! When they've said 'as false
As air, as water, wind or sandy earth,
As fox to lamb, or wolf to heifer's calf,
Pard to the hind, or stepdame[14] to her son',
Yea let them say, to stick the heart of falsehood,
'As false as Cressid'.

---

[12]**characterless are grated** are worn away, leaving no distinctive trace
[13]**upbraid** reproach
[14]**stepdame** step-mother

The Rainbow

by D. H. Lawrence

D. H. Lawrence (1885–1930), the son of a coal-miner, was born in Eastwood, a village outside Nottingham. His first novel, *Sons and Lovers* (1913), is a semi-autobiographical account of his own journey towards sexual maturity. Lawrence's work was always controversial (see *The Trial of Lady Chatterley*, p. 172), and *The Rainbow* was declared obscene and seized by the police. This extract describes one of the most joyful honeymoons in literature – the middle generation of the Brangwen family, Will and Anna. Lawrence suspends his lovers away from time and space, in a new creation of their own.

Will Brangwen had some weeks of holiday after his marriage, so the two took their honeymoon in full hands, alone in their cottage together.

And to him, as the days went by, it was as if the heavens had fallen, and he were sitting with her among the ruins, in a new world, everybody else buried, themselves two blissful survivors, with everything to squander as they would. At first, he could not get rid of a culpable sense of licence on his part. Wasn't there some duty outside, calling him and he did not come?

It was all very well at night, when the doors were locked and the darkness drawn round the two of them. Then they *were* the only inhabitants of the visible earth, the rest were under the flood. And being alone in the world, they were a law unto themselves, they could enjoy and squander and waste like conscienceless gods.

But in the morning, as the carts clanked by, and children shouted down the lane; as the hucksters[1] came calling their wares, and the church clock struck eleven, and he and she had not got up yet, even to breakfast, he could not help feeling

---

[1]**hucksters** pedlars

guilty, as if he were committing a breach of the law – ashamed that he was not up and doing.

'Doing what?' she asked. 'What is there to do? You will only lounge about.'

Still, even lounging about was respectable. One was at least in connection with the world, then. Whereas now, lying so still and peacefully, while the daylight came obscurely through the drawn blind, one was severed from the world, one shut oneself off in tacit denial of the world. And he was troubled.

But it was so sweet and satisfying lying there talking desultorily with her. It was sweeter than sunshine, and not so evanescent. It was even irritating the way the church-clock kept on chiming: there seemed no space between the hours, just a moment, golden and still, whilst she traced his features with her finger-tips, utterly careless and happy, and he loved her to do it.

But he was strange and unused. So suddenly, everything that had been before was shed away and gone. One day, he was a bachelor, living with the world. The next day, he was with her, as remote from the world as if the two of them were buried like a seed in darkness. Suddenly, like a chestnut falling out of a burr, he was shed naked and glistening on to a soft, fecund earth, leaving behind him the hard rind of worldly knowledge and experience. He heard it in the hucksters' cries, the noise of carts, the calling of children. And it was all like the hard, shed rind, discarded. Inside, in the softness and stillness of the room, was the naked kernel, that palpitated in silent activity, absorbed in reality.

Inside the room was a great steadiness, a core of living eternity. Only far outside, at the rim, went on the noise and the destruction. Here at the centre the great wheel was motionless, centred upon itself. Here was a poised, unflawed stillness that was beyond time, because it remained the same, inexhaustible, unchanging, unexhausted.

As they lay close together, complete and beyond the touch of time or change, it was as if they were at the very centre of all the slow wheeling of space and the rapid agitation of life, deep, deep inside them all, at the centre where there is utter radiance, and eternal being, and the silence absorbed in praise: the steady core of all movements, the unawakened sleep of all wakefulness. They found themselves there, and they lay still, in each other's arms; for their moment they were at the heart of eternity, whilst time roared far off, forever far off, towards the rim.

The Song of Songs: Chapter 5

from the Bible

The Song of Songs, also known as *The Song of Solomon*, is the 22nd Book of the Old Testament in the Bible. It reads as a celebration of erotic love, a dialogue between bride and bridegroom, and Biblical scholars have interpreted this text allegorically as representing the relationship between God and his people. In this extract from the 1611 King James version of the Bible, the Bride describes her Beloved.

I am come into my garden, my sister, my spouse: I have gathered my myrrh[1] with my spice; I have eaten my honey-comb with my honey; I have drunk my wine with my milk: eat, O friends; drink, yea, drink abundantly, O beloved.

2 I sleep, but my heart waketh: it is the voice of my beloved that knocketh, saying, Open to me, my sister, my love, my dove, my undefiled: for my head is filled with dew, and my locks with the drops of the night.

3 I have put off my coat; how shall I put it on? I have washed my feet; how shall I defile them?

4 My beloved put in his hand by the hole of the door, and my bowels were moved for him.

5 I rose up to open to my beloved; and my hands dropped with myrrh, and my fingers with sweet smelling myrrh, upon the handles of the lock.

6 I opened to my beloved; but my beloved had withdrawn himself, and was gone: my soul failed when he spake: I sought him, but I could not find him; I called him, but he gave me no answer.

7 The watchmen that went about the city found me, they smote me, they wounded me; the keepers of the walls took away my veil from me.

---

[1]**myrrh** a gum resin used for making incense

8 I charge you, O daughters of Jerusalem, if ye find my beloved, that ye tell him, that I am sick of love.

9 What is thy beloved more than another beloved, O thou fairest among women? what is thy beloved more than another beloved, that thou dost so charge us?

10 My beloved is white and ruddy, the chiefest among ten thousand.

11 His head is as the most fine gold, his locks are bushy, and black as a raven.

12 His eyes are as the eyes of doves by the rivers of waters, washed with milk, and fitly set.

13 His cheeks are as a bed of spices, as sweet flowers: his lips like lilies, dropping sweet smelling myrrh.

14 His hands are as gold rings set with the beryl: his belly is as bright ivory overlaid with sapphires.

15 His legs are as pillars of marble, set upon sockets of fine gold: his countenance is as Lebanon, excellent as the cedars.

16 His mouth is most sweet: yea, he is altogether lovely. This is my beloved, and this is my friend, O daughters of Jerusalem.

Music, When Soft Voices Die

by Percy Bysshe Shelley

Shelley (1792–1822) was one of the leading English Romantic writers and continued the radical beliefs, social and political, which derived from the French Revolution. He also translated classical works, wrote essays, followed Wordsworth as a poet of idealistic philosophy and was an accomplished lyricist.

Music, when soft voices die,
Vibrates in the memory –
Odours, when sweet violets sicken,
Live within the sense they quicken.

Rose leaves, when the rose is dead,
Are heaped for the beloved's bed;
And so thy thoughts, when thou art gone,
Love itself shall slumber on.

Questions

In all of these questions you should consider:

a the ways the writers' choice of form, structure and language shape your responses to the extracts

b how your wider reading in the literature of love has contributed to your understanding and interpretation of the extracts.

1 John Donne was described as the 'monarch of wit'. Consider the impact of witty invention in *The Good-Morrow* and in Carew's *Song*.

2 Examine the relationship between private feelings and public ceremony in the extracts from *Anna Karenina* and *A Pink Wool Knitted Dress*.

3 Consider the effects of questions, confusion and uncertainty in *Two on the Campagna*.

4 Explain any significant differences between the language Shakespeare gives to the man and to the woman in the extract from *Troilus and Cressida*.

5 Which one of the four prose extracts (Wilde, Fitzgerald, Drouet, Plath) and three short poems (McGough, Donne, Carew) gives the strongest impression of a private experience? Which gives the least? Are you influenced by any distinction between the language of prose and verse? Give evidence for your views.

6 Compare the ways in which the extracts from *The Rainbow* and *The Good-Morrow* create a sense of new beginnings. What part do the natural elements play?

7 Compare the relationship between desire and fulfilment in any two or three extracts in this section.

8 Sometimes the ecstatic togetherness of two lovers may be expressed in heightened eloquence; sometimes words seem hesitant or inadequate. Consider some of the extracts in this section in the light of this distinction.

Further reading

- You will find that much writing about love achieved, consummated and celebrated also acknowledges mortality, which may either darken the lovers' happiness or give it an extra intensity, as in Keats's *The Eve of St Agnes* (1819) and his sonnet *Bright Star,* and in Shakespeare's three great love tragedies, *Romeo and Juliet*, *Antony and Cleopatra* and *Othello*. Many of Shakespeare's love sonnets (for example, 18 and 116) celebrate love that defies the passage of time.
- Book 3 of Chaucer's *Troilus and Criseyde* shows the ecstasy of young love, while *The Franklin's Tale*, the most positive of his marriage tales, begins with the calm assurance of two noble lovers deferring to each other's wishes.
- Two often quoted poems, Larkin's *An Arundel Tomb* and Sidney's *My true love hath my heart*, both explore as well as celebrate love. Many anthologies also include Auden's *As I walked out one evening,* his lullaby *Lay your sleeping head*, and Roy Fuller's wittily exuberant *Valentine*.
- Your reading of *Two in the Campagna* (p. 110) may lead you to consider the woman's voice, that of Browning's wife, Elizabeth Barrett Browning. Her *Sonnets from the Portuguese* record her joy at their marriage.
- If you enjoyed *Music, When Soft Voices Die* (p. 128) you might like to read the love poetry of the often overlooked Romantic poet John Clare.
- John Donne and John Wilmot, Earl of Rochester were both frequent and successful lovers and also lively poets; compare, for example, Donne's *The Canonization* with Rochester's *Song: An Age in her Embraces Past*.
- Powerful novels from the 19th century include Turgenev's *The Torrents of Spring* and Flaubert's *Madame Bovary*.
- A. S. Byatt's *Possession*, written in 1990, is set over 100 years earlier, as is Lampedusa's *The Leopard*, which explores the passionate love between a young nobleman and the beautiful daughter of a businessman. D. H. Lawrence, writing in the early 20th century, celebrated love between man and woman: *The Rainbow*, *Women in Love* and *Lady Chatterley's Lover* were bold experiments in exploring sexual and spiritual communion. All these are substantial and thoughtful

novels, as well as being very convincing accounts of passionate love.

- Erotic imagery, seen here in *The Song of Songs*, also characterises two American novels: *Their Eyes were Watching God* by Zora Neale Hurston and *Beloved* by Toni Morrison, both of which also celebrate the spiritual nature of love.
- *Gone with the Wind* is the most iconic of all love films. Many recent films have been influenced by this classic, especially when war is used as a background to a passionate celebration of love. For example, consider *Casablanca* and *Atonement*.

4 Forbidden love

Passionate love is so consuming that it can eclipse all reason, all social and moral discipline and all fear of consequences. Society has always been alarmed by the waywardness of love, the fact that it often can't be explained, predicted or controlled. Religious authorities have been concerned about moral anarchy. The history of Christianity in the West is full of stories about fierce penalties imposed on those who loved outside the permitted area of marriage, and especially those who committed adultery, incest or sodomy.

Literature about love often explores these 'forbidden' areas: partly because there is excitement in flirting with danger (for the writer as well as for the lovers); partly because exploring extremes of behaviour may throw special light on what it means to be human. In Webster's *The Duchess of Malfi* (1614) the heroine conducts a secret affair and marriage with her steward, offending her violent brothers and putting the family reputation at risk. In one of the most gripping scenes in the play she sits at her dressing table speaking, so she thinks, to her husband and jokes at their dangerous predicament: 'Love mixed with fear is sweetest.' She is unaware that her husband is no longer there and that her brother has crept silently into the room behind her.

In the Garden of Eden Adam and Eve fell from their state of grace when they disobeyed God by eating fruit from the forbidden tree. The story has been variously interpreted and has often appeared, directly or allusively, in Western literature. You will find one of the most powerful and seductive in Book 9 of Milton's epic poem *Paradise Lost*. Writers who have a misogynist bias and want to warn against the dangers of carnal love tell of how Adam allowed himself to be seduced by Eve, so that his discipline and reason deserted him. They believe that original sin began with the woman; she and the serpent who first seduced her have been considered equally sinister and devious. Anti-feminist writers often suggest that sexual manipulation is a female weapon, sometimes even associated with witchcraft. They argue that because women have a particular power to trick, confuse and humiliate men, they may be portrayed simultaneously as partners and enemies. You may not be surprised to learn that most of these writers are men!

It is worth noting, however, that a woman in literature who uses her sexuality to manipulate a man is not necessarily the villain of the piece. In *Sir Gawain and the Green Knight* (extract p. 139) the beautiful wife of Gawain's host certainly presents a sexual temptation, though she is no conventional 'femme fatale'. Later in the story we learn that her husband knows of the temptation, and her three visits to Gawain's bedroom have been designed to test his virtue as a true Arthurian knight. He achieves an almost perfect courteous resistance, but in accepting her present of a silk girdle he commits the slightest of errors. Far from being a misogynist story, it has sometimes been read as a feminist adventure, since the woman is at the heart of its controlling moral purpose.

Here are some of literature's most powerful stories about forbidden love:

- Sophocles's *Oedipus Rex* tells of how King Oedipus learns that he killed his father, slept with his mother and had children by her.
- In Greek mythology Phaedra was married to Theseus but fell in love with Hippolytus, her step-son. There are various versions of the disaster that occurred when their illicit love came to light. An extract from Sarah Kane's version is on p. 146.
- The legendary King Arthur and his Round Table of devoted knights have inspired many writers. One of the most morally complicated stories is based on the love triangle of Arthur, his queen Guinevere and Sir Launcelot, the knight most celebrated for his courage and chivalry.

Of course, tastes and restrictions change: what is forbidden in one era may be only mildly disturbing, or even legitimate, in another. Therefore, when you read you should try to project part of your imagination back into the cultural world of the text, even though its values may now seem unfamiliar. Even over the last 100 years attitudes to religion and social class have changed, and to sex perhaps even more so: for example, homosexual relationships are now generally accepted and acknowledged, so that a novel such as E. M. Forster's *Maurice*, which was published only posthumously, in 1971, would now be much less controversial.

The God of Small Things

by Arundhati Roy

Born in 1961, Arundhati Roy won the Booker prize in 1997 for her first novel *The God of Small Things*. She trained as an architect and has also made a living by writing film scripts. She is well known as a political activist.

Her novel takes place in the Kerala state in India. Ammu, the mother of the 7-year-old twins from whose point of view much of the story is narrated, has become deeply attracted to Velutha, an untouchable, the lowest of the low in the caste system. They meet at night by the river.

She moved quickly through the darkness, like an insect following a chemical trail. She knew the path to the river as well as her children did and could have found her way there blindfolded. She didn't know what it was that made her hurry through the undergrowth. That turned her walk into a run. That made her arrive on the banks of the Meenachal breathless. Sobbing. As though she was late for something. As though her life depended on getting there in time. As though she knew he would be there. Waiting. As though *he* knew she would come.

He did.

Know.

That knowledge had slid into him that afternoon. Cleanly. Like the sharp edge of a knife. When history had slipped up. While he had held her little daughter in his arms. When her eyes had told him he was not the only giver of gifts. That she had gifts to give him too, that in return for his boats, his boxes, his small windmills, she would trade her deep dimples when she smiled. Her smooth brown skin. Her shining shoulders. Her eyes that were always somewhere else.

He wasn't there.

Ammu sat on the stone steps that led to the water. She buried her head in her arms, feeling foolish for having been so sure. So *certain*.

Further downstream in the middle of the river, Velutha floated on his back, looking up at the stars. His paralysed brother and his one-eyed father had eaten the dinner he had cooked them and were asleep. So he was free to lie in the river and drift slowly with the current. A log. A serene crocodile. Coconut trees bent into the river and watched him float by. Yellow bamboo wept. Small fish took coquettish liberties with him. Pecked him.

He flipped over and began to swim. Upstream. Against the current. He turned towards the bank for one last look, treading water, feeling foolish for having been so sure. So *certain*.

When he saw her the detonation almost drowned him. It took all his strength to stay afloat. He trod water, standing in the middle of a dark river.

She didn't see the knob of his head bobbing over the dark river. He could have been anything. A floating coconut. In any case she wasn't looking. Her head was buried in her arms.

He watched her. He took his time.

Had he known that he was about to enter a tunnel whose only egress was his own annihilation, would he have turned away?

Perhaps.

Perhaps not.

Who can tell?

He began to swim towards her. Quietly. Cutting through the water with no fuss. He had almost reached the bank when she looked up and saw him. His feet touched the muddy riverbed. As he rose from the dark river and walked up the stone steps, she saw that the world they stood in was his. That he belonged to it. That it belonged to him. The water. The mud. The trees. The fish. The stars. He moved so easily through it. As she watched him she understood the quality of his beauty. How his labour had shaped him. How the wood he fashioned had fashioned him. Each plank he planed, each nail he drove, each thing he made, had moulded him. Had left its stamp on him. Had given him his strength, his supple grace.

He wore a thin white cloth around his loins, looped between his dark legs. He shook the water from his hair. She could see his smile in the dark. His white, sudden smile that he had carried with him from boyhood into manhood. His only luggage.

They looked at each other. They weren't thinking any more. The time for that had come and gone. Smashed smiles lay ahead of them. But that would be later.

Lay Ter.

He stood before her with the river dripping from him. She stayed sitting on the steps, watching him. Her face pale in the moonlight. A sudden chill crept over him. His heart hammered. It was all a terrible mistake. He had misunderstood her. The whole thing was a figment of his imagination. This was a trap. There were people in the bushes. Watching. She was the delectable bait. How could it be otherwise? They had seen him in the march. He tried to make his voice casual. Normal. It came out in a croak.

'Ammukutty . . . what is it?'

She went to him and laid the length of her body against his. He just stood there. He didn't touch her. He was shivering. Partly with cold. Partly terror. Partly aching desire. Despite his fear his body was prepared to take the bait. It wanted her. Urgently. His wetness wet her. She put her arms around him.

He tried to be rational: *What's the worst thing that can happen? I could lose everything. My job. My family. My livelihood. Everything.*

She could hear the wild hammering of his heart.

She held him till it calmed down. Somewhat.

She unbuttoned her shirt. They stood there. Skin to skin. Her brownness against his blackness. Her softness against his hardness. Her nut-brown breasts (that wouldn't support a toothbrush) against his smooth ebony chest. She smelled the river on him. His Particular Paravan smell that so disgusted Baby Kochamma. Ammu put out her tongue and tasted it, in the hollow of his throat. On the lobe of his ear. She pulled his head down towards her and kissed his mouth. A cloudy kiss. A kiss that demanded a kiss-back. He kissed her back. First cautiously. Then urgently. Slowly his arms came up behind her. He stroked her back. Very gently. She could feel the skin on his palms. Rough. Calloused. Sandpaper. He was careful not to hurt her. She could feel how soft she felt to him. She could feel herself through him. Her skin. The way her body existed only where he touched her. The rest of her was smoke. She felt him shudder against her. His hands were on her haunches (that could support a whole array of toothbrushes), pulling her hips against his, to let her know how much he wanted her.

Biology designed the dance. Terror timed it. Dictated the rhythm with which their bodies answered each other. As though they knew already that for each tremor of pleasure they would pay with an equal measure of pain. As though they knew that how far they went would be measured against how far they would be taken. So they held back. Tormented each other. Gave of each other slowly. But that only made it worse. It only raised the stakes. It only cost them more. Because it smoothed the wrinkles, the fumble and rush of unfamiliar love and roused them to fever pitch.

Behind them the river pulsed through the darkness, shimmering like wild silk. Yellow bamboo wept.

Night's elbows rested on the water and watched them.

Sir Gawain and the Green Knight

Anonymous (translated by Simon Armitage)

The young knight Gawain is fulfilling his promise to search out and challenge the mysterious Green Knight who visited King Arthur's court a year before. It is Christmas time in the cold and unfamiliar north country and he is being entertained by a generous and noble host. In the early morning Gawain lies in bed while his host is out hunting. The lady of the house enters his room . . .

This modern translation of the famous 14th-century text is by Simon Armitage.

Yes, he dozes in a daze, dreams and mutters
like a mournful man with his mind on dark matters –
how destiny might deal him a death-blow on the day
when he grapples with the giant in the green chapel;
of how the strike of the axe must be suffered without
        struggle.
But sensing her presence there he surfaces from sleep,
drags himself out of his dreams to address her.
Laughing warmly she walks towards him
and finds his face with the friendliest kiss.
In a worthy style he welcomes the woman
and seeing her so lovely and alluringly dressed,
every feature so faultless, her complexion so fine,
a passionate heat takes hold in his heart.
Speech tripped from their tongues and they traded smiles,
and a bond of friendship was forged there, all blissful
                and bright.
        They talk with tenderness
        and pride, and yet their plight
        is perilous unless
        sweet Mary minds her knight.

For that noble princess pushed him and pressed him,
nudged him ever nearer to a limit where he needed
to allow her love or impolitely reject it.
He was careful to be courteous and avoid uncouthness,
cautious that his conduct might be classed as sinful
and counted as betrayal by the keeper of the castle.
'I shall not succumb,' he swore to himself.
With affectionate laughter he fenced and deflected
all the loving phrases which leapt from her lips.
'You shall bear the blame,' said the beautiful one,
'if you feel no love for the female you lie with,
and wound her, more than anyone on earth, to the heart.
Unless, of course, there is a lady in your life
to whom you are tied and so tightly attached
that you could not begin to break the bond.
So in honesty and trust now tell me the truth;
for the sake of all love, don't be secretive or speak
with guile.'
'You judge wrong, by Saint John,'
he said to her, and smiled.
'There is no other one
and won't be for a while!'

'Those words,' said the woman, 'are the worst insult.
But I asked, and you answered, and now I ache.
Kiss me warmly and then I will walk in the world
in mourning like a lady who loved too much.'
Stooping and sighing she kisses him sweetly,
then withdraws from his side, saying as she stands,
'But before we part will you find me some small favour?
Will you give me some gift – a glove at least,
that might leaven my loss when we meet in my memory?'
'Well it were,' said Gawain. 'I wish I had here
my most priceless possession as a present for your sweetness,
for over and over you deserve and are owed
the highest prize I could hope to offer.

But I would not wish on you a worthless token,
and it strikes me as unseemly that you should receive
nothing greater than a glove as a keepsake from Gawain.
I am here on an errand in an unknown land
without men bearing bags of beautiful gifts,
which I greatly regret through my regard for you;
but man must live by his means, and neither mope
or moan.'
The pretty one replies:
'Nay, noble knight, you mean
you'll pass to me no prize.
No matter. Here is mine.'

She offers him a ring of rich, red gold,
and the stunning stone set upon it stood proud,
beaming and burning with the brightness of the sun;
what wealth it was worth you can well imagine.
But he would not accept it, and said straight away,
'By God, no tokens will I take at this time;
I have nothing to give, so nothing will I gain.'
She insists he receives it but still he resists,
and swears, on his name as a knight, to say no.
Snubbed by his decision, she said to him then,
'You refuse my ring because you find it too fine,
and don't dare to be deeply indebted to me;
so I give you my girdle, a lesser thing to gain.'
From around her body she unbuckled the belt
which tightened the tunic beneath her topcoat,
a green silk girdle trimmed with gold,
exquisitely edged and hemmed by hand.
And she sweetly beseeched Sir Gawain to receive it,
in spite of its slightness, and hoped he would accept.
But still he maintained he intended to take
neither gold nor girdle, until by God's grace

the challenge he had chosen was finally achieved.
'With apologies I pray you are not displeased,
but I must firmly refuse you, no matter how flattered
I am.
For all your grace I owe
a thousand thank-yous, ma'am.
I shall through sun and snow
remain your loyal man.'

'And now he sends back my silk,' the lady responded,
'so simple in itself, or so it appears,
so little and unlikely, worth nothing, or less.
But the knight who knew of the power knitted in it
would pay a high price to possess it, probably.
For the body which is bound within this green belt,
as long as it is buckled robustly about him,
will be safe against those who seek to strike him,
and all the slyness on earth wouldn't see him slain.'
The man mulled it over, and it entered his mind
that this girdle being given could be just the job
to save him from the strike in his challenge at the chapel.
With luck, it might let him escape with his life.
So relenting at last he let her speak,
and promptly she pressed him to take the present,
and he granted her wish, gave in with good grace,
though the woman begged him not to whisper a word
of this gift to her husband, and Gawain agreed;
those words of theirs within those walls
should stay.
His thanks are heartfelt, then.
No sooner can he say
how much it matters, when
three kisses come his way.

Eloisa to Abelard

by Alexander Pope

Alexander Pope (1688–1744) is better known as a great satirist, but some of his early poems were about passionate feelings. This verse letter, published in 1717, is based on the 12th-century love-story of the great scholar Peter Abelard and the much younger Eloisa, daughter to a canon of Paris Cathedral.

When he learns of the love affair, Eloisa's father hires men to break into Abelard's house and emasculate him. Abelard continues to write and teach and founds a nunnery in which Eloisa and others later take refuge. She happens to read a letter in which Abelard tells of his misfortunes, and this prompts her to begin writing to him.

O cursed, dear horrors of all-conscious night!
How glowing guilt exalts the keen delight!
Provoking Dæmons all restraint remove,
And stir within me ev'ry source of love.
I hear thee, view thee, gaze o'er all thy charms,
And round thy phantom glue my clasping arms.
I wake – no more I hear, no more I view,
The phantom flies me, as unkind as you.
I call aloud; it hears not what I say;
I stretch my empty arms; it glides away:
To dream once more I close my willing eyes;
Ye soft illusions, dear deceits, arise!
Alas, no more! – methinks we wand'ring go
Through dreary wastes, and weep each other's woe;
Where round some mould'ring tower pale ivy creeps,
And low-browed rocks hang nodding o'er the deeps.
Sudden you mount! you beckon from the skies;
Clouds interpose, waves roar, and winds arise.
I shriek, start up, the same sad prospect find,
And wake to all the griefs I left behind.
For thee the fates, severely kind, ordain

A cool suspense from pleasure and from pain;
Thy life a long, dead calm of fixed repose;
No pulse that riots, and no blood that glows.
Still as the sea, ere winds were taught to blow,
Or moving spirit bade the waters flow;
Soft as the slumbers of a saint forgiven,
And mild as opening gleams of promised Heaven.
Come, *Abelard*! for what hast thou to dread?
The torch of *Venus* burns not for the dead;
Nature stands check'd; religion disapproves:
Ev'n thou art cold – yet *Eloisa* loves.
Ah hopeless, lasting flames! like those that burn
To light the dead, and warm th' unfruitful urn.
What scenes appear where'er I turn my view!
The dear ideas, where I fly, pursue,
Rise in the grove, before the altar rise,
Stain all my soul, and wanton[1] in my eyes!
I waste the Matin[2] lamp in sighs for thee,
Thy image steals between my God and me,
Thy voice I seem in ev'ry hymn to hear,
With ev'ry bead I drop too soft a tear.
When from the censer clouds of fragrance roll,
And swelling organs lift the rising soul,
One thought of thee puts all the pomp to flight,
Priests, Tapers, Temples, swim before my sight:
In seas of flame my plunging soul is drowned,
While altars blaze, and Angels tremble round.
While prostrate here in humble grief I lie,
Kind, virtuous drops just gath'ring in my eye,
While praying, trembling, in the dust I roll,
And dawning grace is opening on my soul:
Come, if thou dar'st, all charming as thou art!
Oppose thyself to Heaven; dispute my heart;

---

[1]**wanton** play amorously
[2]**Matin** matins, the early morning service

Come, with one glance of those deluding eyes
Blot out each bright Idea of the skies;
Take back that grace, those sorrows, and those tears,
Take back my fruitless penitence and prayers,
Snatch me, just mounting, from the bless'd abode,
Assist the Fiends and tear me from my God!

Phaedra's Love

by Sarah Kane

Sarah Kane (1971–1999) deals explicitly in her plays with themes of death, sex, violence and mental illness. For a time she was artist-in-residence at the innovative Royal Court Theatre. She struggled for many years with depression, which led her to suicide. In *Phaedra's Love* she updated Seneca's version of the Greek myth about the dangerously forbidden relationship between Theseus's wife Phaedra and her step-son Hippolytus, who is seen in the play as squalid, self-indulgent and manipulative. In this scene (scene 3) Phaedra argues with her daughter Strophe.

STROPHE *is working.*
PHAEDRA *enters.*

STROPHE Mother.

PHAEDRA Go away fuck off don't touch me don't talk to me stay with me.

STROPHE What's wrong?

PHAEDRA Nothing. Nothing at all.

STROPHE I can tell.

PHAEDRA Have you ever thought, thought your heart would break?

STROPHE No.

PHAEDRA Wished you could cut open your chest tear it out to stop the pain?

STROPHE That would kill you.

PHAEDRA This is killing me.

STROPHE No. Just feels like it.

PHAEDRA A spear in my side, burning.

STROPHE Hippolytus.

PHAEDRA *(Screams)*

STROPHE You're in love with him.

PHAEDRA *(Laughs hysterically)* What are you talking about?

STROPHE Obsessed.

PHAEDRA No.

STROPHE *(Looks at her)*

PHAEDRA Is it that obvious?

STROPHE I'm your daughter.

PHAEDRA Do you think he's attractive?

STROPHE I used to.

PHAEDRA What changed?

STROPHE I got to know him.

PHAEDRA You don't like him?

STROPHE Not particularly.

PHAEDRA You don't like Hippolytus?

STROPHE No, not really.

PHAEDRA Everyone likes Hippolytus.

STROPHE I live with him.

PHAEDRA It's a big house.

STROPHE He's a big man.

PHAEDRA You used to spend time together.

STROPHE He wore me out.

PHAEDRA You tired of Hippolytus?

STROPHE He bores me.

PHAEDRA Bores you?

STROPHE Shitless.

PHAEDRA Why? Everyone likes him.

STROPHE I know.

PHAEDRA I know what room he's in.

STROPHE He never moves.

PHAEDRA Can feel him through the walls. Sense him. Feel his heartbeat from a mile.

STROPHE Why don't you have an affair, get your mind off him.

PHAEDRA There's a thing between us, an awesome fucking thing, can you feel it? It burns. Meant to be. We were. Meant to be.

STROPHE No.

PHAEDRA Brought together.

STROPHE He's twenty years younger than you.

PHAEDRA Want to climb inside him work him out.

STROPHE This isn't healthy.

PHAEDRA He's not my son.

STROPHE You're married to his father.

PHAEDRA He won't come back, too busy being useless.

STROPHE Mother. If someone were to find out.

PHAEDRA Can't deny something this big.

STROPHE He's not nice to people when he's slept with them. I've seen him.

PHAEDRA Might help me get over him.

STROPHE Treats them like shit.

PHAEDRA Can't switch this off. Can't crush it. Can't. Wake up with it, burning me. Think I'll crack open I want him so much. I talk to him. He talks to me, you know, we, we know each other very well, he tells me things, we're very close. About sex and how much it depresses him, and I know –

STROPHE Don't imagine you can cure him.

PHAEDRA Know if it was someone who loved you, really loved you –

STROPHE He's poison.

PHAEDRA Loved you till it burnt them –

STROPHE They do love him. Everyone loves him. He despises them for it. You'd be no different.

PHAEDRA You could feel such pleasure.

STROPHE Mother. It's me. Strophe, your daughter. Look at me. Please. Forget this. For my sake.

PHAEDRA Yours?

STROPHE You don't talk about anything else any more. You don't work. He's all you care about, but you don't see what he is.

PHAEDRA I don't talk about him that often.

STROPHE No. Most of the time you're with him. Even when you're not with him you're with him. And just occasionally, when you remember that you gave birth to me and not him, you tell me how ill he is.

PHAEDRA I'm worried about him.

STROPHE You've said. See a doctor.

PHAEDRA He –

STROPHE For yourself, not him.

PHAEDRA There's nothing wrong with me. I don't know what to do.

STROPHE Stay away from him, go and join Theseus, fuck someone else, whatever it takes.

PHAEDRA I can't.

STROPHE You can have any man you want.

PHAEDRA I want him.

STROPHE Except him.

PHAEDRA Any man I want except the man I want.

STROPHE Have you ever fucked a man more than once?

PHAEDRA This is different.

STROPHE Mother, this family –

PHAEDRA Oh I know.

STROPHE If anyone were to find out.

PHAEDRA I know, I know.

STROPHE It's the excuse they're all looking for. We'd be torn apart on the streets.

PHAEDRA Yes, yes, no, you're right, yes.

STROPHE Think of Theseus. Why you married him.

PHAEDRA I can't remember.

STROPHE Then think of my father.

PHAEDRA I know.

STROPHE What would he think?

PHAEDRA He'd –

STROPHE Exactly. You can't do it. Can't even think of it.

PHAEDRA No.

STROPHE He's a sexual disaster area.

PHAEDRA Yes, I –

STROPHE No one must know. No one must know.

PHAEDRA You're right, I –

STROPHE No one must know.

PHAEDRA No.

STROPHE Not even Hippolytus.

PHAEDRA No.

STROPHE What are you going to do?

PHAEDRA Get over him.

'Tis Pity She's a Whore

by John Ford

John Ford (1586–c.1639) wrote all or part of 18 plays, 7 of which have been lost. *'Tis Pity She's a Whore* opens with Giovanni confessing to a friar, his former tutor, that he is in love with his sister Annabella. The friar refers to his great fame and potential as a young scholar and urges him to repent of his incestuous thoughts. The second scene shows rivals competing for Annabella's love, but it becomes clear that she is devoted to her brother. This extract (the third scene in the play) brings Giovanni on stage with his private thoughts before his sister enters with her servant.

A Hall in FLORIO*'s House*

Enter GIOVANNI.

GIOVANNI Lost! I am lost! my fates have doomed my death:
The more I strive, I love; the more I love,
The less I hope: I see my ruin certain.
What judgment or endeavours could apply
To my incurable and restless wounds,
I throughly have examined, but in vain.
O, that it were not in religion sin
To make our love a god, and worship it!
I have even wearied Heaven with prayers, dried up
The spring of my continual tears, even starved
My veins with daily fasts: what wit[1] or art
Could counsel, I have practised; but, alas,
I find all these but dreams, and old men's tales,
To fright unsteady youth; I'm still the same:
Or I must speak, or burst. 'Tis not, I know,
My lust, but 'tis my fate that leads me on.
Keep fear and low faint-hearted shame with slaves!

[1]**wit** wisdom

I'll tell her that I love her, though my heart
Were rated at the price of that attempt. –
O me! she comes.

Enter ANNABELLA *and* PUTANA.

ANNABELLA Brother!

GIOVANNI *(Aside)* If such a thing
As courage dwell in men, ye heavenly powers,
Now double all that virtue in my tongue!

ANNABELLA Why, brother,
Will you not speak to me?

GIOVANNI Yes: how d'ye, sister?

ANNABELLA Howe'er I am, methinks you are not well.

PUTANA Bless us! Why are you so sad, sir?

GIOVANNI Let me entreat you, leave us a while, Putana. –
Sister, I would be private with you.

ANNABELLA Withdraw, Putana.

PUTANA I will. – If this were any other company for her, I should think my absence an office of some credit: but I will leave them together.

(Aside, and exit.)

GIOVANNI Come, sister, lend your hand: let's walk together!
I hope you need not blush to walk with me;
Here's none but you and I.

ANNABELLA How's this?

GIOVANNI I'faith,
I mean no harm.

ANNABELLA Harm?

GIOVANNI No, good faith.
How is't with ye?

ANNABELLA *(Aside)* I trust he be not frantic. –
I am very well, brother.

GIOVANNI Trust me, but I am sick; I fear so sick
'Twill cost my life.

ANNABELLA Mercy forbid it! 'tis not so, I hope.

GIOVANNI I think you love me, sister.
ANNABELLA Yes, you know
I do.
GIOVANNI I know't, indeed. – You're very fair.
ANNABELLA Nay, then I see you have a merry sickness.
GIOVANNI That's as it proves. The poets feign, I read,
That Juno for her forehead did exceed
All other goddesses; but I durst swear
Your forehead exceeds hers, as hers did theirs.
ANNABELLA 'Troth, this is pretty!
GIOVANNI Such a pair of stars
As are thine eyes would, like Promethean[2] fire,
If gently glanced, give life to senseless stones.
ANNABELLA Fie upon ye!
GIOVANNI The lily and the rose, most sweetly strange,
Upon your dimpled cheeks do strive for change:
Such lips would tempt a saint; such hands as those
Would make an anchorite[3] lascivious.
ANNABELLA D'ye mock me or flatter me?
GIOVANNI If you would see a beauty more exact
Than art can counterfeit or nature frame,
Look in your glass, and there behold your own.
ANNABELLA O, you are a trim youth!
GIOVANNI Here! *(Offers his dagger to her.)*
ANNABELLA What to do?
GIOVANNI And here's my breast; strike
home!
Rip up my bosom; there thou shalt behold
A heart in which is writ the truth I speak.
Why stand ye?

---

[2]**Promethean** in ancient myth Prometheus stole fire from the gods and reanimated life on earth
[3]**anchorite** hermit

ANNABELLA Are you earnest?
GIOVANNI Yes, most earnest.
You cannot love?
ANNABELLA Whom?
GIOVANNI Me. My tortured soul
Hath felt affliction in the heat of death.
O, Annabella, I am quite undone!
The love of thee, my sister, and the view
Of thy immortal beauty have untuned
All harmony both of my rest and life.
Why d'ye not strike?
ANNABELLA Forbid it, my just fears!
If this be true, 'twere fitter I were dead.
GIOVANNI True, Annabella! 'tis no time to jest.
I have too long suppressed the hidden flames
That almost have consumed me: I have spent
Many a silent night in sighs and groans;
Ran over all my thoughts, despised my fate,
Reasoned against the reasons of my love,
Done all that smoothed-cheeked virtue could advise;
But found all bootless:[4] 'tis my destiny
That you must either love, or I must die.
ANNABELLA Comes this in sadness from you?
GIOVANNI Let some mischief
Befall me soon, if I dissemble aught.
ANNABELLA You are my brother Giovanni.
GIOVANNI You
My sister Annabella; I know this,
And could afford you instance[5] why to love
So much the more for this; to which intent

---

[4]**bootless** pointless
[5]**instance** proof

Wise nature first in your creation meant
To make you mine; else't had been sin and foul
To share one beauty to a double soul.
Nearness in birth and blood doth but persuade
A nearer nearness in affection.
I have asked counsel of the holy church,
Who tells me I may love you; and 'tis just
That, since I may, I should; and will, yes, will.
Must I now live or die?

ANNABELLA Live; thou hast won
The field, and never fought: what thou hast urged
My captive heart had long ago resolved.
I blush to tell thee, – but I'll tell thee now, –
For every sigh that thou hast spent for me
I have sighed ten; for every tear shed twenty:
And not so much for that I loved, as that
I durst not say I loved, nor scarcely think it.

GIOVANNI Let not this music be a dream, ye gods,
For pity's sake, I beg ye!

ANNABELLA On my knees, *(She kneels.)*
Brother, even by our mother's dust, I charge you,
Do not betray me to your mirth or hate:
Love me or kill me, brother.

GIOVANNI On my knees, *(He kneels.)*
Sister, even by my mother's dust, I charge you,
Do not betray me to your mirth or hate:
Love me or kill me, sister.

ANNABELLA You mean good sooth, then?

GIOVANNI In good troth, I do;
And so do you, I hope: say, I'm in earnest.

ANNABELLA I'll swear it, I.

GIOVANNI And I; and by this kiss, –
(Kisses her.)
Once more, yet once more: now let's rise
(They rise), – by this,
I would not change this minute for Elysium.[6]
What must we now do?
ANNABELLA What you will.
GIOVANNI Come, then;
After so many tears as we have wept,
Let's learn to court in smiles, to kiss, and sleep.
(Exeunt)

[6]**Elysium** heaven, where the blessed live (in pre-Christian mythology)

The Gift

by Vicki Feaver

Vicki Feaver (born 1943) studied Music and English and worked as a lecturer and tutor in English and Creative Writing at University College, Chichester, where she later became an Emeritus Professor. In *The Gift* she imagines a woman spurned by her lover and thinking of revenge on her rival. The woman associates herself with Medea, Jason's volatile lover in Greek mythology. Jason was to marry the much calmer Creusa, so Medea sent her a wedding dress soaked in poison.

You see her in the street
and pull a gun out of your handbag.

That's in a dream.

Awake, you're Medea: imagining
your husband's Greek princess
unwrapping your gift
of a wedding dress.

She slips it over her head:
twirling in the mirror, pouting,
swinging her hips, pushing out
her breasts.
            Still happy,
still thinking, *he loves me,*
nothing can ever go wrong;
and loving him more, like meat with salt,
for the wife and children he's left,
she discovers the crown,
its filigree[1] of gold leaves

---

[1]**filigree** delicate ornamental tracery

trembling and tinkling
as she lifts it onto her head.

Then an itch
on her shoulder, and her finger
under the strap, scratching,
making it worse; and a pricking
in her hair, as if she's got lice –
but lice with the teeth of bats;
then on belly and buttocks and back
a stinging like rolling in nettles;
and then everywhere the dress
and crown touch, her flesh burning –
so she's twisting and leaping,
the cool girl he prefers
to his fiery wife, dripping
flame and shrieking.

The Demon Lover

Anonymous

During the time of the first romantic poets (around 1800) there was great enthusiasm for discovering and printing old ballads belonging to the oral tradition of the common people. *The Demon Lover* was first printed by Sir Walter Scott, whose friend William Laidlaw heard it recited.

'O where have you been, my long, long love,
  This long seven years and more?'
'O I'm come to seek my former vows
  Ye granted me before.'

'O hold your tongue of your former vows,
  For they will breed sad strife;
O hold your tongue of your former vows,
  For I am become a wife.'

He turned him right and round about,
  And the tear blinded his ee.
'I wad never hae trodden on Irish ground,
  If it had not been for thee.

'I might hae had a king's daughtèr,
  Far, far beyond the sea;
I might have had a king's daughtèr,
  Had it not been for love o' thee.'

'If ye might have had a king's daughtèr,
  Yer sell ye had to blame;
Ye might have taken the king's daughtèr,
  For ye ken'd[1] that I was nane.'

---

[1]**ken'd** knew

'O fause are the vows of womankind,
  But fair is their fause bodie;
I never wad hae trod on Irish ground,
  Had it not been for love o' thee.'

'If I was to leave my husband dear,
  And my two babes also,
O what have you to take me to,
  If with you I should go?'

'I hae seven ships upon the sea,
  The eighth brought me to land;
With four-and-twenty bold marinèrs,
  And music on every hand.'

She had taken up her two little babes,
  Kiss'd them baith cheek and chin;
'O fare ye weel, my ain two babes,
  For I'll never see you again.'

She set her foot upon the ship
  No mariners could she behold;
But the sails were o' the taffetie,[2]
  And the masts o' the beaten gold.

She had not sail'd a league, a league,
  A league but barely three,
When dismal grew his countenance,
  And drumlie[3] grew his ee.

---

[2]**taffetie** shining silk
[3]**drumlie** turbid, gloomy

The masts that were like the beaten gold
  Bent not on the heaving seas,
And the sails that were o' the taffetie,
  Fill'd not in the east land breeze.

They had not sail'd a league, a league,
  A league but barely three,
Until she espied his cloven foot,
  And she wept right bitterlie.

'O hold your tongue of your weeping,' says he,
  'Of your weeping now let me be;
I will show you how the lilies grow
  On the banks of Italy.'

'O what hills are yon, yon pleasant hills,
  That the sun shines sweetly on?'
'O yon are the hills of heaven,' he said,
  Where you will never win.'

'O whatten a mountain is yon,' she said,
  'All so dreary wi' frost and snow?'
'O yon is the mountain of hell,' he cried,
  'Where you and I will go.'

And aye when she turned her round about,
  Aye taller he seem'd for to be,
Until that the tops o' that gallant ship
  Nae taller were than he.

The clouds grew dark, and the wind grew loud,
  And the levin[4] fill'd her ee;
And waesome wail'd the snaw-white sprites
  Upon the gurlie[5] sea.

He strack the tap-mast wi' his hand,
  The fore-mast wi' his knee;
And he brake that gallant ship in twain
  And sank her in the sea.

---

[4]**levin** lightning
[5]**gurlie** grim

Suite Française

by Irène Némirovsky

The writer Irène Némirovsky (1903–1942) intended her book, *Suite Française*, to be a thousand pages long, composed of five parts; musically, like Beethoven's 5th Symphony and on a par with Tolstoy's literary epic *War and Peace*. The novel's subject was to be France under the German occupation, from the evacuation of Paris onwards. Némirovsky wrote the book as the events unfolded around her. She herself, a Russian-born Jew, was compelled to wear the yellow star and, like characters in her novel, fled Paris to live with her daughters and husband in the country, a precarious sanctuary.

The book was never completed. On 13 July 1942 she was arrested by the French police and deported to Auschwitz. She was gassed on 17 August 1942. Her daughter, Denise, kept her mother's notebooks, supposing they were her diaries, and read them almost 60 years later. They were first published in France in 2004 to tremendous acclaim.

This extract depicts the growing intimacy between Lucile, a Frenchwoman, and Bruno, a German soldier who has taken up residence in her home. Her husband is absent. The novel was translated from French by Sandra Smith.

This friendship between herself and the German, this dark secret, an entire universe hidden in the heart of the hostile house, my God, how sweet it was. Finally she felt she was a human being, proud and free. She wouldn't allow anyone to intrude into her personal world. 'No one. It's no one's business. Let everyone else fight each other, hate each other. Even if his father and mine fought in the past. Even if he himself took my husband prisoner . . .' (an idea that obsessed her unhappy mother-in-law) 'what difference would it make? We're friends.' Friends? She walked through the dim entrance hall and went up to the mirror on the chest of drawers that was framed in black wood; she looked at her dark eyes and trembling lips and smiled. 'Friends? He loves me,' she whispered. She brought her lips to the mirror and gently kissed her reflection. 'Yes, he loves you. You don't owe anything to the husband who betrayed you, deserted you . . . But he's a prisoner of war! Your husband is a prisoner of war and you let a German get close to you, take his place? Well, yes. So what? The one who's gone, the prisoner of war, the husband, I never loved him. I hope he never comes back. I hope he dies!

'But wait . . . think . . .' she continued, leaning her forehead against the mirror. She felt as if she were talking to a part of herself she hadn't known existed until then, who'd been invisible and whom she was seeing now for the first time, a woman with brown eyes, thin, trembling lips, burning cheeks, who was her but not entirely her. 'But wait, think . . . be logical . . . listen to the voice of reason . . . you're a sensible woman . . . you're French . . . where will all this lead? He's a soldier, he's married, he'll go away; where will it lead? Will it be anything more than a moment of fleeting happiness? Not even happiness, just pleasure? Do you even know what that is?' She was fascinated by her reflection in the mirror; it both pleased her and frightened her.

She heard the cook's footsteps in the pantry near the entrance hall; she jumped back in terror and started walking aimlessly through the house. My God, what an enormous empty house! Her mother-in-law, as she had vowed, no longer left her room; her meals were taken up to her. But even though she wasn't there, Lucile could still sense her. This house was a reflection of her, the truest part of her being, just as the truest part of Lucile was the slender young woman (in love, courageous, happy, in despair) who had just been smiling at herself in the mirror with the black frame. (She had disappeared; all that was left of Lucile Angellier was a lifeless ghost, a woman who wandered aimlessly through the rooms, who leaned her face against the windows, who automatically tidied all the useless, ugly objects that decorated the mantelpiece.)

What a day! The air was heavy, the sky grey. The blossoming lime trees had been battered by gusts of cold wind. 'A room, a house of my very own,' thought Lucile, 'a perfect room, almost bare, a beautiful lamp . . . If only I could close these shutters and put on the lights to block out this awful weather. Marthe would ask if I were ill; she'd go and tell my mother-in-law, who would come and open the curtains and turn off the lights because of the cost of electricity. I can't play the piano: it would be seen as an insult to my absent husband. I'd happily go for a walk in the woods in spite of the rain, but everyone would know about it. "Lucile Angellier's gone mad," they'd all say. That's enough to have a woman locked up around here.'

She laughed as she recalled a young girl she'd heard about whose parents had shut her up in a nursing home because she would slip away and run down to the lake whenever there was a full moon. The lake, the night . . . The lake beneath this torrential rain. Oh, anywhere far away! Somewhere else. These horses, these men, these poor resigned people, hunched over in the rain . . . She tore herself away from the window. 'I'm nothing like them,' she told herself, yet she felt bound to them by invisible chains.

She went into Bruno's bedroom. Several times she had slipped quietly into his room in the evening, her heart pounding. He would be propped up on his bed, fully dressed, reading or writing, the metallic blond of his hair glistening beneath the lamp. On an armchair in the corner of the room would be his heavy belt with the motto *Gott mit uns* engraved on the buckle, a black revolver, his cap and almond-green greatcoat; he would take the coat and put it over Lucile's legs because the nights were cold since the week before with its endless storms.

They were alone – they felt they were alone – in the great sleeping house. Not a word of their true feelings was spoken; they didn't kiss. There was simply silence. Silence followed by feverish, passionate conversations about their own countries, their families, music, books . . . They felt a strange happiness, an urgent need to reveal their hearts to each other – the urgency of lovers, which is already a gift, the very first one, the gift of the soul before the body surrenders. 'Know me, look at me. This is who I am. This is how I have lived, this is what I have loved. And you? What about you, my darling?' But up until now, not a single word of love. What was the point? Words are pointless when your voices falter, when your mouths are trembling, amid such long silences. Slowly, gently, Lucile touched the books on the table. The Gothic lettering looked so bizarre, so ugly. The Germans, the Germans . . . A Frenchman wouldn't have let me leave with no gesture of love other than kissing my hand and the hem of my dress . . .

She smiled, shrugging her shoulders slightly; she knew it was neither shyness nor coldness, but that profound, determined German patience – the patience of a wild animal waiting for its hypnotised prey to let itself be taken. 'During the war',[1] Bruno had said, 'we spent a number of nights in wait in the Moeuvre forest. Waiting is erotic . . .' She had laughed at the word. It seemed less amusing now. What did she do now but wait? She waited for him. She wandered through these lifeless rooms. Another two hours, three hours. Then dinner alone. Then the sound of the key locking her mother-in-law's door. Then Marthe crossing the garden with a lantern to close the gate. Then more waiting, feverish and strange . . . and finally the sound of his horse neighing on the road, the clanking of weapons, orders given to the groom who walks away with the horse. The sound of spurs on the doorstep. Then the night, the stormy night, with its great gusts of wind in the lime trees and the thunder rumbling in the distance. She would tell him. Oh, she was no hypocrite, she would tell him in clear, simple French – that the prey he so desired was his. 'And then what? Then what?' she murmured; a mischievous, bold, sensual smile suddenly transformed her expression, just as the reflection of a flame illuminating a face can alter it. Lit up by fire, the softest features can look demonic; they can both repel and attract. She walked quietly out of the room.

[1]**During the war** Bruno is referring to a time earlier in the war

The Lady of the House of Love

by Angela Carter

Angela Carter (1940–1992) collected fairy tales and folk legends for *The Bloody Chamber* and reworked them through her wittily gothic imagination. In *The Lady of the House of Love* a virginal young man is cycling through Romania and is invited into a castle where he meets a strangely beautiful woman, a vampire who intends to feed on him.

He was surprised to find how ruinous the interior of the house was – cobwebs, worm-eaten beams, crumbling plaster; but the mute crone resolutely wound him on the reel of her lantern down endless corridors, up winding staircases, through the galleries where the painted eyes of family portraits briefly flickered as they passed, eyes that belonged, he noticed, to faces, one and all, of a quite memorable beastliness. At last she paused and, behind the door where they'd halted, he heard a faint, metallic twang as of, perhaps, a chord struck on a harpsichord. And then, wonderfully, the liquid cascade of the song of a lark, bringing to him, in the heart – had he but known it – of Juliet's tomb, all the freshness of morning.

The crone rapped with her knuckles on the panels; the most seductively caressing voice he had ever heard in his life softly called out, in heavily accented French, the adopted language of the Romanian aristocracy: 'Entrez.'

First of all, he saw only a shape, a shape imbued with a faint luminosity since it caught and reflected in its yellowed surfaces what little light there was in the ill-lit room; this shape resolved itself into that of, of all things, a hoop-skirted dress of white satin draped here and there with lace, a dress fifty or sixty years out of fashion but once, obviously, intended for a wedding. And then he saw the girl who wore the dress, a girl with the fragility of the skeleton of a moth, so thin, so frail that her dress seemed to him to hang suspended, as if untenanted in the dank air, a fabulous lending, a self-articulated garment in which she lived like a ghost in a machine. All the light in the room came from a low-burning lamp with a thick greenish shade on a distant mantelpiece; the crone who accompanied him shielded her lantern with her hand, as if to protect her mistress from too suddenly seeing, or their guest from too suddenly seeing her.

So that it was little by little, as his eyes grew accustomed to the half-dark, that he saw how beautiful and how very young the bedizened scarecrow was, and he thought of a child dressing up in her mother's clothes, perhaps a child putting on the clothes of a dead mother in order to bring her, however briefly, to life again.

The Countess stood behind a low table, beside a pretty, silly, gilt-and-wire birdcage, hands outstretched in a distracted attitude that was almost one of flight; she looked as startled by their entry as if she had not requested it. With her stark white face, her lovely death's head surrounded by long dark hair that fell down as straight as if it were soaking wet, she looked like a shipwrecked bride. Her huge dark eyes almost broke his heart with their waiflike, lost look; yet he was disturbed, almost repelled, by her extraordinarily fleshy mouth, a mouth with wide, full, prominent lips of a vibrant purplish-crimson, a morbid mouth. Even – but he put the thought away from him immediately – a whore's mouth. She shivered all the time, a starveling chill, a malarial agitation of the bones. He thought she must be only sixteen or seventeen years old, no more, with the hectic, unhealthy beauty of a consumptive. She was the châtelaine[1] of all this decay.

With many tender precautions, the crone now raised the light she held to show his hostess her guest's face. At that, the Countess let out a faint, mewing cry and made a blind, appalled gesture with her hands, as if pushing him away, so that she knocked against the table and a butterfly dazzle of painted cards fell to the floor. Her mouth formed a round 'o' of woe, she swayed a little and then sank into her chair, where she lay as if

---

[1]**châtelaine** mistress of a large house

now scarcely capable of moving. A bewildering reception. Tsk'ing under her breath, the crone busily poked about on the table until she found an enormous pair of dark green glasses, such as blind beggars wear, and perched them on the Countess's nose.

He went forward to pick up her cards for her from a carpet that, he saw to his surprise, was part rotted away, partly encroached upon by all kinds of virulent-looking fungi. He retrieved the cards and shuffled them carelessly together, for they meant nothing to him, though they seemed strange playthings for a young girl. What a grisly picture of a capering skeleton! He covered it up with a happier one – of two young lovers, smiling at one another, and put her toys back into a hand so slender you could almost see the frail net of bone beneath the translucent skin, a hand with fingernails as long, as finely pointed, as banjo picks.

At his touch, she seemed to revive a little and almost smiled, raising herself upright.

'Coffee,' she said. 'You must have coffee.' And scooped up her cards into a pile so that the crone could set before her a silver spirit kettle, a silver coffee pot, cream jug, sugar basin, cups ready on a silver tray, a strange touch of elegance, even if discoloured, in this devastated interior whose mistress ethereally shone as if with her own blighted, submarine radiance.

The crone found him a chair and, tittering noiselessly, departed, leaving the room a little darker.

While the young lady attended to the coffee-making, he had time to contemplate with some distaste a further series of family portraits which decorated the stained and peeling walls of the room; these livid faces all seemed contorted with a febrile madness and the blubber lips, the huge, demented eyes that all had in common bore a disquieting resemblance to those of the hapless victim of inbreeding now patiently filtering her fragrant brew, even if some rare grace has so finely transformed those features when it came to her case. The lark, its chorus done, had long ago fallen silent; no sound but the chink of silver on china. Soon, she held out to him a tiny cup of rose-painted china.

'Welcome,' she said in her voice with the rushing sonorities of the ocean in it, a voice that seemed to come elsewhere than from her white, still throat. 'Welcome to my château. I rarely receive visitors and that's a misfortune since nothing animates me half as much as the presence of a stranger . . . This place is so lonely, now the village is deserted, and my one companion, alas, she cannot speak. Often I am so silent that I think I, too, will soon forget how to do so and nobody here will ever talk any more.'

She offered him a sugar biscuit from a Limoges plate; her fingernails struck carillons[2] from the antique china. Her voice, issuing from those red lips like the obese roses in her garden, lips that do not move – her voice is curiously disembodied; she is like a doll, he thought, a ventriloquist's doll, or, more, like a great, ingenious piece of clockwork. For she seemed inadequately powered by some slow energy of which she was not in control; as if she had been wound up years ago, when she was born, and now the mechanism was inexorably running down and would leave her lifeless. This idea that she might be an automaton, made of white velvet and black fur, that could not move of its own accord, never quite deserted him; indeed, it deeply moved his heart. The carnival air of her white dress emphasized her unreality, like a sad Columbine who lost her way in the wood a long time ago and never reached the fair.

'And the light. I must apologize for the lack of light . . . a hereditary affliction of the eyes . . .'

Her blind spectacles gave him his handsome face back to himself twice over; if he presented himself to her naked face, he would dazzle her like the sun she is forbidden to look at because it would shrivel her up at once, poor night bird, poor butcher bird.

Vous serez ma proie.

---

[2]**carillons** peals like bells

You have such a fine throat, m'sieu, like a column of marble. When you came through the door retaining about you all the golden light of the summer's day of which I know nothing, nothing, the card called 'Les Amoureux' had just emerged from the tumbling chaos of imagery before me; it seemed to me you had stepped off the card into my darkness and, for a moment, I thought, perhaps, you might irradiate it.

I do not mean to hurt you. I shall wait for you in my bride's dress in the dark.

The bridegroom is come, he will go into the chamber which has been prepared for him.

I am condemned to solitude and dark; I do not mean to hurt you.

I will be very gentle.

(And could love free me from the shadows? Can a bird sing only the song it knows, or can it learn a new song?)

See, how I'm ready for you. I've always been ready for you; I've been waiting for you in my wedding dress, why have you delayed for so long . . . it will all be over very quickly.

You will feel no pain, my darling.

She herself is a haunted house. She does not possess herself; her ancestors sometimes come and peer out of the windows of her eyes and that is very frightening. She has the mysterious solitude of ambiguous states; she hovers in a no-man's land between life and death, sleeping and waking, behind the hedge of spiked flowers, Nosferatu's[3] sanguinary rosebud. The beastly forebears on the walls condemn her to a perpetual repetition of their passions.

---

[3]**Nosferatu** the famous vampire of some 20th-century films, based on Bram Stoker's 'Dracula'

The Trial of Lady Chatterley

by C. H. Rolph

In October 1960 Penguin Books was put on trial for publishing D. H. Lawrence's novel *Lady Chatterley's Lover*, a book described as obscene and with 'a tendency to deprave and corrupt'. Lawrence tells of Connie, the young Lady Chatterley, who falls in love with the family's gamekeeper; the fact of their adultery and the details of their love-making were the substance of the case for the prosecution.

In November 1960 the book was acquitted and the case strongly affected future decisions about pornography and writers' freedom to explore sexual relationships. Some social commentators believed that the trial heralded what became known as 'the permissive society' of the 1960s. C. H. Rolph (whose book recorded the day-by-day process of the trial) is the professional name of Cecil Rolph Hewitt (1901–1994) who worked for the City of London Police Force from 1921 to 1946 and later became a journalist and, from 1947 to 1970, a member of the editorial staff of *The New Statesman*. This extract is taken from the closing speech for the defence by Mr Gerald Gardiner QC.

'There has been talk, although the Prosecution have not put it in, of an expurgated edition. It has been suggested that it would be much better if there was a whole lot of asterisks. On the *un*expurgated edition, Professor Muir was asked "What do you take to be the theme of the unexpurgated edition?", and he said, "I should say the redemption of the individual, and hence of society, by what Lawrence calls 'reciprocity of tenderness', and that is why I feel that the expurgated edition is a travesty of the original and ought never to have been published." Mr Connell, when sent an expurgated edition for review, said he found it "(a) trivial, (b) furtive, (c) obscene".

'It was then suggested that perhaps it would have been nice to have published, instead of this book, what has been called the first version, which, apparently many years after Lawrence's death, was published (I think in America) under the title *The First Lady Chatterley*. It is not a "version", properly called, at all. I suppose it might be interesting to students of literature to see the first rough draft of *Sons and Lovers* so as to see how Lawrence's mind progressed and how he carried out his creative function, but the first draft of any of his books is not really a "version" at all; it is merely what he says it was, a first rough draft. It is said that to publish that would be quite all right because that version contains the letters "f . . k" and "c . . t". Have we really descended to this? Are we so frightened of words that while it is perfectly all right to publish a book with "f . . k" it is all wrong to publish a book with the word in its full form? This would in fact have destroyed the whole purpose with which Lawrence was using the words. People in real life do not say "f . . k". After all, these words have been part of spoken English for hundreds and hundreds of years. They are apparently known not only to boys but also to girls at school age.

'When it is said that this is a book about adultery, one wonders how there can be things which people do not see. I suppose it is possible that somewhere there might be a mind which would describe *Antony and Cleopatra* as "a tale about adultery". Antony had a wife in Rome, and I suppose there might be a mind somewhere which would describe this play of Shakespeare's as "the story of a sex-starved man copulating with an Egyptian queen", a parallel with the way this book has been put before you on behalf of the Prosecution. Thus there are minds which are unable to see beauty where it exists, and doubt the integrity of purpose in an author where it is obvious.

'I must deal with what no doubt will be a point sought to be made by the Prosecution. "This is in a book published at 3s. 6d. It will be available to the general public." Of course, that is perfectly true and perfectly obvious. It may well be said that everybody will rush to buy it. You may well think *that* is perfectly true and perfectly obvious, because it happens in every case. Whether it is *The Philanderer* or any other book which is wrongly prosecuted, inevitably people go and buy it. It would be idle to deny it. But whose fault is that? It is always the fact that there has been a wrong prosecution of a book that leads a large number of people to buy it. What was said on this aspect of the case was this. I am most anxious not to do my learned friend any injustice, and so may I quote exactly what he said? He invited you to consider this question after you had read it. "Is it a book that you would even wish your wife or your servants to read?" I cannot help thinking that this was, consciously or unconsciously, an echo from an observation which had fallen from the Bench in an earlier case: "It would never do to let members of the working class read this." I do not want to upset the Prosecution by suggesting that there are a certain number of people nowadays who as a matter of fact don't *have* servants. But of course that whole attitude is one which Penguin Books was formed to fight against, which they always have fought against, and which they will go on fighting against – the attitude that it is all right to publish a special edition at five or ten guineas so that people who are less well off cannot read what other people read. Isn't everybody, whether earning £10 a week or £20 a week, equally interested in the society in which we live, in the problems of human relationships including sexual relationships? In view of the reference made to wives, aren't women equally interested in human relations, including sexual relationships?'

Questions

In all of these questions you should consider:

a the ways the writers' choice of form, structure and language shape your responses to the extracts

b how your wider reading in the literature of love has contributed to your understanding and interpretation of the extracts.

1 Consider the ways in which Roy presents the consummation of a dangerous passion. How erotic do you consider this extract to be?

2 Examine the language of tact and courtesy which the lady and Sir Gawain use to deal with a difficult and potentially embarrassing situation.

3 Compare and contrast the two drama texts by Ford and Kane. Do the different styles of language – elevated in one, blunt in the other – influence your feelings of shock or/and sympathy for the characters in their dangerous predicaments?

4 How does the language of the extract from *Eloisa to Abelard* show a mind tormented by loss, passion and guilt?

5 What effects do writers achieve when they refer to stories from the past? Compare the texts and extracts here by Pope, Feaver, Carter, and the anonymous author of *The Demon Lover*.

6 How does Némirovsky convey the sense that Lucile is thinking through the danger of her desires and actions?

7 What does Angela Carter's richly metaphorical writing contribute to the atmosphere of her story?

8 Compare two or three passages which convey a sense of danger in forbidden areas of love.

9 What do you consider to be the main arguments for and against censorship of books? You could confine yourself to those that include love and lust and in which the language and situations are potentially offensive.

Further reading

- Much great literature explores dangerous borderlines. In the Bible, disobedience is at the centre of the story of Lot and his daughters (Genesis 19) and that of David and Bathsheba (2 Samuel 11–12).
- Mythology too often deals in what is forbidden: Ovid's *Metamorphoses* is a lively and fascinating source of stories about relationships between gods and human beings. See especially the story of Myrrha committing incest with her father.
- The sinister world of Jacobean revenge tragedy is filled with acts of defiant love and their violent consequences; these are often most powerful when committed by women, as in Webster's *The White Devil* and Middleton's *The Changeling*.
- If you are gripped by these plays, try gothic horror – frightening 18th- and 19th-century stories of male obsession and exploited women. Notable examples include Mary Shelley's *Frankenstein*, Ann Radcliffe's *The Mysteries of Udolpho* and Bram Stoker's *Dracula*.
- In *Les Liaisons Dangereuses*, Laclos explores sexual experimentation in stylish French society of the 18th century. Ibsen's *Ghosts* breaks a taboo about an inherited sexual disease; the play scandalised Victorian London.
- Novels set or written in the late 19th century often depend on the contrast between intense love and social rectitude: Hardy's late novels *Tess of the D'Urbervilles* and, especially, *Jude the Obscure* were both fiercely condemned; Fowles's *The French Lieutenant's Woman* (1969) captures the hypocrisy and victimisation of that period.
- In the early 20th century Oscar Wilde's very public disgrace after being put on trial for homosexuality led to his writing *The Ballad of Reading Gaol*, a poem of protest and great suffering.
- More recently, issues of stage censorship were aroused by Arthur Miller's play *A View from the Bridge*, which includes suggestions of both incest and homosexuality. Howard Brenton's play *The Romans in Britain* includes a vivid portrayal of homosexual rape.

- Several of Harold Pinter's plays show unsettling states of mind, notably *The Lover* and *The Homecoming*. Peter Shaffer's *Equus* explores the alarming obsessions of an adolescent boy and Stephen Poliakoff's *Hitting Town* tells a story of incest between brother and sister.
- Novelists whose works deal with incest include Scott Fitzgerald in *Tender is the Night* and Graham Swift in *Waterlands*. Nabokov's *Lolita* explores the forbidden area of paedophilia.

5 Family

So now that all our friends are marrid I will add a few words about their familys. Ethel and Bernard returned from their honeymoon with a son and hair a nice fat baby called Ignatius Bernard. They soon had six more children four boys and three girls and some of them were twins which was very exciting.

This comes from the final chapter of Daisy Ashford's childhood masterpiece, *The Young Visiters*, aptly entitled 'How it ended'. But the marriage, thrilling though the pursuit and the ceremony itself may be, is only the beginning. Children are born (perhaps not as rapidly as the nice fat baby!) and families are created. What kind of love is to be found in the family? The critic C. S. Lewis, writing in *The Four Loves* (1960), defines parental love as 'Affection':

> *The Greeks call this love* storge. *I shall call it simply Affection. My Greek lexicon defines* storge *as 'affection, especially of parents to offspring' but also of offspring to parents. Its qualities include 'warm comfortableness' and a 'satisfaction in being together'. It 'ignores barriers of age, sex, class and education'.*

The Romantic poets saw the child as a gift from God, innocent and holy. Wordsworth writes in the *Ode: Intimations of Immortality from Recollections of Early Childhood* that we enter this world not spiritually naked, 'but trailing clouds of glory'. Blake too believed in the Platonic ideal of childhood: 'the Spiritual Body or Angel as little Children always behold the Face of the heavenly father'.

The novelist George Eliot was influenced by the Romantics: in her novel *Silas Marner* (1861) the toddler Eppie miraculously comes into lonely Silas Marner's life to replace his stolen gold, bringing him lasting joy. Lost children in Shakespeare's final plays are restored to their parents so that a suffering and fragmented family can find happiness: in the last act of *The Winter's Tale* Perdita is reunited with her mother; in *Cymbeline* Imogen with her father and brothers.

In some novels, such as Fielding's *Joseph Andrews* and Dickens's *Bleak House*, orphans discover their true parentage. This is the moment when Esther Summerson (*Bleak House*) recognises her mother and steps into a waking dream: 'I was rendered motionless . . . by a something in her face that I had pined for and dreamed of when I was a little child; something I had never seen in any face.'

But there can be a dark side to love within the family. *Beloved* (1987) by Toni Morrison is based on the story of the slave mother, Margaret Garner, who killed her child when the slave hunters came to catch her at the end of the American Civil War. When questioned, she replied that 'she was unwilling to have her children suffer as she had done'. In Blake's *Songs of Experience* the cruel adult, often a parent, stands for aged ignorance and the children are abused, sold into slavery and denied the natural innocence of their childhood. Family love can be distorted and inappropriate, as hinted in the very title of D. H. Lawrence's semi-autobiographical novel *Sons and Lovers*. This is a reworking of the Oedipus myth, which recurs throughout literature, most famously in the closet scene between Hamlet and his mother Gertrude; it is also suggested at the end of Noel Coward's *The Vortex*.

Yet satisfaction in being together - a desire to celebrate the family and love within the family - cannot be extinguished. It may be expressed through a feast, perhaps in the tradition of a Dickensian Christmas, which derives from the end of *A Christmas Carol,* when the Cratchit family enjoy Mr Scrooge's goose, or in some less formal manner. For example, the family at the end of the short story *First Love and other Sorrows* by Harold Brodkey (1930–1966) mark the sister's engagement with this unexpected midnight feast:

> *To me my mother said, 'Are you eating at this time of night?'*
>
> *My sister said that she was hungry, too.*
>
> *'There's some soup,' my mother said. 'Why don't I heat it up?'*
>
> *And suddenly her eyes filled with tears, and all at once we fell to kissing one another – to embracing and smiling and making cheerful predictions about one another – there in the white, brightly lighted kitchen. We had known each other for so long, and there were so many things we all three remembered. . . . Our smiles, our approving glances, wandered from face to face. There was a feeling of politeness in the air. We were behaving the way we would in railway stations, at my sister's wedding, at the birth of her first child, at my graduation from college. This was the first of many reunions.*

The Young Visiters

by Daisy Ashford

This is extract from 'The Wedding', the penultimate chapter in Daisy Ashford's novel *The Young Visiters* [*sic*]. Ethel has accepted Bernard Clark's proposal and the wedding is due to take place in Westminster Abbey. Mr Salteena is the rejected lover, who has written in a letter 'I am not quite a gentleman but you would hardly notice it'. Daisy Ashford (1881–1972) wrote this masterpiece at the age of 9; the published versions retain her original spellings. Appropriately enough, her talent was discovered by J. M. Barrie, the author of *Peter Pan*.

The Abbey was indeed thronged next day when Ethel and Bernard cantered up in a very fine carrage drawn by two prancing steeds who foamed a good deal. In the porch stood several clean altar boys who conducted the lucky pair up the aile while the organ pealed a merry blast. The mighty edifice was packed and seated in the front row was the Earl of Clincham looking very brisk as he was going to give Ethel away at the correct moment. Beside him sat Mr Salteena all in black and looking bitterly sad and he ground his teeth as Ethel came marching up. There were some merry hymns and as soon as Ethel and Bernard were one the clergyman began a sermon about Adam and Eve and the serpent and Mr Salteena cried into his large handkerchief and the earl kept on nudging him as his sniffs were rarther loud. Then the wedding march pealed fourth and doun the church stepped Ethel and Bernard as husband and wife. Into the cab they got and speedelly dashed off to the Gaierty. The wedding refreshments were indeed a treat to all and even Mr Salteena cheered up when he beheld the wedding cake and sparkling wines. Then the earl got up and made a very fine speech about marrage vows and bliss and he quoted several good bits from the bible which got a lot of applause. Bernard replied in good round terms. I thank your lordship for those kind remarks he said in clear tones I expect we shall be as happy as a lark and I hope you will all be ditto some day. Here Here muttered a stray lady in the crowd and down sat Bernard while Ethel went up to change her wedding garment for a choice pink velvit dress with a golden gurdle and a very chick tocque.[1] Bernard also put on a new suit of blue stripe and some silk socks and clean under clothing. Hurah hurah shouted the guests as the pair reappeard in the aforesaid get ups. Then everybody got a bag of rice and sprinkled on the pair and Mr Salteena sadly threw a white tennis shoe at them wiping his eyes the while. Off drove the happy pair and the guests finished up the food. The happy pair went to Egypt for there Honymoon as they thought it would be a nice warm spot and they had never seen the wondrous land. Ethel was a bit sick on the boat but Bernard braved the storm in manly style. However Ethel had recovered by the time they got to Egypt and here we will leave them for a merry six weeks of bliss while we return to England.

[1]**a very chick tocque** a very elegant small hat

Morning Song

by Sylvia Plath

Sylvia Plath (1932–1963) came to Cambridge from America on a Fulbright scholarship in 1955. She fell in love with the poet Ted Hughes, marrying him in 1956 and having two children with him (Frieda and Nicholas). This poem celebrates the miraculous strangeness of birth and how the poet's sensitivity to the natural world is 'magnified' by the new arrival. It is directly addressed to her child.

Love set you going like a fat gold watch.
The midwife slapped your footsoles, and your bald cry
Took its place among the elements.

Our voices echo, magnifying your arrival. New statue.
In a drafty museum, your nakedness
Shadows our safety. We stand round blankly as walls.

I'm no more your mother
Than the cloud that distills a mirror to reflect its own slow
Effacement at the wind's hand.

All night your moth-breath
Flickers among the flat pink roses. I wake to listen:
A far sea moves in my ear.

One cry, and I stumble from bed, cow-heavy and floral
In my Victorian nightgown.
Your mouth opens clean as a cat's. The window square

Whitens and swallows its dull stars. And now you try
Your handful of notes;
The clear vowels rise like balloons.

Gap Year

by Jackie Kay

One of the most accessible modern writers, Jackie Kay was born in 1961 to a Scottish mother and Nigerian father, and adopted at birth by a Scottish couple. Her novels and poetry are widely published, and she writes for both children and adults. A frequent performer, broadcaster and lecturer, in her poetry Jackie Kay reflects on both her own life and those of others. In her anthology *Darling* she writes to her son who is travelling the world on his gap year. His bed at home is empty, as was his Moses basket in the weeks before birth. 'A flip and a skip ago, you were dreaming in your basket.' Time moves on . . .

(for Mateo)

I

I remember your Moses basket before you were born.
I'd stare at the fleecy white sheet for days, weeks,
willing you to arrive, hardly able to believe
I would ever have a real baby to put in the basket.

I'd feel the mound of my tight tub of a stomach,
and you moving there, foot against my heart,
elbow in my ribcage, turning, burping, awake, asleep.
One time I imagined I felt you laugh.

I'd play you Handel's *Water Music* or Emma Kirkby
singing Pergolesi. I'd talk to you, my close stranger,
call you Tumshie, ask when you were coming to meet me.
You arrived late, the very hot summer of eighty-eight.

You had passed the due date string of eights,
and were pulled out with forceps, blue, floury,
on the fourteenth of August on Sunday afternoon.
I took you home on Monday and lay you in your basket.

II

Now, I peek in your room and stare at your bed
hardly able to imagine you back in there sleeping,
Your handsome face – soft, open. Now you are eighteen,
six foot two, away, away in Costa Rica, Peru, Bolivia.

I follow your trails on my *Times Atlas*:
from the Caribbean side of Costa Rica to the Pacific,
the baby turtles to the massive leatherbacks.
Then on to Lima, to Cuzco. Your grandfather

rings: 'Have you considered altitude sickness,
Christ, he's sixteen thousand feet above sea level.'
Then to the lost city of the Incas, Macchu Picchu,
Where you take a photograph of yourself with the statue

of the original Tupac. You are wearing a Peruvian hat.
Yesterday in Puno before catching the bus for Copacabana,
you suddenly appear on a webcam and blow me a kiss,
you have a new haircut; your face is grainy, blurry.

Seeing you, shy, smiling, on the webcam reminds me
of the second scan at twenty weeks, how at that fuzzy
moment back then, you were lying cross-legged with
an index finger resting sophisticatedly on one cheek.

You started the Inca trail in Arctic conditions
and ended up in subtropical. Now you plan the Amazon
in Bolivia. Your grandfather rings again to say
'There's three warring factions in Bolivia, warn him

against it. He canny see everything. Tell him to come home.'
But you say all the travellers you meet rave about Bolivia.
You want to see the Salar de Uyuni,
the world's largest salt-flats, the Amazonian rainforest.

And now you are not coming home till four weeks after
your due date. After Bolivia, you plan to stay
with a friend's Auntie in Argentina.
Then – to Chile where you'll stay with friends of Diane's.

And maybe work for the Victor Jara Foundation.[1]
I feel like a home-alone mother; all the lights
have gone out in the hall, and now I am
wearing your large black slippers, flip-flopping

into your empty bedroom, trying to imagine you
in your bed. I stare at the photos you send by messenger:
you on the top of the world, arms outstretched, eager.
Blue sky, white snow; you by Lake Tararhua, beaming.

My heart soars like the birds in your bright blue skies.
My love glows like the sunrise over the lost city.
I sing along to Ella Fitzgerald, *A tisket A tasket*
I have a son out in the big wide world.

A flip and a skip ago, you were dreaming in your basket.

---

[1]**Victor Jara Foundation** organisation to perpetuate the memory of a Chilean musician murdered by his government in 1973

The Mill on the Floss

by George Eliot

'George Eliot' is the name under which the Victorian writer Mary Ann Evans, later Marian Evans, sought publication. Like Maggie in *The Mill on the Floss*, in childhood she was close to her brother, Isaac. In many ways she lived an unconventional life – falling in love with the married G. H. Lewes and living with him as 'wife' until his death. She then married a man over twenty years younger than herself, John Walter Cross. This official marriage lasted only seven months as she died in 1880.

A formidable intellect, George Eliot was extremely widely read. In the 1870s she was declared by many, including Queen Victoria, to be the greatest living novelist. In this extract from *The Mill on the Floss*, Tom Tulliver is at boarding school. His sister Maggie comes to visit him with distressing news. This is the point in the novel where 'the golden gates of childhood' are closed forever behind the brother and sister. *The Mill on the Floss* is a *bildungsroman* – a novel depicting Maggie's emotional and often painful journey to womanhood: her life and loves.

Tom had not heard anything from home for some weeks – a fact which did not surprise him, for his father and mother were not apt to manifest their affection in unnecessary letters – when, to his great surprise, on the morning of a dark cold day near the end of November, he was told, soon after entering the study at nine o'clock, that his sister was in the drawing-room. It was Mrs Stelling who had come into the study to tell him, and she left him to enter the drawing-room alone.

Maggie, too, was tall now, with braided and coiled hair: she was almost as tall as Tom, though she was only thirteen; and she really looked older than he did at that moment. She had thrown off her bonnet, her heavy braids were pushed back from her forehead, as if it would not bear that extra load, and her young face had a strangely worn look, as her eyes turned anxiously towards the door. When Tom entered she did not speak, but only went up to him, put her arms round his neck, and kissed him earnestly. He was used to various moods of hers, and felt no alarm at the unusual seriousness of her greeting.

'Why, how is it you're come so early this cold morning, Maggie? Did you come in the gig?' said Tom, as she backed towards the sofa, and drew him to her side.

'No, I came by the coach. I've walked from the turnpike.'[1]

'But how is it you're not at school? The holidays have not begun yet?'

'Father wanted me at home,' said Maggie, with a slight trembling of the lip. 'I came home three or four days ago.'

'Isn't my father well?' said Tom, rather anxiously.

'Not quite,' said Maggie. 'He's very unhappy, Tom. The lawsuit is ended, and I came to tell you because I thought it would be better for you to know it before you came home, and I didn't like only to send you a letter.'

'My father hasn't lost?' said Tom hastily, springing from the sofa, and standing before Maggie with his hands suddenly thrust in his pockets.

'Yes, dear Tom,' said Maggie, looking up at him with trembling.

Tom was silent a minute or two, with his eyes fixed on the floor. Then he said –

'My father will have to pay a good deal of money, then?'

'Yes,' said Maggie, rather faintly.

'Well, it can't be helped,' said Tom, bravely, not translating the loss of a large sum of money into any tangible results. 'But my father's very much vexed, I daresay?' he added, looking at Maggie, and thinking that her agitated face was only part of her girlish way of taking things.

'Yes,' said Maggie, again faintly. Then, urged to fuller speech by Tom's freedom from apprehension, she said loudly and rapidly, as if the words *would* burst from her, 'Oh, Tom, he

---

[1]**turnpike** a road you usually have to pay to use

will lose the mill and the land, and everything; he will have nothing left.'

Tom's eyes flashed out one look of surprise at her, before he turned pale and trembled visibly. He said nothing, but sat down on the sofa again, looking vaguely out of the opposite window.

Anxiety about the future had never entered Tom's mind. His father had always ridden a good horse, kept a good house, and had the cheerful, confident air of a man who has plenty of property to fall back upon. Tom had never dreamed that his father would 'fail'; *that* was a form of misfortune which he had always heard spoken of as a deep disgrace, and disgrace was an idea that he could not associate with any of his relations, least of all with his father. A proud sense of family respectability was part of the very air Tom had been born and brought up in. He knew there were people in St. Ogg's who made a show without money to support it, and he had always heard such people spoken of by his own friends with contempt and reprobation. He had a strong belief, which was a life-long habit, and required no definite evidence to rest on, that his father could spend a great deal of money if he chose; and since his education at Mr. Stelling's had given him a more expensive view of life, he had often thought that when he got older he would make a figure in the world, with his horse and dogs and saddle, and other accoutrements of a fine young man, and show himself equal to any of his contemporaries at St. Ogg's, who might consider themselves a grade above him in society, because their fathers were professional men, or had large oil-mills. As to the prognostics[2] and head-shaking of his aunts and uncles, they had never produced the least effect on him, except to make him think that aunts and uncles were disagreeable society: he had heard them find fault in much the same way as long as he could remember. His father knew better than they did.

---

[2]**prognostics** predictions

The down had come on Tom's lip, yet his thoughts and expectations had been hitherto only the reproduction, in changed forms, of the boyish dreams in which he had lived three years ago. He was awakened now with a violent shock.

Maggie was frightened at Tom's pale, trembling silence. There was something else to tell him – something worse. She threw her arms around him at last, and said, with a half sob –

'Oh, Tom – dear, dear Tom, don't fret too much – try and bear it well.'

Tom turned his cheek passively to meet her entreating kisses, and there gathered a moisture in his eyes, which he just rubbed away with his hand. The action seemed to rouse him, for he shook himself and said, 'I shall go home with you, Maggie. Didn't my father say I was to go?'

'No, Tom, father didn't wish it,' said Maggie, her anxiety about *his* feeling helping her to master her agitation. What *would* he do when she told him all? 'But mother wants you to come – poor mother! – she cries so. Oh, Tom, it's very dreadful at home.'

Maggie's lips grew whiter, and she began to tremble almost as Tom had done. The two poor things clung closer to each other – both trembling – the one at an unshapen fear, the other at the image of a terrible certainty. When Maggie spoke, it was hardly above a whisper.

'And . . . and . . . poor father. . . .'

Maggie could not utter it. But the suspense was intolerable to Tom. A vague idea of going to prison, as a consequence of debt, was the shape his fears had begun to take.

'Where's my father?' he said, impatiently. '*Tell* me, Maggie.'

'He's at home,' said Maggie, finding it easier to reply to that question. 'But,' she added, after a pause, 'not himself. . . . He fell off his horse. . . . He has known nobody but me ever since. . . . He seems to have lost his senses. . . . Oh, father, father. . . .'

With these last words, Maggie's sobs burst forth with the more violence for the previous struggle against them. Tom felt that pressure of the heart which forbids tears: he had no distinct vision of their troubles as Maggie had, who had been at home: he only felt the crushing weight of what seemed unmitigated misfortune. He tightened his arm almost convulsively round Maggie as she sobbed, but his face looked rigid and tearless – his eyes blank – as if a black curtain of cloud had suddenly fallen on his path.

But Maggie soon checked herself abruptly: a single thought had acted on her like a startling sound.

'We must set out, Tom – we must not stay – father will miss me – we must be at the turnpike at ten to meet the coach.' She said this with hasty decision, rubbing her eyes, and rising to seize her bonnet. Tom at once felt the same impulse, and rose too. 'Wait a minute, Maggie,' he said. 'I must speak to Mr. Stelling, and then we'll go.'

He thought he must go to the study where the pupils were, but on his way he met Mr. Stelling, who had heard from his wife that Maggie appeared to be in trouble when she asked for her brother; and, now that he thought the brother and sister had been alone long enough, was coming to inquire and offer his sympathy.

'Please, sir, I must go home,' Tom said, abruptly, as he met Mr. Stelling in the passage. 'I must go back with my sister directly. My father's lost his lawsuit – he's lost all his property – and he's very ill.'

Mr. Stelling felt like a kind-hearted man; he foresaw a probable money loss for himself, but this had no appreciable share in his feeling, while he looked with grave pity at the brother and sister for whom youth and sorrow had begun together. When he knew how Maggie had come, and how eager she was to get home again, he hurried their departure, only whispering something to Mrs. Stelling, who had followed him, and who immediately left the room.

Tom and Maggie were standing on the door-step, ready to set out, when Mrs. Stelling came with a little basket, which she hung on Maggie's arm, saying, 'Do remember to eat something on the way, dear.' Maggie's heart went out towards this woman whom she had never liked, and she kissed her silently. It was the first sign within the poor child of that new sense which is the gift of sorrow – that susceptibility to the bare offices of humanity which raises them into a bond of loving fellowship, as to haggard men among the icebergs the mere presence of an ordinary comrade stirs the deep fountains of affection.

Mr. Stelling put his hand on Tom's shoulder and said, 'God bless you, my boy: let me know how you get on.' Then he pressed Maggie's hand; but there were no audible goodbyes. Tom had so often thought how joyful he should be the day he left school 'for good!' And now his school-years seemed like a holiday that had come to an end.

The two slight youthful figures soon grew indistinct on the distant road – were soon lost behind the projecting hedgerow.

They had gone forth together into their new life of sorrow, and they would never more see the sunshine undimmed by remembered cares. They had entered the thorny wilderness, and the golden gates of their childhood had for ever closed behind them.

To My Brothers

by John Keats

Perhaps the most attractive and iconic of the Romantic poets, John Keats lived a life (1795–1821) that seems to the 21st-century reader to be blighted with tragedy. Both parents died by the time he was 14; he was deeply attached to his brothers and his sister, and had to witness his brother Tom's death from tuberculosis in 1818. He fell passionately in love with his neighbour Fanny Brawne, but he died in Rome from tuberculosis in 1821, having never married her.

His poetry is rich and sensuous, a celebration of life as much as an acknowledgement of the ever-present shadow of death. His letters display his warmth, wit and generous humanity. This affectionate sonnet on 18 November 1816 was written as a birthday present for his brother Tom.

Small, busy flames play through the fresh laid coals,
   And their faint cracklings o'er our silence creep
   Like whispers of the household gods that keep
A gentle empire o'er fraternal souls.
And while, for rhymes, I search around the poles,
   Your eyes are fix'd, as in poetic sleep,
   Upon the lore[1] so voluble and deep,
That aye at fall of night our care condoles.
This is your birth-day Tom, and I rejoice
   That thus it passes smoothly, quietly.
Many such eves of gently whisp'ring noise
   May we together pass, and calmly try
What are this world's true joys, – ere the great voice,
   From its fair face, shall bid our spirits fly.

[1]**lore** body of tradition and knowledge

A Handful of Dust

by Evelyn Waugh

Evelyn Waugh (1903–1966) is equally famous as a writer of wittily satiric novels such as *Vile Bodies* (1930) and *Decline and Fall* (1928), and as the author of *Brideshead Revisited* (1945), a novel which begins and ends during World War II, but which is better known for its passionate treatment of Roman Catholicism and its nostalgic yearning for a golden past never to be recovered. *A Handful of Dust* (1934) was written four years after Waugh had been divorced from his first wife and then received as a convert into the Roman Catholic Church. This novel may be read as a social satire, and in some ways it also anticipates *Brideshead Revisited* through the importance placed by Tony Last on English tradition, epitomised by his much-loved country house Hetton Manor, and through the significance of the family – particularly the child John Andrew, who is adored by his father and virtually ignored by his mother, Brenda. In order to stave off boredom, Brenda has begun an affair with John Beaver, an idle and feckless young man living in London. Here John Andrew and his father, Tony, meet Brenda off the London train.

'Is mummy coming back today?'

'I hope so.'

'That monkey-woman's party has lasted a long time. Can I come in to the station and meet her?'

'Yes, we'll both go.'

'She hasn't seen Thunderclap for four days. She hasn't seen me jump the new post and rail, has she, daddy?'

She was coming by the 3.18. Tony and John Andrew were there early. They wandered about the station looking at things, and bought some chocolate from a slot machine. The station-master came out to talk to them. 'Her ladyship coming back today?' He was an old friend of Tony's.

'I've been expecting her every day. You know what it is when ladies get to London.'

'Sam Brace's wife went to London and he couldn't get her back. Had to go up and fetch her himself. And then she give him a hiding.'

Presently the train came in and Brenda emerged exquisitely from her third class carriage. 'You've *both* come. What angels you are. I don't at all deserve it.'

'Oh mummy, have you brought the monkey-lady?'

'What *does* the child mean?'

'He's got it into his head that your chum Polly has a tail.'

'Come to think of it, I shouldn't be surprised if she had.'

Two little cases held all her luggage. The chauffeur strapped them on behind the car, and they drove to Hetton.

'What's all the news?'

'Ben's put the rail up ever so high and Thunderclap and I jumped it six times yesterday and six times again today and two more of the fish in the little pond are dead, floating upside down all swollen and nanny burnt her finger on the kettle yesterday and daddy and I saw a fox just as near as anything and he sat quite still and then went away into the wood and I began drawing a picture of a battle only I couldn't finish it because the paints weren't right and the grey carthorse the one that had worms is quite well again.'

'Nothing much has happened,' said Tony. 'We've missed you. What did you find to do in London all this time?'

'Me? Oh I've been behaving rather badly to tell you the truth.'

'Buying things?'

'Worse. I've been carrying on madly with young men and I've spent heaps of money and I've enjoyed it very much indeed. But there's one awful thing.'

'What's that?'

'No, I think it had better keep. It's something you won't like at all.'

'You've bought a Pekingese.'

'Worse, far worse. Only I haven't done it yet. But I *want* to dreadfully.'

'Go on.'

'Tony, I've found a flat.'

'Well, you'd better lose it again, quick.'

'All right. I'll attack you about it again later. Meanwhile try not to brood about it.'

'I shan't give it another thought.'

'What's a flat, daddy?'

The Vortex

by Noël Coward

Noël Coward (1899–1973) is known for his elegant comedies of manners, but he achieved special fame (and some notoriety) with this early play about family tension. Nicky Lancaster, a drug-addict, has been abandoned by his fiancée, who is moving towards an affair with Tom Veryan, who is betraying his lover, Florence (Nicky's mother). Nicky is distressed by his mother's adulteries and her obsessive need to stay glamorously young. This extract is taken from the end of the play.

NICKY I'm sorry, mother. I felt I had to talk to you alone.

FLORENCE At this hour of the night – you're mad!

NICKY No, I'm not, I think I'm probably more unhappy than I've ever been in my life.

FLORENCE You're young – you'll get over it.

NICKY I hope so.

FLORENCE I knew the first moment I saw her – what sort of a girl she was.

NICKY Oh, mother!

FLORENCE It's true. I had an *instinct* about her.

NICKY It's all been rather a shock, you know –

FLORENCE *(Becoming motherly)* Yes, dear – I know – I know – but you mustn't be miserable about her – she isn't worth it. *(She goes to kiss him.)*

NICKY *(Gently pushing her away)* Don't, mother!

FLORENCE Listen, Nicky – go back to bed now – there's a dear – my head's splitting.

NICKY I can't yet.

FLORENCE Take some aspirin – that'll calm your nerves.

NICKY I'm afraid I'm a little beyond aspirin.

FLORENCE I don't want you to think I don't sympathise with you, darling – my heart *aches* for you – I know so well what you're going through.

NICKY Do you?

FLORENCE It's agony – absolute agony – but, you see – it will wear off – it always does in time. *(*NICKY *doesn't answer.)* Nicky, please go now!

NICKY I want to talk to you.

FLORENCE To-morrow – we'll talk to-morrow.

NICKY No, now – *now*!

FLORENCE You're inconsiderate and cruel – I've told you my head's bursting.

NICKY I want to sympathise with you, too – and try to understand everything – as well as I can –

FLORENCE Understand everything?

NICKY Yes, please.

FLORENCE I don't know what you mean –

NICKY Will you tell me things – as though I were somebody quite different?

FLORENCE What kind of things?

NICKY Things about you – your life.

FLORENCE Really, Nicky – you're ridiculous – asking me to tell you stories at this hour!

NICKY *(With dead vehemence)* Mother – sit down quietly. I'm not going out of this room until I've got everything straight in my mind.

FLORENCE *(Sinking down – almost hypnotised)* Nicky – please – I –

NICKY Tom Veryan has been your lover, hasn't he?

FLORENCE *(Almost shrieking)* Nicky – how dare you!

NICKY Keep calm – it's our only chance – keep calm.

FLORENCE *(Bursting into tears)* How dare you speak to me like that – suggest such a thing – I –

NICKY It's true, isn't it?

FLORENCE Go away – go away!

NICKY It's true, isn't it?

FLORENCE No – no!

NICKY It's true, isn't it?

FLORENCE No – I tell you – no – no – no!

NICKY You're lying to me, mother. What's the use of that?

FLORENCE You're mad – mad –

NICKY Does father know?

FLORENCE Go away!

NICKY Does father know?

FLORENCE Your father knows nothing – he doesn't understand me any more than you do.

NICKY Then it's between us alone.

FLORENCE I tell you I don't know what you're talking about.

NICKY Mother – don't go on like that, it's useless – we've arrived at a crisis, wherever we go – whatever we do we can't escape from it. I know we're neither of us very strong-minded or capable, and we haven't much hope of coming through successfully – but let's try – it's no good pretending any more.

[. . .]

You've had other lovers besides Tom Veryan – haven't you?

FLORENCE Yes, I have – I have. Now then!

NICKY Well, anyhow – that's the truth – at last –

He rises, turns his back on her and stands looking out of the window.

FLORENCE *(After a pause – going to him)* Nicky – don't be angry – please don't be angry with me.

NICKY I'm not angry a bit – I realise that I'm living in a world where things like this happen – and they've got to be faced and given the right value. If only I'd had the courage to realise everything before – it wouldn't be so bad now – it's the sudden shock that's thrown the whole thing out of focus for me – but I mean to get it right – please help me!

FLORENCE *(Dully)* I don't know what to do.

NICKY It's your life, and you've lived it as you've wanted to live it – that's fair –

FLORENCE Yes – yes.

NICKY You've wanted love always – passionate love, because you were made like that – it's not your fault – it's the fault of circumstances and civilisation – civilisation makes rottenness so much easier – we're utterly rotten – both of us –

FLORENCE Nicky – don't – don't –

NICKY How can we help ourselves? – We swirl about in a vortex of beastliness – this is a chance – don't you see – to realise the truth – our only chance.

FLORENCE Oh, Nicky, do stop – go away!

NICKY Don't keep on telling me to stop when our only hope is to hammer it out.

FLORENCE You're overwrought – it isn't as bad as you think.

NICKY Isn't it?

FLORENCE No, no. Of course it isn't. To-morrow morning you'll see things quite differently.

NICKY You haven't understood.

FLORENCE Yes, I have – I have.

NICKY You haven't understood. Oh, my God, you haven't understood! You're building up silly defences in your mind. I'm overwrought. To-morrow morning I shall see things quite differently. That's true – that's the tragedy of it, and you won't see – To-morrow morning I *shall* see things differently. All this will seem unreal – a nightmare – the machinery of our lives will go on again and gloss over the truth as it always does – and our chance will be gone for ever.

FLORENCE Chance – chance? What are you talking about – what chance?

NICKY I must make you see somehow.

FLORENCE You're driving me mad.

NICKY Have patience with me – please – please –

FLORENCE *(Wildly)* How can I have patience with you? – You exaggerate everything.

NICKY No I don't – I wish I did.

FLORENCE Listen – let me explain something to you.

NICKY Very well – go on.

FLORENCE You're setting yourself up in judgment on me – your own mother.

NICKY No, I'm not.

FLORENCE You are – you are – let me speak – you don't understand my temperament in the least – nobody does – I –

NICKY You're deceiving yourself – your temperament's no different from thousands of other women, but you've been weak and selfish and given way all along the line –

FLORENCE Let me speak, I tell you –!

NICKY What's the use – you're still pretending – you're building up barriers between us instead of helping me to break them down.

FLORENCE What are you accusing me of having done?

NICKY Can't you see yet?

FLORENCE No, I can't. If you're preaching morality you've no right to – that's my affair – I've never done any harm to anyone.

NICKY Look at me.

FLORENCE Why – what do you mean?

NICKY You've given me *nothing* all my life – nothing that counts.

FLORENCE Now you're pitying yourself.

NICKY Yes, with every reason.

FLORENCE You're neurotic and ridiculous – just because Bunty broke off your engagement you come and say wicked, cruel things to me –

NICKY You forget what I've seen to-night, mother.

FLORENCE I don't care what you've seen.

NICKY I've seen you make a vulgar, disgusting scene in your own house, and on top of that humiliate yourself before a boy half your age. The misery of losing Bunty faded away when that happened – everything is comparative after all.

FLORENCE I didn't humiliate myself –

NICKY You ran after him up the stairs because your vanity wouldn't let you lose him – it isn't that you love him – that would be easier – you never love anyone, you only love them loving you – all your so-called passion and temperament is false – your whole existence had degenerated into an endless empty craving for admiration and flattery – and then you say you've done no harm to anybody – Father used to be a clever man, with a strong will and a capacity for enjoying everything – I can remember him like that, and now he's nothing – a complete nonentity because his spirit's crushed. How could it be otherwise? You've let him down consistently for years – and God knows I'm nothing for him to look forward to – but I might have been if it hadn't been for you –

FLORENCE Don't talk like that. Don't – don't – it can't be such a crime being loved – it can't be such a crime being happy –

NICKY You're not happy – you're never happy – you're fighting – fighting all the time to keep your youth and your looks – because you can't bear the thought of living without them – as though they mattered in the end.

FLORENCE *(Hysterically)* What does anything matter – ever?

NICKY That's what I'm trying to find out.

FLORENCE I'm still young inside – I'm still beautiful – why shouldn't I live my life as I choose?

NICKY You're not young or beautiful; I'm seeing for the first time how old you are – it's horrible – your silly fair hair – and your face all plastered and painted –

FLORENCE Nicky – Nicky – stop – stop – stop!

She flings herself face downwards on the bed. NICKY *goes over to her.*

NICKY Mother!

FLORENCE Go away – go away – I hate you – go away –

NICKY Mother – sit up –

FLORENCE *(Pulling herself together)* Go out of my room –

NICKY Mother –

FLORENCE I don't ever want to see you again – you're insane – you've said wicked, wicked things to me – you've talked to me as though I were a woman off the streets. I can't bear any more – I can't bear any more!

NICKY I have a slight confession to make –

FLORENCE Confession?

NICKY Yes.

FLORENCE Go away – go away –

NICKY *(Taking a small gold box[1] from his pocket)* Look –

FLORENCE What do you mean – what is it – ?

NICKY Don't you know?

FLORENCE *takes the box with trembling fingers and opens it. She stares at it for a moment. When she speaks again her voice is quite dead.*

---

[1]**a small gold box** where Nicky keeps his drugs

FLORENCE Nicky, it isn't – you haven't – ?

NICKY Why do you look so shocked?

FLORENCE *(Dully)* Oh, my God!

NICKY What does it matter?

FLORENCE *suddenly rises and hurls the box out of the window.*

That doesn't make it any better.

FLORENCE *(Flinging herself on her knees beside him)* Nicky, promise me, oh, promise you'll never do it again – never in your life – it's frightful – horrible –

NICKY It's only just the beginning.

FLORENCE What can I say to you – what can I say to you?

NICKY Nothing – under the circumstances.

FLORENCE What do you mean?

NICKY It can't possibly matter – now.

FLORENCE Matter – but it's the finish of everything – you're young, you're just starting on your life – you must stop – you must swear never to touch it again – swear to me on your oath. Nicky – I'll help you – I'll help you –

NICKY You!

He turns away.

FLORENCE *(Burying her face in her hands and moaning)* Oh – oh – oh!

NICKY How could you possibly help me?

FLORENCE *(Clutching him)* Nicky!

NICKY *(Almost losing control)* Shut up – shut up – don't touch me –

FLORENCE *(Trying to take him in her arms)* Nicky – Nicky –

NICKY I'm trying to control myself, but you won't let me – you're an awfully rotten woman, really.

FLORENCE Nicky – stop – stop – stop –

She beats him with her fists.

NICKY Leave go of me!

He breaks away from her, and going up to the dressing-table he sweeps everything off on to the floor with his arm.

FLORENCE *(Screaming)* Oh – oh – Nicky – !

NICKY Now then! Now then! You're not to have any more lovers; you're not going to be beautiful and successful ever again – you're going to be my mother for once – it's about time I had one to help me, before I go over the edge altogether –

FLORENCE Nicky – Nicky –

NICKY Promise me to be different – you've got to promise me!

FLORENCE *(Sinking on to the end of couch, facing audience)* Yes – yes – I promise – *(The tears are running down her face.)*

NICKY I love you, really – that's why it's so awful.

He falls on his knees by her side and buries his face in her lap.

FLORENCE No. No, not awful – don't say that – I love you, too.

NICKY *(Sobbing hopelessly)* Oh, mother – !

FLORENCE *(Staring in front of her)* I wish I were dead!

NICKY It doesn't matter about death, but it matters terribly about life.

FLORENCE I know –

NICKY *(Desperately)* Promise me you'll be different – promise me you'll be different –

FLORENCE Yes, yes – I'll try –

NICKY We'll both try.

FLORENCE Yes, dear. – Oh, my dear – !

She sits quite still, staring in front of her – the tears are rolling down her cheeks, and she is stroking NICKY*'s hair mechanically in an effort to calm him.*

CURTAIN

Letter to Lady Elizabeth Ralegh, 1603

from Sir Walter Ralegh

This letter was sent from the Tower, where Ralegh (1554–1618) was imprisoned by James I on a bogus charge of high treason. He writes to his wife anticipating his execution. He was eventually put to death on 29 October 1618. He was an active man of the world: an explorer, politician, courtier, soldier. In his writings he was a poet, historian and philosopher – in fact, a true 'Renaissance man'.

You shall now receive (my deare wife) my last words in these my last lines. My love I send you that you may keep it when I am dead, and my councell that you may remember it when I am no more. I would not by my will present you with sorrowes (dear Besse) let them go to the grave with me and be buried in the dust. And seeing that it is not Gods will that I should see you any more in this life, beare it patiently, and with a heart like thy selfe.

First, I send you all the thankes which my heart can conceive, or my words can reherse for your many travailes, and care taken for me, which though they have not taken effect as you wished, yet my debt to you is not the lesse: but pay it I never shall in this world.

Secondly, I beseech you for the love you beare me living, do not hide your selfe many dayes, but by your travailes seeke to helpe your miserable fortunes and the right of your poor childe. Thy mourning cannot availe me, I am but dust.

Thirdly, you shall understand, that my land was conveyed *bona fide* to my childe; the writings were drawne at midsummer was twelve months, my honest cosen Brett can testify so much, and Dolberry too, can remember somewhat therein. And I trust my blood will quench their malice that have cruelly murthered me: and that they will not seek also to kill thee and thine with extreame poverty.

To what friend to direct thee I know not, for all mine have left me in the true time of tryall. And I perceive that my death was determined from the first day. Most sorry I am God knowes that being thus surprised with death I can leave you in no better estate. God is my witnesse I meant you all my office of wines or all that I could have purchased by selling it, halfe of my stuffe, and all my jewels, but some one for the boy, but God hath prevented all my resolutions. That great God that ruleth all in all, but if you live free from want, care for no more, for the rest is but vanity. Love God, and begin betimes to repose your selfe upon him, and therein shall you finde true and lasting riches, and endlesse comfort: for the rest when you have travailed and wearied your thoughts over all sorts of worldly cogitations, you shall but sit downe by sorrowe in the end.

Teach your son also to love and feare God while he is yet young, that the feare of God may grow with him, and then God will be a husband to you, and a father to him; a husband and a father which cannot be taken from you.

Baily oweth me 200 pounds, and Adrian Gilbert 600. In Jersey I also have much owing me besides. The arrearages of the wines will pay my debts. And howsoever you do, for my soules sake, pay all poore men. When I am gone, no doubt you shall be sought for by many, for the world thinkes that I was very rich. But take heed of the pretences of men, and their affections, for they last not but in honest and worthy men, and no greater misery can befall you in this life, than to become a prey, and afterwards to be despised. I speake not this (God knowes) to dissuade you from marriage, for it will be best for you, both in respect of the world and of God. As for me, I am no more yours, nor you mine, death hath cut us asunder: and God hath divided me from the world, and you from me.

Remember your poor childe for his father's sake, who chose you, and loved you in his happiest times. Get those letters (if it be possible) which I writ to the Lords, wherein I sued for my life: God is my witnesse it was for you and yours that I desired life, but it is true that I disdained my self for begging of it: for know it (my deare wife) that your son is the son of a true man, and one who in his owne respect despiseth death and all his misshapen & ugly formes.

I cannot write much, God he knows how hardly I steale this time while others sleep, and it is also time that I should separate my thoughts from the world. Begg my dead body which living was denied thee; and either lay it at Sherburne (and if the land continue) or in Exeter-Church, by my Father and Mother; I can say no more, time and death call me away.

The everlasting God, powerfull, infinite, and omnipotent God, That Almighty God, who is goodnesse it selfe, the true life and true light keep thee and thine: have mercy on me, and teach me to forgive my persecutors and false accusers, and send us to meet in his glorious Kingdome. My deare wife farewell. Blesse my poore boy. Pray for me, and let my good God hold you both in his armes.

Written with the dying hand of sometimes thy Husband, but now alasse overthrowne.

Yours that was, but now not my own.

Walter Rawleigh

Questions

In all of these questions you should consider:

a the ways the writers' choice of form, structure and language shape your responses to the extracts

b how your wider reading in the literature of love has contributed to your understanding and interpretation of the extracts.

1 In what ways does a child's perception influence the description of the wedding ceremony in the extract from *The Young Visiters*?

2 Compare the attitudes to childbirth and new life as expressed by Sylvia Plath and Jackie Kay.

3 Compare the effects of time and place on family relationships in any two of these extracts.

4 How does George Eliot depict distress in childhood?

5 In what ways do Keats and George Eliot communicate love between siblings?

6 Compare the ways in which Ashford and Waugh achieve comic effects in their writing. How seriously should the reader take either extract?

7 Which of the passages do you think most powerfully conveys love between parent and child? Give reasons for your choice.

8 Compare the extracts from *The Vortex* and *A Handful of Dust*. In what ways may both passages be said to disturb?

9 Compare the ways in which lasting love is communicated in any two passages.

Further reading

- In Shakespeare's comedies angry fathers harangue their daughters: Leonato insults Hero in church (*Much Ado about Nothing*); Egeus is enraged that Hermia loves Lysander (*A Midsummer Night's Dream*). At the end familial harmony is restored in the dance of marriage, but in the tragedies it is a different story. Daughters die: Cordelia, King Lear's favourite daughter, is hanged (*King Lear*); Juliet takes her own life (*Romeo and Juliet*); Ophelia drowns (*Hamlet*); Desdemona is murdered (*Othello*).
- 20th-century drama centring on family relationships includes Eugene O'Neill's *Long Day's Journey into Night*, Tennessee Williams's *The Glass Menagerie* and *A Street Car Named Desire*, Shelagh Delaney's *A Taste of Honey*, Edward Albee's *Who's Afraid of Virginia Woolf* and Arthur Miller's *Death of a Salesman*, *View from the Bridge* and *All my Sons*.
- The young playwright Polly Stenham explores dysfunctional family relationships in her two plays *The Face* (2007) and *Tusk Tusk* (2008).Three children are playing hide and seek and waiting for a mobile phone to come alive . . . .
- Families and their place within society are the mainstay of all Jane Austen's novels. You might like to consider the various film versions of her novels currently available. Which Mr Darcy do you feel is most true to Jane Austen's depiction of him in *Pride and Prejudice*?
- Charles Dickens's novels were serialised in magazines. His readers were like audiences of today's soap-operas: the next episode was eagerly anticipated. Would true parentage be discovered? Would Esther be reunited with her mother in *Bleak House*? Would Mr Dombey in *Dombey and Son* ever learn to love his faithful and tender-hearted daughter, Florence?
- If you enjoyed the extract from *The Mill on the Floss*, try *Middlemarch*, George Eliot's greatest novel, which depicts many aspects of family life.
- *The Young Visiters* was written by a nine-year-old child. If you enjoyed this extract, try researching children's literature of the 19th century. *The History of the Fairchild Family* by Mary Martha Sherwood and *The Daisy Chain* by Charlotte M. Yonge are particularly famous examples of family life.

- The families in the writings of the Brontë sisters are often abusive and violent: for example, compare the Reeds in *Jane Eyre* and the Earnshaws in *Wuthering Heights*. For light relief, you may enjoy Stella Gibbons' *Cold Comfort Farm*, where an absurdly dysfunctional family is brought into the 20th century by the efficiency of their niece, Flora Poste.
- Children suffer too at the hands of adults in recent fiction; consider the events in *The God of Small Things* by Arundhati Roy and *Atonement* by Ian McEwan. But is the child completely innocent here?
- As we have seen, the extract from *The Vortex* owes much to the closet scene from *Hamlet*. Another significant intertextual link may be made between the novels *On Beauty* by Zadie Smith and *Howard's End* by E. M. Forster, both of which explore tensions within apparently loving and close-knit families. *A Thousand Acres* by Jane Smiley is based on Shakespeare's political and familial tragedy *King Lear*.
- If you enjoyed Jackie Kay's affectionate poem to her son, try her first collection *The Adoption Papers* (1991), which was dramatised and broadcast by the BBC. *Chapter 4, Baby Lazarus* is particularly moving, and may owe something to the poetry of Sylvia Plath, who herself writes so tenderly about motherhood.

6 Friendship

The poet Emily Dickinson (in poem 1391) sums up friendship as follows:

They might not need me, but they might.
I'll let my head be just in sight;
A smile as small as mine might be
Precisely their necessity.

It is often said that friendship should rank higher than romantic love, because, at its best, it is disinterested and not possessive; Mary Wollstonecraft (extract p. 229) argues on these lines. The 16th-century French philosopher Montaigne similarly rated friendship higher than family love, because we can choose our friends but not our parents or siblings. Duty has no part in our deciding who we choose to love as a friend. He spoke of an ideal friendship as

so perfect a union that the seam which has joined them is effaced and disappears. If I were pressed to say why I love him, I feel that my only reply could be: 'Because it was he, because it was I.'

In 1939, at the outbreak of world war, the novelist E. M. Forster famously declared: 'if I had to choose between betraying my country and betraying my friend, I hope I should have the guts to betray my country.'

In romantic literature, friendships may sometimes appear hidden, unvoiced, as the plot interest centres on the trials of the lovers. Yet friends have an important part to play; the female friend may support the heroine through the joys and sorrows of life: in *Jane Eyre* Helen Burns teaches Jane how to love; Amy delivers Sethe's baby in *Beloved*; and Susan Nipper in *Dombey and Son* is a strong and devoted friend to Florence Dombey, rejected by her father until the last pages of the book. Endurance is thus a characteristic of these female friendships.

Intellectual stimulus has often enriched friendships: in George Eliot's *The Mill on the Floss* the shared interests of Maggie and Philip help them both to survive their difficult circumstances. Historically,

World War I isolated many women at home, but also provided them with new opportunities for independent work and friendships. This is clearly seen in *Testament of Friendship* by Vera Brittain where she describes the importance of her friendship with the author Winifred Holtby. The Virago Press, set up in 1973 to promote the work of unknown or forgotten female writers, is a rewarding source of literature on this subject.

Ideas about deep friendship as a type of love have a long history, from Plato and the Bible's story of David and Jonathan, to Shakespeare's sonnets addressed to a young nobleman. In some of Shakespeare's plays, bonds of loyalty and affection often challenge other relationships: see, for example, *The Merchant of Venice*, in which Bassanio's love for Antonio causes awkward conflict in his courtship of Portia. However, in some 20th-century cultures male friends have sometimes felt inhibited about using the word 'love' when speaking or writing to each other. Perhaps these men preferred to be seen as stoical and immune to erratic emotional impulses.

More recently it has become again acceptable for men to acknowledge their feelings of love in friendship. A celebrated instance occurred in August 2008 in relation to a great Victorian friendship. Cardinal John Henry Newman, who died in 1890, was to be canonised by the Catholic Church and his remains moved to the Oratory in Birmingham, with some to be retained as sacred relics. However, he had been buried, at his own request, in the same grave as his close friend Ambrose St John, with whom he lived for many years. After St John's death in 1875 Newman wrote: 'I have ever thought no bereavement was equal to that of a husband's or a wife's, but I feel it difficult to believe that any can be greater, or any one's sorrow greater, than mine.' Disturbing the remains would violate Newman's wish and, as some critics believe, show disrespect for the depth of their friendship. Nevertheless, the grave was opened – but Newman's remains were found to have completely decomposed.

The Thing in the Forest

by A. S. Byatt

A. S. Byatt (born 1936) often writes about female friendships and about the interaction of life and art. Her best work is both accessible and scholarly, notably *Possession* (1990) which won the Booker Prize. She included *The Thing in the Forest*, an unsettling narrative, written in fairy-tale style, as the first of five in *The Little Black Book of Stories*.

There were once two little girls who saw, or believed they saw, a thing in a forest. The two little girls were evacuees, who had been sent away from the city by train, with a large number of other children. They all had their names attached to their coats with safety-pins, and they carried little bags or satchels, and the regulation gas-mask. They wore knitted scarves and bonnets or caps, and many had knitted gloves attached to long tapes which ran along their sleeves, inside their coats, and over their shoulders and out, so that they could leave their ten woollen fingers dangling, like a spare pair of hands, like a scarecrow. They all had bare legs and scuffed shoes and wrinkled socks. Most had wounds on their knees in varying stages of freshness and scabbiness. They were at the age when children fall often and their knees were unprotected. With their suitcases, some of which were almost too big to carry, and their other impedimenta, a doll, a toy car, a comic, they were like a disorderly dwarf regiment, stomping along the platform.

The two little girls had not met before, and made friends on the train. They shared a square of chocolate, and took alternate bites at an apple. One gave the other the inside page of her *Beano*.[1] Their names were Penny and Primrose. Penny was thin and dark and taller, possibly older, than Primrose, who was plump and blonde and curly. Primrose had bitten nails, and a

[1]**Beano** a children's comic, published weekly from 1938

velvet collar to her dressy green coat. Penny had a bloodless transparent paleness, a touch of blue in her fine lips. Neither of them knew where they were going, nor how long the journey might take. They did not even know why they were going, since neither of their mothers had quite known how to explain the danger to them. How do you say to your child, I am sending you away, because enemy bombs may fall out of the sky, because the streets of the city may burn like forest fires of brick and timber, but I myself am staying here, in what I believe may be daily danger of burning, burying alive, gas, and ultimately perhaps a grey army rolling in on tanks over the suburbs, or sailing its submarines up our river, all guns blazing? So the mothers (who did not resemble each other at all) behaved alike, and explained nothing, it was easier. Their daughters they knew were little girls, who would not be able to understand or imagine.

The girls discussed on the train whether it was a sort of holiday or a sort of punishment, or a bit of both. Penny had read a book about Boy Scouts, but the children on the train did not appear to be Brownies or Wolf Cubs, only a mongrel battalion of the lost. Both little girls had the idea that these were all perhaps *not very good* children, possibly being sent away for that reason. They were pleased to be able to define each other as 'nice'. They would stick together, they agreed. Try to sit together, and things.

The train crawled sluggishly further and further away from the city and their homes. It was not a clean train – the upholstery of their carriage had the dank smell of unwashed trousers, and the gusts of hot steam rolling backwards past their windows were full of specks of flimsy ash, and sharp grit, and occasional fiery sparks that pricked face and fingers like hot needles if you opened the window. It was very noisy too, whenever it picked up a little speed. The engine gave great bellowing sighs, and the invisible wheels underneath clicked rhythmically and monotonously, tap-tap-tap-CRASH, tap-tap-tap-CRASH. The window-panes were both grimy and misted up. The train stopped frequently, and when it stopped, they used their gloves to wipe rounds, through which they peered out at flooded fields, furrowed hillsides and tiny stations whose names were carefully blacked out, whose platforms were empty of life.

The children did not know that the namelessness was meant to baffle or delude an invading army. They felt – they did not think it out, but somewhere inside them the idea sprouted – that the erasure was because of them, because they were not meant to know where they were going or, like Hansel and Gretel, to find the way back. They did not speak to each other of this anxiety, but began the kind of conversation children have about things they really disliked, things that upset, or disgusted, or frightened them. Semolina pudding with its grainy texture, mushy peas, fat on roast meat. Listening to the stairs and the window-sashes creaking in the dark or the wind. Having your head held roughly back over the basin to have your hair washed, with cold water running down inside your liberty bodice. Gangs in playgrounds. They felt the pressure of all the other alien children in all the other carriages as a potential gang. They shared another square of chocolate, and licked their fingers, and looked out at a great white goose flapping its wings beside an inky pond.

The sky grew dark grey and in the end the train halted. The children got out, and lined up in a crocodile, and were led to a mud-coloured bus. Penny and Primrose managed to get a seat together, although it was over the wheel, and both of them began to feel sick as the bus bumped along snaking country lanes, under whipping branches, dark leaves on dark wooden arms on a dark sky, with torn strips of thin cloud streaming across a full moon, visible occasionally between them.

They were billeted temporarily in a mansion commandeered from its owner, which was to be arranged to hold a hospital for the long-term disabled, and a secret store of artworks and other valuables. The children were told they were there temporarily, until families were found to take them all into their homes. Penny and Primrose held hands, and said to each other that it would be wizard if they could go to the same family, because at least they would have each other. They didn't say anything to the rather tired-looking ladies who were ordering them about, because with the cunning of little children, they knew that requests were most often counter-productive, adults liked saying no. They imagined possible families into which they might be thrust. They did not discuss what they imagined, as these pictures, like the black station signs, were too frightening, and words might make some horror solid, in some magical way. Penny, who was a reading child, imagined Victorian dark pillars of severity, like Jane Eyre's Mr Brocklehurst, or David Copperfield's Mr Murdstone. Primrose imagined – she didn't know why – a fat woman with a white cap and round red arms who smiled nicely but made the children wear sacking aprons and scrub the steps and the stove. 'It's like we were orphans,' she said to Penny. 'But we're not,' Penny said. 'If we manage to stick together . . . '

The Kite Runner

by Khaled Hosseini

Khaled Hosseini was born in Kabul, Afghanistan, in 1965. His father was a diplomat with the Afghan Foreign Ministry. After the Soviet invasion, the family, then in Paris, was granted political asylum in the United States. They moved to San Jose, California. After high school Hosseini studied Biology and Medicine at Santa Clara University. The early chapters of *The Kite Runner* describe the friendship between two boys, Amir, who lives with his father in a prosperous part of Kabul, and Hassan, the son of Amir's father's servant, Ali.

One day, in July 1973, I played another little trick on Hassan. I was reading to him, and suddenly I strayed from the written story. I pretended I was reading from the book, flipping pages regularly, but I had abandoned the text altogether, taken over the story, and made up my own. Hassan, of course, was oblivious to this. To him, the words on the page were a scramble of codes, indecipherable, mysterious. Words were secret doorways and I held all the keys. After, I started to ask him if he'd liked the story, a giggle rising in my throat, when Hassan began to clap.

'What are you doing?' I said.

'That was the best story you've read me in a long time,' he said, still clapping.

I laughed. 'Really?'

'Really.'

'That's fascinating,' I muttered. I meant it too. This was . . . wholly unexpected. 'Are you sure, Hassan?'

He was still clapping. 'It was great, Amir agha. Will you read me more of it tomorrow?'

'Fascinating,' I repeated, a little breathless, feeling like a man who discovers a buried treasure in his own backyard. Walking down the hill, thoughts were exploding in my head like the fireworks at *Chaman. Best story you've read me in a long time*, he'd said. I had read him a *lot* of stories. Hassan was asking me something.

'What?' I said.

'What does that mean, "fascinating"?'

I laughed. Clutched him in a hug and planted a kiss on his cheek.

'What was that for?' he said, startled, blushing.

I gave him a friendly shove. Smiled. 'You're a prince, Hassan. You're a prince and I love you.'

That same night, I wrote my first short story. It took me thirty minutes. It was a dark little tale about a man who found a magic cup and learned that if he wept into the cup, his tears turned into pearls. But even though he had always been poor, he was a happy man and rarely shed a tear. So he found ways to make himself sad so that his tears could make him rich. As the pearls piled up, so did his greed grow. The story ended with the man sitting on a mountain of pearls, knife in hand, weeping helplessly into the cup with his beloved wife's slain body in his arms.

That evening, I climbed the stairs and walked into Baba's smoking room, in my hands the two sheets of paper on which I had scribbled the story. Baba and Rahim Khan were smoking pipes and sipping brandy when I came in.

'What is it, Amir?' Baba said, reclining on the sofa and lacing his hands behind his head. Blue smoke swirled around his face. His glare made my throat feel dry. I cleared it and told him I'd written a story.

Baba nodded and gave a thin smile that conveyed little more than feigned interest. 'Well, that's very good, isn't it?' he said. Then nothing more. He just looked at me through the cloud of smoke.

I probably stood there for under a minute, but, to this day, it was one of the longest minutes of my life. Seconds plodded by, each separated from the next by an eternity. Air grew heavy, damp, almost solid. I was breathing bricks. Baba went on staring me down, and didn't offer to read.

As always, it was Rahim Khan who rescued me. He held out his hand and favored me with a smile that had nothing feigned about it. 'May I have it, Amir jan? I would very much like to read it.' Baba hardly ever used the term of endearment *jan* when he addressed me.

Baba shrugged and stood up. He looked relieved, as if he too had been rescued by Rahim Khan. 'Yes, give it to *Kaka* Rahim. I'm going upstairs to get ready.' And with that, he left the room. Most days I worshiped Baba with an intensity approaching the religious. But right then, I wished I could open my veins and drain his cursed blood from my body.

An hour later, as the evening sky dimmed, the two of them drove off in my father's car to attend a party. On his way out, Rahim Khan hunkered before me and handed me my story and another folded piece of paper. He flashed a smile and winked. 'For you. Read it later.' Then he paused and added a single word that did more to encourage me to pursue writing than any compliment any editor has ever paid me. That word was *Bravo*.

When they left, I sat on my bed and wished Rahim Khan had been my father. Then I thought of Baba and his great big chest and how good it felt when he held me against it, how he smelled of Brut in the morning, and how his beard tickled my face. I was overcome with such sudden guilt that I bolted to the bathroom and vomited in the sink.

Later that night, curled up in bed, I read Rahim Khan's note over and over. It read like this:

Amir jan,

I enjoyed your story very much. Mashallah, *God has granted you a special talent. It is now your duty to hone that talent, because a person who wastes his God-given talents is a donkey. You have written your story with sound grammar and interesting style. But the most impressive thing about your story is that it has irony. You may not even know what that word means. But you will someday. It is something that some writers reach for their entire careers and never attain. You have achieved it with your first story.*

My door is and always will be open to you, Amir jan. I shall hear any story you have to tell. Bravo.

Your friend,
Rahim

Buoyed by Rahim Khan's note, I grabbed the story and hurried downstairs to the foyer where Ali and Hassan were sleeping on a mattress. That was the only time they slept in the house, when Baba was away and Ali had to watch over me. I shook Hassan awake and asked him if he wanted to hear a story.

He rubbed his sleep-clogged eyes and stretched. 'Now? What time is it?'

'Never mind the time. This story's special. I wrote it myself,' I whispered, hoping not to wake Ali. Hassan's face brightened.

'Then I *have* to hear it,' he said, already pulling the blanket off him.

I read it to him in the living room by the marble fireplace. No playful straying from the words this time; this was about me! Hassan was the perfect audience in many ways, totally immersed in the tale, his face shifting with the changing tones in the story. When I read the last sentence, he made a muted clapping sound with his hands.

'*Mashallah*, Amir agha. Bravo!' He was beaming.

'You liked it?' I said, getting my second taste – and how sweet it was – of a positive review.

'Some day, *Inshallah*, you will be a great writer,' Hassan said. 'And people all over the world will read your stories.'

'You exaggerate, Hassan,' I said, loving him for it.

'No. You will be great and famous,' he insisted. Then he paused, as if on the verge of adding something. He weighed his words and cleared his throat. 'But will you permit me to ask a question about the story?' he said shyly.

'Of course.'

'Well . . .' he started, broke off.

'Tell me, Hassan,' I said. I smiled, though suddenly the insecure writer in me wasn't so sure he wanted to hear it.

'Well,' he said, 'if I may ask, why did the man kill his wife? In fact, why did he ever have to feel sad to shed tears? Couldn't he have just smelled an onion?'

I was stunned. That particular point, so obvious it was utterly stupid, hadn't even occurred to me. I moved my lips soundlessly. It appeared that on the same night I had learned about one of writing's objectives, irony, I would also be introduced to one of its pitfalls: the Plot Hole. Taught by Hassan, of all people. Hassan who couldn't read and had never written a single word in his entire life. A voice, cold and dark, suddenly whispered in my ear, *What does he know, that illiterate Hazara? He'll never be anything but a cook. How dare he criticize you?*

'Well,' I began. But I never got to finish that sentence.

Because suddenly Afghanistan changed forever.

The Keepsake

by Fleur Adcock

Fleur Adcock was born in New Zealand in 1934, and was partly educated in England, where she settled in 1963. Her collections of poems include descriptions of public events, travel and various landscapes, though she is better known as a poet on a more domestic scale. She wrote *The Keepsake* as an elegy in memory of her friend Pete Laver.

'To Fleur from Pete, on loan perpetual.'
It's written on the flyleaf of the book
I wouldn't let you give away outright:
'Just make it permanent loan' I said – a joke
between librarians, professional
jargon. It seemed quite witty, on a night

when most things passed for wit. We were all hoarse
by then, from laughing at the bits you'd read
aloud – the heaving bosoms, blushing sighs,
demoniac lips. 'Listen to this!' you said:
'"Thus rendered bold by frequent intercourse
I dared to take her hand."' We wiped our eyes.

'"Colonel, what mean these stains upon your dress?"'
We howled. And then there was Lord Ravenstone
faced with Augusta's dutiful rejection
in anguished prose; or, for a change of tone,
a touch of Gothic: Madame la Comtesse
's walled-up lover. An inspired collection:

The Keepsake, 1835; the standard
drawing-room annual, useful as a means
for luring ladies into chaste flirtation
in early 19th century courtship scenes.

I'd never seen a copy; often wondered.
Well, here it was – a pretty compilation

of tales and verses: stanzas by Lord Blank
and Countess This and Mrs That; demure
engravings, all white shoulders, corkscrew hair
and swelling bosoms; stories full of pure
sentiments, in which gentlemen of rank
urged suits upon the nobly-minded fair.

You passed the volume round, and poured more wine.
Outside your cottage lightning flashed again:
a Grasmere storm, theatrically right
for stories of romance and terror. Then
somehow, quite suddenly, the book was mine.
The date in it's five weeks ago tonight.

'On loan perpetual.' If that implied
some dark finality, some hint of 'nox
perpetua', something desolate and bleak,
we didn't see it then, among the jokes.
Yesterday, walking on the fells, you died.
I'm left with this, a trifling, quaint antique.

You'll not reclaim it now; it's mine to keep:
a keepsake, nothing more. You've changed the 'loan
perpetual' to a bequest by dying.
Augusta, Lady Blanche, Lord Ravenstone –
I've read the lot, trying to get to sleep.
The jokes have all gone flat. I can't stop crying.

The Grasshopper

by Richard Lovelace

Richard Lovelace (1618–1658) was a wealthy, handsome courtier serving Charles I during the dangerous period of the English Civil War. He was imprisoned at least twice and died in poverty. *The Grasshopper* is addressed 'To My Noble Friend, Mr Charles Cotton.'

O thou that swing'st upon the waving hair
Of some well-filled oaten beard,
Drunk ev'ry night with a delicious tear
Dropt thee from heav'n, where now th' art rear'd:

The joys of earth and air are thine entire,
That with thy feet and wings dost hop and fly;
And when thy poppy works thou dost retire
To thy carv'd acorn-bed to lie.

Up with the day, the sun thou welcom'st then,
Sport'st in the gilt plats of his beams,
And all these merry days mak'st merry men,
Thyself, and melancholy streams.

But ah the sickle! golden ears are cropt;
Ceres[1] and Bacchus[2] bid good night;
Sharp frosty fingers all your flow'rs have topt,
And what scythes spar'd, winds shave off quite.

Poor verdant fool, and now green ice! thy joys.
Large and as lasting as thy perch of grass,
Bid us lay in 'gainst winter rain, and poise
Their floods with an o'erflowing glass.

---

[1]**Ceres** the Roman goddess of crops and vegetation
[2]**Bacchus** the Roman god of wine and revelry

Thou best of men and friends! we will create
  A genuine Summer in each other's breast;
And spite of this cold Time and frozen Fate,
  Thaw us a warm seat to our rest.

Our sacred hearths shall burn eternally
  As vestal flames;[3] the North-wind, he
Shall strike his frost-stretch'd wings; dissolve, and fly
  This Etna[4] in epitome.

Dropping December shall come weeping in,
  Bewail th' usurping of his reign;
But when in show'rs of old Greek[5] we begin,
  Shall cry he hath his crown again.

Night as clear Hesper[6] shall our tapers whip
  From the light casements where we play,
And the dark hag from her black mantle strip,
  And stick there everlasting day.

Thus richer than untempted kings are we,
  That asking nothing, nothing need:
Though lord of all what seas embrace, yet he
  That wants himself is poor indeed.

---

[3]**vestal flames** sacred flames in the temple of Vesta, goddess of the household hearth

[4]**Etna** Mount Etna, a volcano in Sicily

[5]**old Greek** a type of fine matured wine

[6]**Hesper** the evening star (Greek)

Sonnet 104

by William Shakespeare

Shakespeare (1564–1616) wrote his 154 sonnets during the 1590s. The first 126 were written in loving tribute to a young man, a wealthy patron, possibly the Earl of Southampton. The remaining 28 are about the poet's complicated love for a woman, the 'dark lady'. However, there has been much scholarly dispute about both the male recipient and the nature of the relationships. One of the teasing mysteries about Shakespeare is his reticence about his own life compared with the rich detail in the lives and loves of his characters.

To me fair friend you never can be old,
For as you were when first your eye I eyed,
Such seems your beauty still: three winters cold,
Have from the forests shook three summers' pride,
Three beauteous springs to yellow autumn turned,
In process of the seasons have I seen,
Three April perfumes in three hot Junes burned,
Since first I saw you fresh which yet are green.
Ah yet doth beauty like a dial hand,
Steal from his figure, and no pace perceived,
So your sweet hue, which methinks still doth stand
Hath motion, and mine eye may be deceived.
   For fear of which, hear this thou age unbred,
   Ere you were born was beauty's summer dead.

A Vindication of the Rights of Woman

by Mary Wollstonecraft

Mary Wollstonecraft (1759–1797) wrote reviews and translations, met many of London's leading intellectuals, travelled to Paris immediately after the French Revolution, and married William Godwin in 1797. She died soon after giving birth to their daughter, Mary, who later married the poet Percy Shelley and became an author herself. This extract urges a more mature attitude towards the way men and women relate to each other in marriage: a true and lasting marriage becomes a friendship.

The most holy band of society is friendship. It has been well said, by a shrewd satirist, 'that rare as true love is, true friendship is still rarer.'

This is an obvious truth, and, the cause not lying deep, will not elude a slight glance of inquiry.

Love, the common passion, in which chance and sensation take place of choice and reason, is, in some degree, felt by the mass of mankind; for it is not necessary to speak, at present, of the emotions that rise above or sink below love. This passion, naturally increased by suspense and difficulties, draws the mind out of its accustomed state, and exalts the affections; but the security of marriage, allowing the fever of love to subside, a healthy temperature is thought insipid only by those who have not sufficient intellect to substitute the calm tenderness of friendship, the confidence of respect, instead of blind admiration, and the sensual emotions of fondness.

This is, must be, the course of nature. Friendship or indifference inevitably succeeds love. And this constitution seems perfectly to harmonise with the system of government which prevails in the moral world. Passions are spurs to action, and open the mind; but they sink into mere appetites, become a personal and momentary gratification when the object is gained, and the satisfied mind rests in enjoyment. The man who had some virtue whilst he was struggling for a crown, often becomes a voluptuous tyrant when it graces his brow; and, when the lover is not lost in the husband, the dotard, a prey to childish caprices and fond jealousies, neglects the serious duties of life, and the caresses which should excite confidence in his children are lavished on the overgrown child, his wife.

In order to fulfil the duties of life, and to be able to pursue with vigour the various employments which form the moral character, a master and mistress of a family ought not to continue to love each other with passion. I mean to say that they ought not to indulge those emotions which disturb the order of society, and engross the thoughts that should be otherwise employed. The mind that has never been engrossed by one object wants vigour, – if it can long be so, it is weak.

Waiting for Godot

by Samuel Beckett

Samuel Beckett (1906–1989) was born near Dublin and went to teach in Paris, where he formed a friendship with fellow Irishman James Joyce in 1928. He reviewed, translated, wrote poems, novels and articles and published his most famous play, *En Attendant Godot*, in French in 1952. Its first performance in English came three years later.

This extract is taken from the opening of Act 2 and concerns the strange interdependency of Vladimir and Estragon. This bleak and comic play contains few events; in fact, one critic described it as a play where 'nothing happens – twice'.

ESTRAGON*'s boots front centre, heels together, toes splayed.* LUCKY*'s hat at same place.*
The tree has four or five leaves.
Enter VLADIMIR *agitatedly. He halts and looks long at the tree, then suddenly begins to move feverishly about the stage. He halts before the boots, picks one up, examines it, sniffs it, manifests disgust, puts it back carefully. Comes and goes. Halts extreme right and gazes into distance off, shading his eyes with his hand. Comes and goes. Halts extreme left, as before. Comes and goes. Halts suddenly and begins to sing loudly.*

VLADIMIR A dog came in –
Having begun too high he stops, clears his throat, resumes.

A dog came in the kitchen
And stole a crust of bread.
Then cook up with a ladle
And beat him till he was dead.

Then all the dogs came running
And dug the dog a tomb –
He stops, broods, resumes:

Then all the dogs came running
And dug the dog a tomb
And wrote upon the tombstone
For the eyes of dogs to come:

A dog came in the kitchen
And stole a crust of bread.
Then cook up with a ladle
And beat him till he was dead.

Then all the dogs came running
And dug the dog a tomb –
He stops, broods, resumes:

Then all the dogs came running
And dug the dog a tomb –
He stops, broods. Softly.

And dug the dog a tomb . . .

He remains a moment silent and motionless, then begins to move feverishly about the stage. He halts before the tree, comes and goes, before the boots, comes and goes, halts extreme right, gazes into distance, extreme left, gazes into distance. Enter ESTRAGON *right, barefoot, head bowed. He slowly crosses the stage.* VLADIMIR *turns and sees him.*

VLADIMIR You again! *(*ESTRAGON *halts, but does not raise his head.* VLADIMIR *goes towards him.)* Come here till I embrace you.

ESTRAGON Don't touch me!

VLADIMIR *holds back, pained.*

VLADIMIR Do you want me to go away? *(Pause.)* Gogo! *(Pause.* VLADIMIR *observes him attentively.)* Did they beat you? *(Pause.)* Gogo! *(*ESTRAGON *remains silent, head bowed.)* Where did you spend the night?

ESTRAGON Don't touch me! Don't question me! Don't speak to me! Stay with me!

VLADIMIR Did I ever leave you?

ESTRAGON You let me go.

VLADIMIR Look at me. *(*ESTRAGON *does not raise his head. Violently.)* Will you look at me!

ESTRAGON *raises his head. They look long at each other, then suddenly embrace, clapping each other on the back. End of the embrace.* ESTRAGON, *no longer supported, almost falls.*

ESTRAGON What a day!

VLADIMIR Who beat you? Tell me.

ESTRAGON Another day done with.

VLADIMIR Not yet.

ESTRAGON For me it's over and done with, no matter what happens. *(Silence.)* I heard you singing.

VLADIMIR That's right, I remember.

ESTRAGON That finished me. I said to myself, he's all alone, he thinks I'm gone for ever, and he sings.

VLADIMIR One isn't master of one's moods. All day I've felt in great form. *(Pause.)* I didn't get up in the night, not once!

ESTRAGON *(sadly).* You see, you piss better when I'm not there.

VLADIMIR I missed you . . . and at the same time I was happy. Isn't that a queer thing?

ESTRAGON *(shocked).* Happy?

VLADIMIR Perhaps it's not the right word.

ESTRAGON And now?

VLADIMIR Now? . . . *(Joyous.)* There you are again . . . *(Indifferent.)* There we are again . . . *(Gloomy.)* There I am again.

ESTRAGON You see, you feel worse when I'm with you. I feel better alone, too.

VLADIMIR *(vexed).* Then why do you always come crawling back?

ESTRAGON I don't know.

VLADIMIR No, but I do. It's because you don't know how to defend yourself. I wouldn't have let them beat you.

ESTRAGON You couldn't have stopped them.

VLADIMIR Why not?

ESTRAGON There were ten of them.

VLADIMIR No, I mean before they beat you. I would have stopped you from doing whatever it was you were doing.

ESTRAGON I wasn't doing anything.

VLADIMIR Then why did they beat you?

ESTRAGON I don't know.

VLADIMIR Ah no, Gogo, the truth is there are things escape you that don't escape me, you must feel it yourself.

ESTRAGON I tell you I wasn't doing anything.

VLADIMIR Perhaps you weren't. But it's the way of doing it that counts, the way of doing it, if you want to go on living.

ESTRAGON I wasn't doing anything.

VLADIMIR You must be happy, too, deep down, if you only knew it.

ESTRAGON Happy about what?

VLADIMIR To be back with me again.

ESTRAGON Would you say so?

VLADIMIR Say you are, even if it's not true.

ESTRAGON What am I to say?

VLADIMIR Say, I am happy.

ESTRAGON I am happy.

VLADIMIR So am I.

ESTRAGON So am I.

VLADIMIR We are happy.

ESTRAGON We are happy. *(Silence.)* What do we do now, now that we are happy?

Stuart, a Life Backwards

by Alexander Masters

The author of this book, Alexander Masters, met Stuart Shorter whilst working for WinterComfort, a day centre for the homeless in Cambridge. The son of two writers, Masters originally came to Cambridge in the late 1990s to study for a PhD in Physics. This book charts the friendship between the author and Stuart Shorter, 'thief, hostage taker, psycho and sociopathic street-raconteur: a man with an important life'. Stuart's life story is narrated in reverse by Alexander. This extract concludes the book, which at this point lacks a title.

'How about – I mean for the title now – think about it for a moment once I've said it, Stuart, because I think it has a nice ring to it, I mean, it'll make people perk up when they read it, and think "I wonder what this is about?", which is what we want, after all, so don't just dismiss it out of hand . . . '

'Get on with it, Alexander.'

'*Stuart Shorter: Stabbing my Stepfather*. You've got to admit, it has shock value.'

Stuart shakes his head emphatically. 'Definitely not. Me and him are getting on really well at the moment. He's had enough of me stabbing him in real life without me doing it on the front of a book as well.

'Something with "madness" in the title, I reckon,' he proffers. '*Living with Madness*.'

'Too bleak. *Life and Deaths on Level D*.'

'That's cheerful?'

'I can't bear books called "Madness",' I admit, determined to cure him of this weakness. 'They're such types. Like books with "Daddy" in the title, which drone on about how the author's father was too busy with his prize dahlias to notice them during their youth. I know: *Stuart Shorter: Lock Him Up!*'

Warming to the theme I sip my coffee and stick my feet on the table. 'Then we could have a sequel: *Keep Him Locked Up!*'

Stuart laughs once more. He has a good, dirty laugh, like Sid James, except it's a short burst rather than a continued lewdness. I have decided to put his drinking (an unusual thing for him to do in my room) down to tension, though heaven knows why at this time, when he says he's happy and 'getting it all together' and just about to go out to his little sister's house to try on some shirts. To his delight, he's to be best man at her wedding later this month.

Encouraged that he is starting to relax at last I get carried away. 'What about *The Ten Best Solitary Confinement Cells of Great Britain* or *How to Screw Your Life Up in Three Easy Lessons?* I know: *Knives I Have Known.*'

Why I Dangle Me Little 'Un Out of Me Kitchen Window – I manage to stop myself in time before I say that one.

'Nah, don't like any of them. Let me think about it. I'll write some down for when we next meet, OK?'

Out comes the squashy diary and we decide on next Wednesday. 'I'll tell you what, I wanted to ask if I could borrow £20.'

'Of course you can.'

'I'll pay you back.'

'Of course you will.' He always does.

'It's just I need . . . '

'No need to explain, Stuart. You borrow money off me when you need it. I borrow money off you when I need it. What's the fuss about?'

'Thanks. Appreciated.'

I hand over the cash and he stands up to go through his usual departing ritual of returning the odds and ends of cigarette papers and tobacco and diary into his pocket, together with the items that have spilt on to the armchair seat during his stay, then in goes the opened beer can, too, into the other pocket.

I offer to give him a lift.

'Yes, if you don't mind. Thanks. Feeling a bit weak today. Not too much trouble?'

'Depends where you need to go.'

He knows full well I'd drive him to Edinburgh if he asked. This is not just friendship speaking, but the fact that I now own his old car with the sticky blobs, which he has sold to me for £275, plus alloy wheels, a £25 discount on what he was planning to raise.

'Only into town. The King's Street Run.' A pub.

Going outside, Stuart grapples down the steps through my buddleia, edges into the car and drops the last few inches with a bounce.

'You know, Alexander, I don't know meself how I got to be like this,' he remarks as we drive beside the river, then cross the bridge past the Wintercomfort Day Centre where, at that Ruth and John campaign meeting, years ago, Stuart first encountered his 'middle-class people'. 'It's too easy to blame, in'it? Sometimes, I think I'm the child of the Devil. Honestly, I do believe that. I've invited the Devil in, and now I can't get him out. I've tried burning him out and cutting him out and he don't take no notice. Why should he? He doesn't want to be homeless. He's got me. Little, skinny, violent me.'

We drive by the public toilets where Keith Laverack was once caught soliciting, at just about the time when he was headmaster of Stuart's old school. Stupid man, he tried it on with an undercover policeman. Not that that stopped the council employing him as an overseer of young boys.

'Do you think,' I ask, not knowing quite how to phrase the question at first, 'do you think – is your unpleasant lifestyle due to something particular about you?'

Stuart juts out his jaw to consider the idea. 'I don't know. It's something I'm quite philosophical about. Some people have grown up, have learnt to cope and accept and have been very successful, and led a very, in brackets, normal competitive life. And then I've met so many people who've led the same sort of lifestyle as I have and had the same sort of childhood and experiences and they're torn to pieces.'

'So, if you had to change one thing, just one thing to make it right, what would it be?'

'Same answer. Don't know. Changing one thing? How much is one thing? Change me brother – does that change me getting rageous? The muscular dystrophy? That don't change the nonces, the System, do it? It's such a mess. Not being funny, change one and you got to change them all. Be easier just to change me.'

We reach the pub down a couple of backstreets and I pull over as near to the door as possible.

I turn to face him, rather hoping that he'll suddenly remember that his sister has invited me to the wedding too. I'd like to see him got up in shirt and tails like a penguin, tattoos poking out beyond the cuff links. But if she has asked him to invite me, he's forgotten about it.

'You know,' I remark as he prepares to haul himself back on to the pavement, 'we have come to the end of this book, and there's still one question left.'

'What's that, mate?'

'Can't you guess?'

'No, mate,' he says, squeezing around on the seat to pick up the infernal Rizlas[1] that have dropped out of his pocket once again. I love that word, 'mate'. Stuart uses it with me very rarely.

'What's your date of birth?'

'Right,' he says, cheerfully, as if our hundreds of hours of conversation are about to start at the beginning again. 'Right. I'm Stuart Clive Shorter, born 19th of the 9th, 1968 . . .'

'So you're thirty-three, aren't you?'

'I'm thirty-three. Getting older, as they say. I lead a very controversial, unpleasant life.'

---

[1]**Rizlas** papers for rolling tobacco

Beloved

by Toni Morrison

This novel has been described as the most important text to have emerged from the African-American literary tradition. Morrison (born 1931) describes how Sethe escaped out of slavery, to be reunited with her children. In this extract, she is telling her youngest daughter Denver about when she was about to give birth whilst fleeing from slavery, and met Amy, a white girl. Sethe is in great pain . . .

She told Denver that a *something* came up out of the earth into her – like a freezing, but moving too, like jaws inside. 'Look like I was just cold jaws grinding,' she said. Suddenly she was eager for his eyes, to bite into them; to gnaw his cheek.

'I was hungry,' she told Denver, 'just as hungry as I could be for his eyes. I couldn't wait.'

So she raised up on her elbow and dragged herself, one pull, two, three, four, toward the young white voice talking about 'Who that back in there?'

'Come see,' I was thinking. 'Be the last thing you behold,' and sure enough here come the feet so I thought well that's where I'll have to start God do what He would, I'm gonna eat his feet off. I'm laughing now, but it's true. I wasn't just set to do it. I was hungry to do it. Like a snake. All jaws and hungry.

'It wasn't no whiteboy at all. Was a girl. The raggediest-looking trash you ever saw saying, "Look there. A nigger. If that don't beat all."'

And now the part Denver loved the best:

Her name was Amy and she needed beef and pot liquor like nobody in this world. Arms like cane stalks and enough hair for four or five heads. Slow-moving eyes. She didn't look at anything quick. Talked so much it wasn't clear how she could breathe at the same time. And those cane-stalk arms, as it turned out, were as strong as iron.

'You 'bout the scariest-looking something I ever seen. What you doing back up in here?'

Down in the grass, like the snake she believed she was, Sethe opened her mouth, and instead of fangs and a split tongue, out shot the truth.

'Running,' Sethe told her. It was the first word she had spoken all day and it came out thick because of her tender tongue.

'Them the feet you running on? My Jesus my.' She squatted down and stared at Sethe's feet. 'You got anything on you, gal, pass for food?'

'No.' Sethe tried to shift to a sitting position but couldn't.

'I like to die I'm so hungry.' The girl moved her eyes slowly, examining the greenery around her. 'Thought there'd be huckleberries. Look like it. That's why I come up in here. Didn't expect to find no nigger woman. If they was any, birds ate em. You like huckleberries?'

'I'm having a baby, miss.'

Amy looked at her. 'That mean you don't have no appetite? Well I got to eat me something.'

Combing her hair with her fingers, she carefully surveyed the landscape once more. Satisfied nothing edible was around, she stood up to go and Sethe's heart stood up too at the thought of being left alone in the grass without a fang in her head.

'Where you on your way to, miss?'

She turned and looked at Sethe with freshly lit eyes. 'Boston. Get me some velvet. It's a store there called Wilson. I seen the pictures of it and they have the prettiest velvet. They don't believe I'm a get it, but I am.'

Sethe nodded and shifted her elbow. 'Your ma'am know you on the lookout for velvet?'

The girl shook her hair out of her face. 'My mama worked for these here people to pay for her passage. But then she had me and since she died right after, well, they said I had to work for em to pay it off. I did, but now I want me some velvet.'

They did not look directly at each other, not straight into the eyes anyway. Yet they slipped effortlessly into yard chat about nothing in particular – except one lay on the ground.

'Boston,' said Sethe. 'Is that far?'

'Ooooh, yeah. A hundred miles. Maybe more.'

'Must be velvet closer by.'

'Not like in Boston. Boston got the best. Be so pretty on me. You ever touch it?'

'No, miss. I never touched no velvet.' Sethe didn't know if it was the voice, or Boston or velvet, but while the whitegirl talked, the baby slept. Not one butt or kick, so she guessed her luck had turned.

'Ever see any?' she asked Sethe. 'I bet you never even seen any.'

'If I did I didn't know it. What's it like, velvet?'

Amy dragged her eyes over Sethe's face as though she would never give out so confidential a piece of information as that to a perfect stranger.

'What they call you?' she asked.

However far she was from Sweet Home, there was no point in giving out her real name to the first person she saw. 'Lu,' said Sethe. 'They call me Lu.'

'Well, Lu, velvet is like the world was just born. Clean and new and so smooth. The velvet I seen was brown, but in Boston they got all colors. Carmine. That means red but when you talk about velvet you got to say "carmine".' She raised her eyes to the sky and then, as though she had wasted enough time away from Boston, she moved off saying, 'I gotta go.'

Picking her way through the brush she hollered back to Sethe, 'What you gonna do, just lay there and foal?'

'I can't get up from here,' said Sethe.

'What?' She stopped and turned to hear.

'I said I can't get up.'

Amy drew her arm across her nose and came slowly back to where Sethe lay. 'It's a house back yonder,' she said.

'A house?'

'Mmmmm. I passed it. Ain't no regular house with people in it though. A lean-to, kinda.'

'How far?'

'Make a difference, does it? You stay the night here snake get you.'

'Well he may as well come on. I can't stand up let alone walk and God help me, miss, I can't crawl.'

'Sure you can, Lu. Come on,' said Amy and, with a toss of hair enough for five heads, she moved toward the path.

So she crawled and Amy walked alongside her, and when Sethe needed to rest, Amy stopped too and talked some more about Boston and velvet and good things to eat. The sound of that voice, like a sixteen-year-old boy's, going on and on and on, kept the little antelope quiet and grazing. During the whole hateful crawl to the lean-to, it never bucked once.

Nothing of Sethe's was intact by the time they reached it except the cloth that covered her hair. Below her bloody knees, there was no feeling at all; her chest was two cushions of pins. It was the voice full of velvet and Boston and good things to eat that urged her along and made her think that maybe she wasn't, after all, just a crawling graveyard for a six-month baby's last hours.

The lean-to was full of leaves, which Amy pushed into a pile for Sethe to lie on. Then she gathered rocks, covered them with more leaves and made Sethe put her feet on them, saying: 'I know a woman had her feet cut off they was so swole.' And she made sawing gestures with the blade of her hand across Sethe's ankles. 'Zzz Zzz Zzz Zzz.'

'I used to be a good size. Nice arms and everything. Wouldn't think it, would you? That was before they put me in the root cellar. I was fishing off the Beaver once. Catfish in Beaver River sweet as chicken. Well I was just fishing there and a nigger floated right by me. I don't like drowned people, you? Your feet remind me of him. All swole like.'

Then she did the magic: lifted Sethe's feet and legs and massaged them until she cried salt tears.

'It's gonna hurt, now,' said Amy. 'Anything dead coming back to life hurts.'

Questions

In all of these questions you should consider:

a the ways the writers' choice of form, structure and language shape your responses to the extracts

b how your wider reading in the literature of love has contributed to your understanding and interpretation of the extracts.

1 In *The Thing in the Forest*, how does A. S. Byatt mingle the way children think and behave with the way an adult (author) looks at children?

2 Compare *The Grasshopper* and *The Keepsake* as poems about affectionate friendship.

3 How does awareness of time passing and the natural world contribute to Shakespeare's feeling for his friend in his *Sonnet 104*?

4 How does Wollstonecraft aim to make her arguments convincing in the extract from *The Rights of Woman*? Explain why you are - or are not - convinced.

5 In productions of *Waiting for Godot*, some directors emphasise the comedy in the friendship of Vladimir and Estragon, others the pathos. Which seems to you to be the stronger in this extract? Give reasons for your answer.

6 Compare the relative impact of dialogue as distinct from narrative and description in the extract from *Stuart, a Life Backwards*.

7 Compare the friendship between Stuart and Alexander with that between Vladimir and Estragon. What do they have in common? What is the place of comedy?

8 Among these extracts, in what ways can you sense a gender difference between the way women and men feel and express their friendships?

9 Compare any two extracts which describe friendship at its best. How do the writers achieve their effects?

Further reading

- Friendships - and especially the challenges to such close bonds - dominate many books: from ancient tales such as the love between David and Jonathan in the Bible (1 Samuel), to the early medieval *Chanson de Roland*, to Conan Doyle's stories about Sherlock Holmes in Edwardian London.
- You can find entertaining mixtures of comedy and social observation in stories of master/servant friendships, with the master depending on his servant's witty resourcefulness: Shakespeare's *The Taming of the Shrew* and Cervantes's *Don Quixote* are enduring classics; P. G. Wodehouse's Jeeves stories have become 20th-century favourites.
- Farquhar's *The Beaux' Stratagem* focuses on the friendship of two male fortune-hunters and that of the women they marry. Congreve's *The Way of the World* is an equally witty but more unsettling account of how passionate love and possible betrayal put friendships under strain.
- If you enjoyed the childhood extract from *The Kite Runner*, try *A Thousand Splendid Suns* by the same author.
- You will find descriptions of female friendships flourishing and under pressure in Thackeray's novel *Vanity Fair*, Jane Austen's *Emma* and Elizabeth Gaskell's *Wives and Daughters*.
- The pressure of war may make friendships more intense and more precious, as in Faulks's *Birdsong* and Susan Hill's *Strange Meeting*. *Mrs Dalloway* by Virginia Woolf, though set in London, is haunted by the shadow of the Great War.
- You can find a classic comic treatment of a struggle between friends in Wilde's *The Importance of being Earnest*. More seriously, Forster's *A Passage to India* describes a close friendship complicated by cultural differences.
- Alan Bennett's *The History Boys* depicts relationships among teachers and pupils. If you enjoyed the extract from *Stuart, a Life Backwards*, try Bennett's *The Lady in the Van*, a comic, moving story about an unusual friendship of his own.
- Adam Sisman's *Wordsworth and Coleridge: The Friendship* shows how the two great poets influenced each other's life and writing. *Possession* by A. S. Byatt invents a fictional literary friendship between two poets.

7 Loss and betrayal

In his sonnet 116 Shakespeare makes the bold claim that love 'is an ever-fixed mark / That looks on tempests and is never shaken.' This is a high ideal in a very optimistic poem. However, in real life most people in love also suffer times of disorientation, pain and loss. For example, the intense feelings in love's early days may fade, and lovers drift apart. Sometimes there is betrayal that can lead to the harsher pains of guilt, shame and anger.

Love is also subject to mortality: a partner dies and the other feels stranded and alone. Loneliness and grief often eclipse the joy of once-shared love so that only pain is left and memory seems to be the only – and doubtful – benefit of having been in love. C. S. Lewis, in *A Grief Observed*, his autobiography of loss (1961), describes his process through suffering, the various thoughts, feelings and moods he had to endure; an extract from *Shadowlands*, a play about his loss, appears on p. 272. Tennyson, the 19th-century poet-laureate, who mourns his friend Arthur Hallam through the 132 poems of *In Memoriam*, also finds that love lost, like love enjoyed and celebrated, is not a single experience, but a bewildering mixture of many.

It is revealing to compare prose and poetry about loss by examining the language and form that the writers have chosen. Often the larger canvas of a novel or autobiography can more easily mingle reflection and analysis with feeling, as in Henry James's *Washington Square* (extract p. 261) and Blake Morrison's memoir *And When Did You Last See Your Father?* (1993). Vera Brittain's *Testament of Youth* (extract p. 268) suggests in its very title that she is writing something full and final about her early life, which was so profoundly affected by the Great War. In telling her painful story she is also speaking for a generation, not just of men who were killed, so often the focus of literature about war, but also about the women who had to wait at home and cope with devastating news.

On the whole (and this is a very broad generalisation), a short poem aims to capture a moment of feeling, especially when its language and form bring it close to music. In fact, many poems about loss have been written to be sung: from Wyatt's 16th-century poems (see p. 259), which were often accompanied by the lute, to our contemporary song lyrics.

Ballads usually have a strong narrative line too and their effect is often to give the suffering heroine or hero a legendary status. Examples range from the traditional *Barbara Allen*, to poems by Keats and Hardy, to more contemporary works, such as those by the Cornish poet Charles Causley.

Suffering often brings loneliness to an individual, and the feeling that an acute problem is unique. In recent times many newspapers and magazines have invited those suffering loss and betrayal in love to share their problems. It can be helpful for these readers to know that they are joining what amounts to a community of grief. This is also one of the benefits often attributed to tragedy, perhaps even more so when performed than when read, whether the play is a doomed love story like *Romeo and Juliet* or a narrative on a grander and more philosophical scale like *Medea*, *King Lear* or *Oedipus Rex*. Most tragedies face the inescapable fact that suffering is widespread and a part of being human.

Poem 1789

by Emily Dickinson

Emily Dickinson (1830–1886) wrote almost 2000 poems, very few of which were published in her lifetime. She grew up in New England in a restricted Puritan culture. Though well educated and extremely well read, she led a secluded life. Her writing sounds personal, even autobiographical, but she warned against reading it in this way: 'When I state myself as the Representative of the Verse – it does not mean – me – but a supposed person.'

The saddest noise, the sweetest noise,
The maddest noise that grows, –
The birds, they make it in the spring,
At night's delicious close

Between the March and April line –
That magical frontier
Beyond which summer hesitates,
Almost too heavenly near.

It makes us think of all the dead
That sauntered with us here,
By separation's sorcery
Made cruelly more dear.

It makes us think of what we had,
And what we now deplore.
We almost wish those siren throats
Would go and sing no more.

An ear can break a human heart
As quickly as a spear.
We wish the ear had not a heart
So dangerously near.

A Doll's House

by Henrik Ibsen

The Norwegian playwright Henrik Ibsen (1828–1906) wrote this ground-breaking play in 1879. Nora is about to leave her husband Torvald and their children. Eight years before she borrowed from Krogstad, a money-lender, so that she could pay to take her husband on a recuperative holiday. Torvald assumed that the money came from Nora's father; in fact, she had forged her father's signature and Krogstad is now blackmailing her. Torvald, a bank manager of high reputation, was horrified to read in Krogstad's letter of Nora's 'crime'; he attacked her for being irresponsible, and then tried to withdraw his bitter remarks when he read a second letter in which Krogstad returned the forged signature, promising to take the matter no further.

Nora is shaken by the attack: she realises that the 'miracle' of her husband's support is impossible. She also sees that she has lived in 'a doll's house', being cherished and patronised by Torvald, who believes that husbands should be strong and masterful and women should be no more than charmingly decorative. This translation is by James MacFarlane.

NORA You have never understood me . . . I've been greatly wronged, Torvald. First by my father, and then by you.

HELMER What! Us two! The two people who loved you more than anybody?

NORA *(Shakes her head)* You two never loved me. You only thought how nice it was to be in love with me.

HELMER But, Nora, what's this you are saying?

NORA It's right, you know, Torvald. At home, Daddy used to tell me what he thought, then I thought the same. And if I thought differently, I kept quiet about it, because he wouldn't have liked it. He used to call me his baby doll, and he played with me as I used to play with my dolls. Then I came to live in your house. . . .

HELMER What way is that to talk about our marriage?

NORA *(Imperturbably)* What I mean is: I passed out of Daddy's hands into yours. You arranged everything to your tastes, and I acquired the same tastes. Or I pretended to . . . I don't really know . . . I think it was a bit of both, sometimes one thing and sometimes the other. When I look back, it seems to me I have been living here like a beggar, from hand to mouth. I lived by doing tricks for you, Torvald. But that's the way you wanted it. You and Daddy did me a great wrong. It's your fault that I've never made anything of my life.

HELMER Nora, how unreasonable . . . how ungrateful you are! Haven't you been happy here?

NORA No, never. I thought I was, but I wasn't really.

HELMER Not . . . not happy!

NORA No, just gay. And you've always been so kind to me. But our house has never been anything but a play-room. I have been your doll wife, just as at home I was Daddy's doll child. And the children in turn have been my dolls. I thought it was fun when you came and played with me, just as they thought it was fun when I went and played with them. That's been our marriage, Torvald.

HELMER There is some truth in what you say, exaggerated and hysterical though it is. But from now on it will be different. Play-time is over; now comes the time for lessons.

NORA Whose lessons? Mine or the children's?

HELMER Both yours and the children's, my dear Nora.

NORA Ah, Torvald, you are not the man to teach me to be a good wife for you.

HELMER How can you say that?

NORA And what sort of qualifications have I to teach the children?

HELMER Nora!

NORA Didn't you say yourself, a minute or two ago, that you couldn't trust me with that job.

HELMER In the heat of the moment! You shouldn't pay any attention to that.

NORA On the contrary, you were quite right. I'm not up to it. There's another problem needs solving first. I must take steps to educate myself. You are not the man to help me there. That's something I must do on my own. That's why I'm leaving you.

HELMER *(Jumps up)* What did you say?

NORA If I'm ever to reach any understanding of myself and the things around me, I must learn to stand alone. That's why I can't stay here with you any longer.

HELMER Nora! Nora!

NORA I'm leaving here at once. I dare say Kristine will put me up for tonight. . . .

HELMER You are out of your mind! I won't let you! I forbid you!

NORA It's no use forbidding me anything now. I'm taking with me my own personal belongings. I don't want anything of yours, either now or later.

HELMER This is madness!

NORA Tomorrow I'm going home – to what used to be my home, I mean. It will be easier for me to find something to do there.

HELMER Oh, you blind, inexperienced . . .

NORA I must set about *getting* experience, Torvald.

HELMER And leave your home, your husband and your children? Don't you care what people will say?

NORA That's no concern of mine. All I know is that this is necessary for *me*.

HELMER This is outrageous! You are betraying your most sacred duty.

NORA And what do you consider to be my most sacred duty?

HELMER Does it take me to tell you that? Isn't it your duty to your husband and your children?

NORA I have another duty equally sacred.

HELMER You have not. What duty might *that* be?

NORA My duty to myself.

HELMER First and foremost, you are a wife and mother.

NORA That I don't believe any more. I believe that first and foremost I am an individual, just as much as you are – or at least I'm going to try to be. I know most people agree with you, Torvald, and that's also what it says in books. But I'm not content any more with what most people say, or with what it says in books. I have to think things out for myself, and get things clear.

HELMER Surely you are clear about your position in your own home? Haven't you an infallible guide in questions like these? Haven't you your religion?

NORA Oh, Torvald, I don't really know what religion is.

HELMER What do you say!

NORA All I know is what Pastor Hansen said when I was confirmed. He said religion was this, that and the other. When I'm away from all this and on my own, I'll go into that, too. I want to find out whether what Pastor Hansen told me was right – or at least whether it's right for *me*.

HELMER This is incredible talk from a young woman! But if religion cannot keep you on the right path, let me at least stir your conscience. I suppose you do have some moral sense? Or tell me – perhaps you don't?

NORA Well, Torvald, that's not easy to say. I simply don't know. I'm really very confused about such things. All I know is my ideas about such things are very different from yours. I've also learnt that the law is different from what I thought; but I simply can't get it into my head that that particular law is right. Apparently a woman has no right to spare her old father on his death-bed, or to save her husband's life, even. I just don't believe it.

HELMER You are talking like a child. You understand nothing about the society you live in.

NORA No, I don't. But I shall go into that too. I must try to discover who is right, society or me.

HELMER You are ill, Nora. You are delirious. I'm half inclined to think you are out of your mind.

NORA Never have I felt so calm and collected as I do tonight.

HELMER Calm and collected enough to leave your husband and children?

NORA Yes.

HELMER Then only one explanation is possible.

NORA And that is?

HELMER You don't love me any more.

NORA Exactly.

HELMER Nora! Can you say that!

NORA I'm desperately sorry, Torvald. Because you have always been so kind to me. But I can't help it. I don't love you any more.

HELMER *(Struggling to keep his composure)* Is that also a 'calm and collected' decision you've made?

NORA Yes, absolutely calm and collected. That's why I don't want to stay here.

HELMER And can you also account for how I forfeited your love?

NORA Yes, very easily. It was tonight, when the miracle didn't happen. It was then I realized you weren't the man I thought you were.

HELMER Explain yourself more clearly. I don't understand.

NORA For eight years I have been patiently waiting. Because, heavens, I knew miracles didn't happen every day. Then this devastating business started, and I became absolutely convinced the miracle *would* happen. All the time Krogstad's letter lay there, it never so much as crossed my mind that you would ever submit to that man's conditions. I was absolutely convinced you would say to him: Tell the whole wide world if you like. And when that was done . . .

HELMER Yes, then what? After I had exposed my own wife to dishonour and shame . . . !

NORA When that was done, I was absolutely convinced you would come forward and take everything on yourself, and say: I am the guilty one.

HELMER Nora!

NORA You mean I'd never let you make such a sacrifice for my sake? Of course not. But what would my story have counted for against yours? – That was the miracle I went in hope and dread of. It was to prevent it that I was ready to end my life.

HELMER I would gladly toil day and night for you, Nora, enduring all manner of sorrow and distress. But nobody sacrifices his *honour* for the one he loves.

NORA Hundreds and thousands of women have.

HELMER Oh, you think and talk like a stupid child.

NORA All right. But you neither think nor talk like the man I would want to share my life with. When you had got over your fright – and you weren't concerned about me but only about what might happen to you – and when all danger was past, you acted as though nothing had happened. I was your little sky-lark again, your little doll, exactly as before; except you would have to protect it twice as carefully as before, now that it had shown itself to be so weak and fragile. *(Rises.)* Torvald, that was the moment I realised that for eight years I'd been living with a stranger, and had borne him three children. . . . Oh, I can't bear to think about it! I could tear myself to shreds.

HELMER *(Sadly)* I see. I see. There is a tremendous gulf dividing us. But, Nora, is there no way we might bridge it?

NORA As I am now, I am no wife for you.

HELMER I still have it in me to change.

NORA Perhaps . . . if you have your doll taken away.

HELMER And be separated from you! No, no, Nora, the very thought of it is inconceivable.

NORA *(Goes into the room, right)* All the more reason why it must be done.

She comes back with her outdoor things and a small travelling bag which she puts on the chair beside the table.

HELMER Nora, Nora, not now! Wait till the morning.

NORA *(Putting on her coat)* I can't spend the night in a strange man's room.

HELMER Couldn't we go on living here like brother and sister . . . ?

NORA *(Tying on her hat)* You know very well that wouldn't last. *(She draws the shawl round her.)* Goodbye, Torvald. I don't want to see the children. I know they are in better hands than mine. As I am now, I can never be anything to them.

HELMER But some day, Nora, some day. . . ?

NORA How should I know? I've no idea what I might turn out to be.

HELMER But you are my wife, whatever you are.

NORA Listen, Torvald, from what I've heard, when a wife leaves her husband's house as I am doing now, he is absolved by law of all responsibility for her. I can at any rate free you from all responsibility. You must not feel in any way bound, any more than I shall. There must be full freedom on both sides. Look, here's your ring back. Give me mine.

HELMER That too?

NORA That too.

HELMER There it is.

NORA Well, that's the end of that. I'll put the keys down here. The maids know where everything is in the house – better than I do, in fact. Kristine will come in the morning after I've left to pack up the few things I brought with me from home. I want them sent on.

HELMER The end! Nora, will you never think of me?

NORA I dare say I'll often think about you and the children and this house.

HELMER May I write to you, Nora?

NORA No, never. I won't let you.

HELMER But surely I can send you . . .

NORA Nothing, nothing.

HELMER Can't I help you if ever you need it?

NORA I said 'no'. I don't accept things from strangers.

HELMER Nora, can I never be anything more to you than a stranger?

NORA *(Takes her bag)* Ah, Torvald, only by a miracle of miracles. . . .

HELMER Name it, this miracle of miracles!

NORA Both you and I would have to change to the point where . . . Oh, Torvald, I don't believe in miracles any more.

HELMER But I *will* believe. Name it! Change to the point where. . . ?

NORA Where we could make a real marriage of our lives together. Goodbye!

She goes out through the hall door.

HELMER *(Sinks down on a chair near the door, and covers his face with his hands.)* Nora! Nora! *(He rises and looks round.)* Empty! She's gone! *(With sudden hope.)* The miracle of miracles. . . ?

(The heavy sound of a door being slammed is heard from below.)

In Memoriam

by Alfred Lord Tennyson

Tennyson (1809–1892) met his great friend Arthur Hallam when they were both undergraduates at Trinity College Cambridge. In 1833 Hallam died abroad and Tennyson began a sequence of 132 poems, entitled *In Memoriam*, to describe his various thoughts and feelings during the long period of his grief. These were published in 1850 and were widely read and praised. Queen Victoria also found comfort in them after the death of her husband Prince Albert in 1861.

2

Old Yew, which graspest at the stones
  That name the underlying dead,
  Thy fibres net the dreamless head,
Thy roots are wrapped about the bones.

The seasons bring the flower again,
  And bring the firstling to the flock;
  And in the dusk of thee, the clock
Beats out the little lives of men.

O not for thee the glow, the bloom,
  Who changest not in any gale,
  Nor branding summer suns avail
To touch thy thousand years of gloom:

And gazing on thee, sullen tree,
  Sick for thy stubborn hardihood,
  I seem to fail from out my blood
And grow incorporate into thee.

54

Oh yet we trust that somehow good
Will be the final goal of ill,
To pangs of nature, sins of will,
Defects of doubt, and taints of blood;

That nothing walks with aimless feet;
That not one life shall be destroyed,
Or cast as rubbish to the void,
When God hath made the pile complete;

That not a worm is cloven in vain;
That not a moth with vain desire
Is shrivelled in a fruitless fire,
Or but subserves another's gain.

Behold, we know not anything;
I can but trust that good shall fall
At last – far off – at last, to all,
And every winter change to spring.

So runs my dream: but what am I?
An infant crying in the night:
An infant crying for the light:
And with no language but a cry.

With Serving Still . . .

by Sir Thomas Wyatt

Sir Thomas Wyatt (1503–1542) was a courtier and diplomat in the service of Henry VIII. After his visit to Italy in 1527 he translated Petrarch's love poems. He was a lover of Anne Boleyn before her marriage to the king. His love poems, many of them laments about loss, betrayal and uncertainty in love, convey the sense of living in dangerous times and the excitement of seizing happiness in the brief time available.

With serving still
  This have I won,
For my goodwill
  To be undone.

And for redress
  Of all my pain,
Disdainfulness
  I have again.

And for reward
  Of all my smart,
Lo, thus unheard
  I must depart!

Wherefore all ye
  That after shall
By fortune be,
  As I am, thrall,

Example take
  What I have won,
Thus for her sake
  To be undone!

The Apparition

by John Donne

John Donne (1572–1631) was a leading practitioner of what became known as 'metaphysical poetry'. Many of his earlier poems are about love but, after he was ordained in 1615, he became one of the most famous preachers in London and wrote a number of religious poems and sermons. Whether secular or religious, his work is passionate, intellectual and self-dramatising. He often catches the moment of strong feeling: *The Apparition* conveys the bitter sense of betrayal in love.

When by thy scorn, O murdress, I am dead
And that thou thinkst thee free
From all solicitation from me,
Then shall my ghost come to thy bed,
And thee, fain'd vestal,[1] in worse arms shall see;
Then thy sick taper will begin to wink,[2]
And he, whose thou art then, being tyr'd before,
Will, if thou stir, or pinch to wake him, think
        Thou call'st for more,
And in false sleep will from thee shrink,
And then poor aspen[3] wretch, neglected thou
Bath'd in a cold quicksilver sweat wilt lie
        A veryer ghost than I;
What I will say, I will not tell thee now,
Lest that preserve thee; and since my love is spent,
I'had rather thou shouldst painfully repent,
Than by my threatnings rest still innocent.[4]

---

[1]**vestal** virgin (in Ancient Rome the Vestal Virgins served Vesta, the goddess of the hearth)
[2]**wink** flicker
[3]**aspen** leaves on the aspen tree are pale on the underside and quiver in a breeze
[4]**innocent** free from harm

Washington Square

by Henry James

Henry James (1843–1916) was born in New York and settled in London in 1875. Many of his novels explore the interaction of American and European cultures. In *Washington Square* he tells the story of Catherine, the daughter of Dr Sloper, a wealthy New York doctor. He is ashamed of her because she is shy and plain-looking, and so she receives very little love or respect. Morris Townsend, a charming and handsome young man, begins to court her. Dr Sloper is convinced that he loves her money more than he loves her; she falls in love with him and tries to defy her father. When Morris comes to realise that he will not receive any of Sloper's wealth he decides to slide out of the love affair.

'Are you sick?' she asked of Morris. 'You seem so restless, and you look pale.'

'I am not at all well,' said Morris; and it occurred to him that, if he could only make her pity him enough, he might get off.

'I am afraid you are overworked; you oughtn't to work so much.'

'I must do that.' And then he added, with a sort of calculated brutality, 'I don't want to owe you everything.'

'Ah, how can you say that?'

'I am too proud,' said Morris.

'Yes – you are too proud.'

'Well, you must take me as I am,' he went on; 'you can never change me.'

'I don't want to change you,' she said, gently; 'I will take you as you are.' And she stood looking at him.

'You know people talk tremendously about a man's marrying a rich girl,' Morris remarked. 'It's excessively disagreeable.'

'But I am not rich,' said Catherine.

'You are rich enough to make me talked about.'

'Of course you are talked about. It's an honour.'

'It's an honour I could easily dispense with.'

She was on the point of asking him whether it was not a compensation for this annoyance that the poor girl who had the misfortune to bring it upon him loved him so dearly and believed in him so truly; but she hesitated, thinking that this would perhaps seem an exacting speech, and, while she hesitated, he suddenly left her.

The next time he came, however, she brought it out, and she told him again that he was too proud. He repeated that he couldn't change, and this time she felt the impulse to say that with a little effort he might change.

Sometimes he thought that if he could only make a quarrel with her it might help him; but the question was how to quarrel with a young woman who had such treasures of concession. 'I suppose you think the effort is all on your side,' he broke out. 'Don't you believe that I have my own effort to make?'

'It's all yours now,' she said; 'my effort is finished and done with.'

'Well, mine is not.'

'We must bear things together,' said Catherine. 'That's what we ought to do.'

Morris attempted a natural smile. 'There are some things which we can't very well bear together – for instance, separation.'

'Why do you speak of separation?'

'Ah! you don't like it; I knew you wouldn't.'

'Where are you going, Morris?' she suddenly asked.

He fixed his eye on her a moment, and for a part of that moment she was afraid of it. 'Will you promise not to make a scene?'

'A scene! – do I make scenes?'

'All women do!' said Morris, with the tone of large experience.

'I don't. Where are you going?'

'If I should say I was going away on business, should you think it very strange?'

She wondered a moment, gazing at him. 'Yes – no. Not if you will take me with you.'

'Take you with me – on business?'

'What is your business? Your business is to be with me.'

'I don't earn my living with you,' said Morris. 'Or, rather,' he cried, with a sudden inspiration, 'that's just what I do – or what the world says I do!'

This ought perhaps to have been a great stroke, but it miscarried. 'Where are you going?' Catherine simply repeated.

'To New Orleans – about buying some cotton.'

'I am perfectly willing to go to New Orleans,' Catherine said.

'Do you suppose I would take you to a nest of yellow-fever?' cried Morris. 'Do you suppose I would expose you at such a time as this?'

'If there is yellow-fever, why should you go? Morris, you must not go.'

'It is to make six thousand dollars,' said Morris. 'Do you grudge me that satisfaction?'

'We have no need of six thousand dollars. You think too much about money.'

'You can afford to say that. This is a great chance; we heard of it last night.' And he explained to her in what the chance consisted; and told her a long story, going over more than once several of the details, about the remarkable stroke of business which he and his partner had planned between them.

But Catherine's imagination, for reasons best known to herself, absolutely refused to be fired. 'If you can go to New Orleans, I can go,' she said. 'Why shouldn't you catch yellow-fever quite as easily as I? I am every bit as strong as you, and not in the least afraid of any fever. When we were in Europe we were in very unhealthy places; my father used to make me take some pills. I never caught anything, and I never was nervous. What will be the use of six thousand dollars if you die of a fever? When persons are going to be married they oughtn't to think so much about business. You shouldn't think about cotton; you should think about me. You can go to New Orleans some other time – there will always be plenty of cotton. It isn't the moment to choose: we have waited too long already.' She spoke more forcibly and volubly than he had ever heard her, and she held his arm in her two hands.

'You said you wouldn't make a scene,' cried Morris. 'I call this a scene.'

'It's you that are making it. I have never asked you anything before. We have waited too long already.' And it was a comfort to her to think that she had hitherto asked so little; it seemed to make her right to insist the greater now.

Morris bethought himself a little. 'Very well, then; we won't talk about it any more. I will transact my business by letter.' And he began to smooth his hat, as if to take leave.

'You won't go?' and she stood looking up at him.

He could not give up his idea of provoking a quarrel; it was so much the simplest way. He bent his eyes on her upturned face with the darkest frown he could achieve. 'You are not discreet; you mustn't bully me.'

But, as usual, she conceded everything. 'No, I am not discreet; I know I am too pressing. But isn't it natural? It is only for a moment.'

'In a moment you may do a great deal of harm. Try and be calmer the next time I come.'

'When will you come?'

'Do you want to make conditions?' Morris asked. 'I will come next Saturday.'

'Come tomorrow,' Catherine begged; 'I want you to come tomorrow. I will be very quiet,' she added; and her agitation had by this time become so great that the assurance was not unbecoming. A sudden fear had come over her; it was like the solid conjunction of a dozen disembodied doubts, and her imagination, at a single bound, had traversed an enormous distance. All her being, for the moment, was centred in the wish to keep him in the room.

Morris bent his head and kissed her forehead. 'When you are quiet, you are perfection,' he said; 'but when you are violent, you are not in character.'

It was Catherine's wish that there should be no violence about her save the beating of her heart, which she could not help; and she went on, as gently as possible, 'Will you promise to come tomorrow?'

'I said Saturday!' Morris answered, smiling. He tried a frown at one moment, a smile at another; he was at his wit's end.

'Yes, Saturday too,' she answered, trying to smile. 'But tomorrow first.' He was going to the door, and she went with him quickly. She leaned her shoulder against it; it seemed to her that she would do anything to keep him.

'If I am prevented from coming tomorrow, you will say I have deceived you,' he said.

'How can you be prevented? You can come if you will.'

'I am a busy man – I am not a dangler!' cried Morris, sternly.

His voice was so hard and unnatural that, with a helpless look at him, she turned away; and then he quickly laid his hand on the door knob. He felt as if he were absolutely running away from her. But in an instant she was close to him again, and murmuring in a tone none the less penetrating for being low, 'Morris, you are going to leave me.'

'Yes, for a little while.'

'For how long?'

'Till you are reasonable again.'

'I shall never be reasonable, in that way.' And she tried to keep him longer; it was almost a struggle. 'Think of what I have done!' she broke out. 'Morris, I have given up everything.'

'You shall have everything back.'

'You wouldn't say that if you didn't mean something. What is it? – what has happened? – what have I done? – what has changed you?'

'I will write to you – that is better,' Morris stammered.

'Ah, you won't come back!' she cried, bursting into tears.

'Dear Catherine,' he said, 'don't believe that. I promise you that you shall see me again.' And he managed to get away, and to close the door behind him.

Neutral Tones

by Thomas Hardy

Thomas Hardy (1840–1928) has gained a world-wide reputation as a poet and novelist. Most of his work is set in the fictional area of 'Wessex', based on the archaic name for the south-western English counties of Dorset, Wiltshire and Somerset. In 1911 Hardy's wife died and he explored his complicated feelings of loss in a collection of poems written during the following year.

Neutral Tones was written much earlier, in 1867, when Hardy was a young man struggling with doubts about his religious faith. There is no clear evidence as to who the woman at the centre of the poem might have been. Hardy published *Neutral Tones* in his 1898 collection entitled *Wessex Poems and Other Verses.*

We stood by a pond that winter day,
And the sun was white, as though chidden of[1] God,
And a few leaves lay on the starving sod;
– They had fallen from an ash and were gray.

Your eyes on me were as eyes that rove
Over tedious riddles of years ago;
And some words played between us to and fro
On which lost the more by our love.

The smile on your mouth was the deadest thing
Alive enough to have strength to die;
And a grin of bitterness spread thereby
Like an ominous bird a-wing . . .

Since then keen lessons that love deceives,
And wrings with wrong, have shaped to me
Your face, and the God-curst sun, and a tree,
And a pond edged with grayish leaves.

---

[1]**chidden of** rebuked by

Testament of Youth

by Vera Brittain

Vera Brittain (1893–1970), a feminist and pacifist writer, wrote her autobiographical *Testament of Youth* about her experiences in World War I, during which she served as a Voluntary Aid Detachment nurse, and suffered the losses of her fiancé Roland Leighton, her brother Edward, and two other close friends.

In Sussex, by the end of January, the season was already on its upward grade; catkins hung bronze from the bare, black branches, and in the damp lanes between Hassocks and Keymer the birds sang loudly. How I hated them as I walked back to the station one late afternoon, when a red sunset turned the puddles on the road into gleaming pools of blood, and a new horror of mud and death darkened my mind with its dreadful obsession. Roland, I reflected bitterly, was now part of the corrupt clay into which war had transformed the fertile soil of France; he would never again know the smell of a wet evening in early spring.

I had arrived at the cottage that morning to find his mother and sister standing in helpless distress in the midst of his returned kit, which was lying, just opened, all over the floor. The garments sent back included the outfit that he had been wearing when he was hit. I wondered, and I wonder still, why it was thought necessary to return such relics – the tunic torn back and front by the bullet, a khaki vest dark and stiff with blood, and a pair of blood-stained breeches slit open at the top by someone obviously in a violent hurry. Those gruesome rags made me realise, as I had never realised before, all that France really meant. Eighteen months afterwards the smell of Étaples village, though fainter and more diffused, brought back to me the memory of those poor remnants of patriotism.

'Everything,' I wrote later to Edward, 'was damp and worn and simply caked with mud. And I was glad that neither you nor Victor nor anyone who may some day go to the front was there to see. If you had been, you would have been overwhelmed by the horror of war without its glory. For though he had only worn the things when living, the smell of those clothes was the smell of graveyards and the Dead. The mud of France which covered them was not ordinary mud; it had not the usual clean pure smell of earth, but it was as though it were saturated with dead bodies – dead that had been dead a long, long time . . . There was his cap, bent in and shapeless out of recognition – the soft cap he wore rakishly on the back of his head – with the badge thickly coated with mud. He must have fallen on top of it, or perhaps one of the people who fetched him in trampled on it.'

Edward wrote gently and humbly in reply, characteristically emphasising the simple, less perturbing things that I had mentioned in another part of my letter.

'I expect he had only just received the box of cigarettes and the collars and braces I gave him for Christmas and I feel glad that he did get them because he must have thought of me then.'

So oppressively at length did the charnel-house smell pervade the small sitting-room, that Roland's mother turned desperately to her husband:

'Robert, take those clothes away into the kitchen and don't let me see them again: I must either burn or bury them. They smell of death; they are not Roland; they even seem to detract from his memory and spoil his glamour. I won't have anything more to do with them!'

What actually happened to the clothes I never knew, but, incongruously enough, it was amid this heap of horror and decay that we found, surrounded by torn bills and letters, the black manuscript note-book containing his poems. On the fly-leaf he had copied a few lines written by John Masefield on the subject of patriotism:

It is not a song in the street and a wreath on a column and a flag flying from a window and a pro-Boer[1] *under a pump. It is a thing very holy and very terrible, like life itself. It is a burden to be borne, a thing to labour for and to suffer for and to die for, a thing which gives no happiness and no pleasantness – but a hard life, an unknown grave, and the respect and bowed heads of those who follow.*

The poems were few, for he had always been infinitely dissatisfied with his own work, but 'Nachklang' was there, and 'In the Rose Garden', as well as the roundel 'I Walk Alone', and the villanelle[2] 'Violets', which he had given me during his leave. The final entry represented what must have been the last, and was certainly the most strangely prophetic, of all his writings. It evidently belonged to the period of our quarrel, when he was away from his regiment with the Somerset Light Infantry, for it was headed by the words:

HÉDAUVILLE. ***November 1915:***

The sunshine on the long white road
That ribboned down the hill,
The velvet clematis that clung
Around your window-sill,
Are waiting for you still.

Again the shadowed pool shall break
In dimples round your feet,
And when the thrush sings in your wood,
Unknowing you may meet
Another stranger, Sweet.

And if he is not quite so old
As the boy you used to know,
And less proud, too, and worthier,

---

[1]**pro-Boer** someone who opposed government policy to fight the Boer War of 1899–1902
[2]**villanelle** a rhyming poem written in five tercets and a quatrain

You may not let him go –
(And daisies are truer than passion-flowers)
It will be better so.

What did he mean, I wondered, as I read and re-read the poem, puzzled and tormented. What could he have meant?

Five years afterwards, as I motored from Amiens through the still disfigured battlefields to visit Roland's grave at Louvencourt, I passed, with a sudden shock, a white board inscribed briefly: 'HÉDAUVILLE'.

The place was then much as it must have looked after a year or two's fighting, with only the stumpy ruins of farmhouses crumbling into the tortured fields to show where once a village had been. But over the brow of a hill the shell-torn remnants of a road turned a corner and curved steeply downwards. As the car lurched drunkenly between the yawning shell-holes I looked back, and it seemed to me that perhaps in November 1915, this half-obliterated track had still retained enough character and dignity to remind Roland of the moorland road near Buxton where we had walked one spring evening before the war.

Shadowlands

by William Nicholson

Shadowlands is a play about the deep love between the Oxford scholar C. S. Lewis (1898–1963), apparently a confirmed bachelor, and an American divorcée Joy Davidson. Their brief marriage was cut short by her death from cancer and Lewis found himself with her son Douglas to look after, while coping with his emotional grief, his intellectual problems about the nature of suffering and his belief in God being deeply shaken. This experience of love achieved so late then brutally lost led Lewis to explore his feelings in *A Grief Observed*. Both the story and Lewis's book led William Nicholson (born 1948) to write this play.

LEWIS I love you, Joy. I love you so much. You've made me so happy. I didn't know I could be so happy. You're the truest person I've ever known. Sweet Jesus, be with my beloved wife, Joy. Forgive me if I love her too much. Have mercy on us both.

JOY *(Her eyes open. She speaks very faintly.)* Get some sleep, Jack.

LEWIS How's the pain?

JOY Not too good. Only shadows.

LEWIS Only shadows.

Her eyes close again. LEWIS *rises, stoops and kisses her, and walks softly out of the pool of light.*

The light on JOY *fades slowly to black as the screen comes in.*

HARRINGTON Naturally I wouldn't say this to Jack, but better sooner than later. Better quick than slow. After all, there was no question about it. The writing was on the wall.

GREGG Is he taking it very hard?

HARRINGTON He's a remarkable man, Jack. Faith solid as a rock.

RILEY Harry, those few well-chosen words at the church – did I hear you correctly? It seemed to me that you said something like 'All who knew her loved her.'

HARRINGTON Something like that.

RILEY Not quite God's own truth, was it?

HARRINGTON Good grief, Christopher, what was I supposed to say? That nobody could stand her?

RILEY Jack loved her. That's what's true, and that's what matters. But I didn't and you didn't.

HARRINGTON She is dead.

RILEY Death does not improve the character.

The screen goes up and they join WARNIE *and* GREGG, *who are seated at the college high table.*

GREGG You don't love anyone, Christopher, as far as I can see.

RILEY That may well be true, but Harry still shouldn't tell whoppers.

HARRINGTON Jack was standing six feet away.

RILEY Jack wouldn't have minded. He's changed. She did that. She was a remarkable woman. But I'm damned if I'm going to start liking her just because she's dead.

HARRINGTON Did you like her, Warnie?

WARNIE Not at first. But oh, yes.

LEWIS *enters. An awkward silence falls as he comes to his place at table.*

LEWIS I wasn't going to come. Then I thought I would. *(He sits. He sounds perfectly calm.)*

HARRINGTON Life must go on.

LEWIS I don't know that it must. But it certainly does.

GREGG I'm sorry I wasn't able to be at the church.

LEWIS Not important, Alan.

HARRINGTON My little address, Jack. Was it . . . ?

LEWIS Please forgive me, Harry. I haven't the slightest idea what you said in church. I didn't hear a word.

HARRINGTON Fine. Fine. Perfectly understandable.

RILEY Are you alright, Jack?

LEWIS No.

HARRINGTON Thank God for your faith, Jack. Where would you be without that?

LEWIS I'd be here, drinking my port.

HARRINGTON What I mean to say, Jack, is that it's only faith that makes any sense of times like this.

LEWIS *(Puts down his glass.)* No, I'm sorry, Harry, but it won't do. This is a mess, and that's all there is to it.

HARRINGTON A mess?

LEWIS What sense do you make of it? You tell me.

HARRINGTON But, Jack – we have to have faith that God knows –

LEWIS God knows. Yes, God knows. I don't doubt that. God knows. But does God care? Did He care about Joy?

HARRINGTON Why are you talking like this, Jack? We can't see what's best for us. You know that. We're not the Creator.

LEWIS No. We're the creatures. We're the rats in the cosmic laboratory. I've no doubt the great experiment is for our own good, eventually, but that still makes God the vivisectionist.

HARRINGTON This is your grief talking.

LEWIS What was talking before? My complacency?

HARRINGTON Please, Jack. Please.

LEWIS I'm sorry, Harry. You're a good man. I don't mean to distress you. But the fact is, I've come up against a bit of experience recently. Experience is a brutal teacher, but you learn fast. I'm sorry. I shouldn't have come this evening. I'm not fit company. *(He rises.)* If you'll forgive me. *(He leaves the table.)*

WARNIE Excuse me.

WARNIE *follows* LEWIS *to where he stands, frowning, by himself. The screen falls.*

LEWIS Sorry about that, Warnie. Not necessary.

WARNIE Everybody understands, Jack.

LEWIS I can't see her anymore. I can't remember her face. What's happening to me?

WARNIE I expect it's shock.

LEWIS I'm so terribly afraid. Of never seeing her again. Of thinking that suffering is just suffering after all. No cause. No purpose. No pattern. No sense. Just pain, in a world of pain.

WARNIE I don't know what to tell you, Jack.

LEWIS Nothing. There's nothing to say.

They are silent for a few moments.

DOUGLAS *enters on the far side of the stage. He is profoundly hurt by his mother's death but is refusing to show it.*

WARNIE Jack.

LEWIS Yes.

WARNIE About Douglas.

LEWIS Yes.

WARNIE Your grief is your business. Maybe you feel life is a mess. Maybe it is. But he's only a child.

LEWIS What am I supposed to do about it?

WARNIE Talk to him.

LEWIS I don't know what to say to him.

WARNIE Just talk to him. *(*WARNIE *exits.)*

LEWIS *(Walks across to* DOUGLAS*. He speaks to the boy in a matter-of-fact way, as if they are equals.)* When I was your age, my mother died. That was cancer too. I thought that if I prayed for her to get better, and if I really believed she'd get better, then she wouldn't die. But she did.

DOUGLAS It doesn't work.

LEWIS No. It doesn't work.

DOUGLAS I don't care.

LEWIS I do. When I'm alone, I start crying. Do you cry?

DOUGLAS No.

LEWIS I didn't when I was your age. *(A brief pause.)* I loved your mother very much.

DOUGLAS That's okay.

LEWIS I loved her too much. She knew that. She said to me, 'Is it worth it?' She knew how it would be later. *(Pause.)* It doesn't seem fair, does it? If you want the love, you have to have the pain.

DOUGLAS I don't see why she had to get sick.

LEWIS Nor I. *(Pause.)* You can't hold on to things. You have to let them go.

DOUGLAS Jack?

LEWIS Yes.

DOUGLAS Do you believe in heaven?

LEWIS Yes.

DOUGLAS I don't believe in heaven.

LEWIS That's okay.

DOUGLAS I sure would like to see her again.

LEWIS Me too.

DOUGLAS *can't take any more. He reaches out for comfort, pressing himself against* LEWIS. LEWIS *wraps his arms around the boy, and at last his own tears break through, in heart-breaking sobs, unloosing the grief of a lifetime. His emotion releases the tears that have been waiting in the boy.*

As they fall quiet, DOUGLAS *detaches himself and exits.*

LEWIS *turns to face the audience and begins to speak quietly. His words are a version of the talk he has given earlier, now transformed by his own suffering.*

LEWIS We are like blocks of stone, out of which the
sculptor carves the forms of men. The blows
of his chisel, which hurt us so much, are what
make us perfect.
No shadows here. Only darkness, and silence,
and the pain that cries like a child.
It ends, like all affairs of the heart, with
exhaustion. Only so much pain is possible.
Then, rest.
So it comes about that, when I am quiet, when
I am quiet, she returns to me. There she is, in
my mind, in my memory, coming towards me,
and I love her again as I did before, even though
I know I will lose her again, and be hurt again.
So you can say if you like that Jack Lewis has
no answer to the question after all, except this: I
have been given the choice twice in my life. The
boy chose safety. The man chooses suffering.

He now speaks to her, in his memory.

LEWIS I went to my wardrobe this morning. I was
looking for my old brown jacket, the one I
used to wear before – I'd forgotten that you'd
carried out one of your purges there. Just
before we went to Greece, I think it was. I
find I can live with the pain, after all. The
pain, now, is part of the happiness, then.
That's the deal.
Only shadows, Joy.

Final Curtain

Out of Danger

by James Fenton

James Fenton (born 1949), a journalist, critic and academic, was Professor of Poetry at Oxford between 1994 and 1999. His poems have strong musical qualities and some read almost like ballads. This poem appears in his collection *Out of Danger*, which won the Whitbread award for poetry.

Heart be kind and sign the release
As the trees their loss approve
Learn as leaves must learn to fall
Out of danger, out of love.

What belongs to frost and thaw
Sullen winter will not harm.
What belongs to wind and rain
Is out of danger from the storm.

Jealous passion, cruel need
Betray the heart they feed upon.
But what belongs to earth and death
Is out of danger from the sun.

I was cruel, I was wrong –
Hard to say and hard to know.
You do not belong to me.
You are out of danger now –

Out of danger from the wind,
Out of danger from the wave,
Out of danger from the heart,
Falling, falling out of love.

Questions

In all of these questions you should consider:

a the ways the writers' choice of form, structure and language shape your responses to the extracts

b how your wider reading in the literature of love has contributed to your understanding and interpretation of the extracts.

1 Compare the language used in *Neutral Tones* and poem 2 from *In Memoriam* to describe a sense of place. How does it convey the writer's feelings of grief and loss?

2 In the four poems *The Apparition*, *Neutral Tones*, *With Serving Still* and *Out of Danger*, do you find the poets' attitudes bitter, regretful, relieved or resigned? Compare the language used by the poets to explain your responses.

3 In the extract from *Washington Square*, how does the author make Morris's language of betrayal seem reasonable?

4 Examine the arguments put forward by both husband and wife in the extract from *A Doll's House*. Do you think the playwright wants us to find one more convincing than the other?

5 In the extract from *Testament of Youth* examine the connection between what the author observes and how she reflects.

6 At the end of *Shadowlands*, Jack says: 'The pain, now, is part of the happiness, then.' How convincing do you find this comment?

7 Explore the ways in which any two of these extracts express the relationship between loss and time passing.

8 'Much writing about lost love is likely to be self-indulgent, concentrating as it does on the victim left behind rather than on the loved one who has died.' To what extent do you find this to be the case in the extracts included here?

Further reading

- This anthology includes extracts from two versions of the legendary story of Troilus and Cressida (by Chaucer (p. 6) and Shakespeare (p. 119)). The story ends in betrayal and bitterness and was so well known that the Scottish poet Robert Henryson (1424?–1506?) wrote a moving sequel, *The Testament of Cresseid*.
- Among Shakespeare's late plays, *Cymbeline* and *The Winter's Tale* tell stories of love lost and regained.
- If you enjoyed Emily Dickinson's oblique poem of loss, try the haunting poetry of Christina Rossetti. Some moving 20th-century poems about loss include *Absence* by Elizabeth Jennings, Tony Harrison's sonnet *Though My Mother Was Already Two Years Dead* and Causley's *Ballad of the Faithless Wife*.
- For more about love and loss during war time, try *The English Patient* by Michael Ondatje, *The End of the Affair* by Graham Greene or the *Regeneration* trilogy by Pat Barker.
- From the 19th century, you might enjoy Flaubert's great novel of betrayal, *Madame Bovary*. Many of Thomas Hardy's novels also show the suffering of lovers, deserted and betrayed: *The Woodlanders* and *Far from the Madding Crowd* are among the best known.
- Writing in the 20th century, Graham Greene conveys a cruel form of betrayal in *Brighton Rock*. In John Banville's *The Sea*, the hero tries to come to terms with disturbing events from his past. *On Chesil Beach* by Ian McEwan tells of lovers whose sexual anxieties lead them to mutual recrimination.
- The death of a child can be particularly disturbing: powerful examples are Ben Jonson's poem *On My First Son* and Paul's death in Dickens's *Dombey and Son*. Alice Sebold, in *The Lovely Bones*, imagines how a murdered child might continue to observe the living.
- *To the Lighthouse* by Virginia Woolf is an elegy to the memory of the dead – Woolf's own parents. Famous elegies include Milton's *Lycidas* and Henry King's *Exequy* for his wife (both from the 17th century). Andrew Motion's memoir *In the Blood* is not strictly an elegy, but begins and ends with a moving account of his mother's death. *In the Springtime of the Year* by Susan Hill reflects upon the shock of sudden bereavement.

Acknowledgements

The volume editor and publishers acknowledge the following sources of copyright material and are grateful for the permissions granted. While every effort has been made, it has not always been possible to identify the sources of all the material used, or to trace all copyright holders. If any omissions are brought to our notice we will be happy to include the appropriate acknowledgement on reprinting.

p. xi: 'Twelve Songs XII' by W. H. Auden, published by Faber & Faber Ltd; p. 4: 'All in green went my love riding' is reprinted from *Complete Poems 1904–1962* by E. E. Cummings, edited by George J. Firmage, by permission of W. W. Norton & Company, copyright © 1991 by the Trustees for the E. E. Cummings Trust and George James Firmage; p. 9 *Free Fall* by William Golding, published by Faber & Faber Ltd; p. 18: *The True History of the Kelly Gang* by Peter Carey, published by Faber & Faber Ltd, copyright © 2000 by Peter Carey, reproduced by permission of the author c/o Rogers, Coleridge & White Ltd., 20 Powis Mews, London W11 1JN and Random House Canada; p. 28: *Samuel Pepys The Unequalled Self* by Claire Tomalin (Viking, 2002), copyright © Claire Tomalin, 2002, reproduced by permission of Penguin Books Ltd; p. 32: *Betrayal* by Harold Pinter, published by Faber & Faber Ltd; p. 37: *Half of a Yellow Sun* by Chimamanda Ngozi Adichie, published by HarperCollins Publishers Ltd © 2006 Chimamanda Ngozi Adichie; p. 44: *The Line of Beauty* by Alan Hollinghurst, copyright © Alan Hollinghurst, 2005; p. 61: *Tales from Ovid* by Ted Hughes, published by Faber & Faber Ltd; p. 68: *Dusty Answer* by Rosamond Lehmann, by permission of The Society of Authors as the literary representative of the Estate of Rosamond Lehmann; p. 73: *The Glass Menagerie* by Tennessee Williams, copyright © 1945, renewed 1973 The University of the South, reprinted by permission of Georges Borchardt, Inc. for the Estate of Tennessee Williams; p. 82: *The Waves* by Virginia Woolf, by permission of The Society of Authors as the literary representative of the Estate of Virginia Woolf; p. 87: *Cold Comfort Farm* by Stella Gibbons, reproduced with permission of Curtis Brown Group Ltd, London on behalf of the Estate of Stella Gibbons, copyright © Stella Gibbons 1932; p. 92: 'Warming Her Pearls' is taken from *Selling Manhattan* by Carol Ann Duffy, published by Anvil Press Poetry in 1987; p. 97: 'East Coker' by T. S. Eliot, published by Faber & Faber Ltd; p. 100: 'Comeclose and Sleepnow' by

Roger McGough from *The Mersey Sound* (© Roger McGough 1967) is reproduced by permission of PFD (www.pfd.co.uk) on behalf of Roger McGough; p. 105: letter from Zelda Fitzgerald, from *Love Letters* edited by Antonia Fraser, published by Penguin, reprinted by permission; p. 107: extract from *The Journals of Sylvia Plath 1950–1962*, edited by Karen Kukil, published by Faber & Faber Ltd; p. 108: 'A Pink Wool Knitted Dress' from *Birthday Letters* by Ted Hughes, published by Faber & Faber Ltd; p. 113: 'I Like it to Rain' by Nii Parkes, copyright © Nii Parkes, 2004; p. 135: *The God of Small Things* by Arundhati Roy, published by HarperCollins Publisher Ltd © 1997, Arundhati Roy; p. 139: *Sir Gawain and the Green Knight* translated by Simon Armitage, published by Faber & Faber Ltd; p. 146: *Phaedra's Love* by Sarah Kane, published by Methuen Drama, an imprint of A&C Black Publishers Ltd; p. 157: 'The Gift' from *The Book of Blood* by Vicki Feaver, published by Jonathan Cape, reprinted by permission of The Random House Group Ltd; p. 163: from *Suite Française* by Irène Némirovsky, translated by Sandra Smith, published by Chatto & Windus, reprinted by permission of The Random House Group Ltd, copyright © 2004 by Editions Denoel, license arranged by the French Publishers' Agency in New York, translation copyright © 2006 by Sandra Smith, reprinted by permission of Knopf Canada; p. 167: *The Lady of the House of Love* by Angela Carter, copyright © 1980 Angela Carter, reproduced by permission of the author c/o Rogers, Coleridge & White Ltd, 20 Powis Mews, London W11 1JN; p. 172: *Lady Chatterley's Trial – Regina v Penguin Books*, published by Penguin; p. 179: *The Four Loves* by C. S. Lewis © Copyright C. S. Lewis Pte Ltd, 1960; p. 180: *First Love and Other Sorrows* by Harold Brodkey, copyright © Harold Brodkey, 1958; p. 181: from *The Young Visiters* by Daisy Ashford, published by Chatto & Windus, reprinted by permission of The Random House Group Ltd; p. 183: 'Morning Song' from *Ariel* by Sylvia Plath, published by Faber & Faber Ltd; p. 184: 'Gap Year' by Jackie Kay, from *Darling: New & Selected Poems* (Bloodaxe Books, 2007); p. 194: *A Handful of Dust* by Evelyn Waugh, edited with an introduction and notes by Robert Murray Davis (first published by Chapman and Hall 1934, Penguin Classics 2000), copyright © Evelyn Waugh, 1934, introduction and notes copyright © Robert Murray Davis, 1997, reproduced by permission of Penguin Books Ltd; p. 197: *The Vortex* by Noël Coward, published by Methuen Drama, an imprint of A&C Black Publishers Ltd, permission granted by Alan Brodie Representation Ltd on behalf of NC Aventales AG, successor in title to the Estate of Noël Coward; p. 215: from 'The Thing in the Forest' from *The Little Black Book of Stories* by A. S. Byatt, published by Chatto & Windus, reprinted by permission of The Random House Group Ltd; p. 219: *The Kite Runner* by Khaled Hosseini, published by Bloomsbury, copyright © Khaled Hosseini 2003, reprinted by permission of Doubleday Canada, used by permission of Riverhead Books, an imprint of Penguin Group (USA) Inc; p. 224: *The Keepsake* by Fleur Adcock, from *Poems 1955–2000* (Bloodaxe Books, 2000); p. 231: *Waiting for Godot* by Samuel Beckett, published by Faber & Faber Ltd; p. 235: *Stuart: A Life Backwards* by Alexander Masters, published by HarperCollins Publishers Ltd © 2005 Alexander Masters; p. 239: from *Beloved* by Toni Morrison, copyright © 1987 by Toni Morrison, used by permission of Alfred A. Knopf, a division of Random House, Inc, and International Creative Management, Inc; p. 248: *A Doll's House* by Henrik Ibsen, translated by James McFarlane; p. 268: The extract from *Testament of Youth* by Vera Brittain (1933) is included by permission of Mark Bostridge and Timothy Brittain-Catlin, Literary Executors for the Vera Brittain Estate 1970; p. 272 *Shadowlands* by William Nicholson; p. 278: 'Out of Danger' by James Fenton, published by Faber & Faber Ltd.

The publishers would like to thank the following for permission to reproduce photographs and illustrations:

p. xiv: Pictorial Press Ltd / Alamy; p. xvi: Francesca da Rimini, 1835 (oil on canvas) by Scheffer, Ary (1795–1858) © Wallace Collection, London, UK / The Bridgeman Art Library; p. 72: 'Raining In My Heart (Longing)', image copyright The Singh Twins (www.singhtwins.co.uk).